Hosting the Stranger: Between Religions

Hosting the Stranger: Between Religions

Edited by
Richard Kearney and James Taylor

continuum

The Continuum International Publishing Group
80 Maiden Lane, New York, NY 10038
The Tower Building, 11 York Road, London SE1 7NX

www.continuumbooks.com

Library of Congress Cataloging-in-Publication Data
A catalog record for this book is available from the Library of Congress.

ISBN: HB: 978-0-8264-2737-3
PB: 978-1-4411-5808-6

Typeset by Pindar NZ, Auckland, New Zealand
Printed and bound in the United States of America

CONTENTS

LIST OF CONTRIBUTORS

Francis X. Clooney, S.J. is Parkman Professor of Divinity and Director of the Center for the Study of World Religions at Harvard Divinity School. He works primarily on theological commentarial writings in the Sanskrit and Tamil traditions of Hindu India, and in comparative theology. He has also written on the Jesuit missionary tradition, particularly in India, and on the dynamics of dialogue in the contemporary world. The author of numerous articles and books, including *Beyond Compare: St. Francis and Sri Vedanta Desika on Loving Surrender to God* (Georgetown University Press, 2008), *The Truth, the Way, the Life: Christian Commentary on the Three Holy Mantras of the Srivaisnava Hindus* (Peeters, 2008) and *Comparative Theology: Deep Learning Across Religious Borders* (Wiley-Blackwell, 2010), Professor Clooney's current projects include an exercise in dramatic theology, the reading of Bernard of Clairvaux's sermons on the Song of Songs as well as Nampillai's commentary on Satakopan's *Tiruvaymoli*.

Catherine Cornille is Associate Professor of Comparative Theology and Chair of the Department of Theology at Boston College. Her teaching and research focus mainly on methodological and theological questions in the study of religions, inculturation and interreligious dialogue. Her books include *The Guru in Indian Catholicism: Ambiguity or Opportunity of Inculturation* (Peeters, 1991); ed., *Many Mansions? Multiple Religious Belonging and Christian Identity* (Orbis Books, 2002); ed., *Song Divine: Christian Commentaries on the Bhagavad Gita* (Peeters, 2006); and most recently *The Im-Possibility of Interreligious Dialogue* (Crossroad, 2008) and ed., *Criteria of Discernment in Interreligious Dialogue* (Wipf & Stock, 2009). She is also the managing editor of the series *Christian Commentaries on non-Christian Sacred Texts*.

Hugh Cummins is currently completing his PhD thesis on the theme of home and homelessness in the thought of Emmanuel Levinas at University College, Dublin, Ireland. He works as a part-time tutor and lecturer in philosophy and psychoanalysis. From 2001 until 2009 he was also a full-time employee in a centre for homeless people in Dublin.

Mark Patrick Hederman is Abbot of Glenstal Abbey, Limerick, Ireland. Author of a number of books, including *The Haunted Inkwell* (Columba Press, 2001), *Walkabout: Life as the Holy Spirit* (Columba Press, 2005), *I Must be Talking to Myself: Dialogue in the Roman Catholic Church since Vatican II* (Veritas, 2005) and most recently *Symbolism: Glory of Escutcheoned Doors* (Veritas, 2007), and a founding editor of the cultural journal *The Crane Bag* and of the *Journal of Irish Studies*, Abbot Hederman is an active voice in Ireland and abroad on matters of culture, art and religion and is a frequent guest on Irish National Television. He has also lectured on philosophy in Africa, the United States and Europe.

Edward Kaplan is the Kaiserman Professor in the Humanities at Brandeis University, where he has been teaching French, comparative literature, and religious studies for over 30 years. In addition to books and articles on French authors, he has written on Thomas Merton and published a prize-winning biography of Abraham Joshua Heschel.

Richard Kearney holds the Charles Seelig Chair of Philosophy at Boston College and is visiting professor at University College Dublin. He has authored more than 20 books on European philosophy and literature, two novels and a volume of poetry. His most recent philosophical works include *Anatheism: Returning to God after God* (Columbia University Press, 2009), and the "Philosophy at the Limits" trilogy: *Strangers, Gods, and Monsters: Ideas of Otherness* (Routledge, 2002), *The God Who May Be* (Indiana University Press, 2001), and *On Stories (Thinking in Action)* (Routledge, 2001). Richard Kearney is the founder and the international director of the Guestbook Project, a multi-media interdisciplinary collaboration that facilitates cross-cultural and interreligious dialogue by hosting seminars, conferences and performances on the themes of host and guest, violence and reconciliation, and on the role of the embodied imagination in religious discourse.

Joseph Lumbard is an Assistant Professor of Classical Islam. His research is focused on Islamic intellectual traditions with an emphasis on Sufism and Islamic philosophy, and most recently, on the development of Sufi theories of love in the early Islamic period. Professor Lumbard is the editor of *Islam, Fundamentalism, and the Betrayal of Tradition* (World Wisdom, 2004), a collection of essays that examines the religious, political and historical factors that have led to the rise of Islamic fundamentalism.

John Makransky is Associate Professor of Buddhism and Comparative Theology at Boston College and a Senior Faculty Advisor at the Centre for Buddhist Studies, Kathmandu University, Ka-Nying Shedrub Ling Monastery in Bodhanath, Nepal. He was Visiting Lecturer in Buddhist Studies from 2009–2011 at the Harvard Divinity School and is currently a guiding meditation teacher at the Foundation for Active Compassion. His publications include *Buddhahood Embodied: Sources of Controversy in India and Tibet* (State University of New York Press, 1997), "Buddhist Perspectives on Truth in Other Religions: Past and Present," in *Theological Studies Journal* (2003), and "Buddhist Analogues of Sin and Grace: A Dialogue with Augustine," forthcoming in *Augustinian*

Heritage. His most recent book is titled *Awakening Through Love: A Buddhist guide for Unveiling Deepest Goodness* (Wisdom, 2007).

Jacob Meskin is Academic Director of the Me'ah and Ikkarim Programs (in adult Jewish education) and Assistant Professor of Jewish Thought and Education at Hebrew College in Newton, Massachusetts. He served as Ruderman Visiting Professor of Jewish Studies at Northeastern University in 2009–2010 and has published widely in the fields of modern Jewish philosophy and philosophy of religion.

Marianne Moyaert is a post-doctoral researcher at the Interdisciplinary Centre for the Study of Religion and Interreligious Dialogue (Research Foundation—Flanders) at the Faculty of Theology, K.U.Leuven, Belgium. Her research focuses on the hermeneutical, ethical and theological presuppositions of inter-religious dialogue. She is currently preparing a book entitled *A Certain Fragility: Interreligious Dialogue between Openness and Identity* (Rodopi, 2010). She has published articles in *Horizons, Exchange, Ethical Perspectives, Studies for Interreligious Dialogue* and *The Heythrop Journal*.

Joseph S. O'Leary teaches English literature at Sophia University, and received his PhD from the Pontifical University of Maynooth (1976). He is the author of *Questioning Back: The Overcoming of Metaphysics in Christian Tradition* (Winton/Seabury, 1985), *Religious Pluralism and Christian Truth* (Edinburgh University Press, 1996) and *L'art du jugement en théologie* (forthcoming). His research is focused on philosophical theology and East/West dialogue. He has also written extensively on Henry James, George Moore, Yeats, Joyce and Beckett.

Andy Rotman is Associate Professor of Religion at Smith College. His research concerns the ways in which seeing and what is seen in South Asia function as part of social history and material culture. This interest is apparent in his research on Indian Buddhism, South Asian media, and the North Indian bazaar. He recently published *Divine Stories* (Wisdom, 2008), the first part of a two-part translation of the *Divyāvadā na*, one of the most important collections of ancient Buddhist narratives. His second book, *Thus Have I Seen: Visualizing Faith in Early Indian Buddhism* (Oxford University Press, 2008), considers the construction of faith as a visual practice in Buddhism, and how seeing and faith function as part of overlapping visual and moral systems.

Dana Sajdi is Assistant Professor in the History Department at Boston College. Her research focuses on the social and cultural history of the early modern Levant. She is currently completing a book on the "life and work" of an eighteenth-century barber entitled *The Barber of Damascus: Nouveau Literacy in the 18th-Century Ottoman Levant*. Her next project is on an eight-century-long tradition of literary topographies of the city of Damascus.

Kalpana Seshadri is Associate Professor in the Department of English at Boston College. Her primary areas of research are philosophy of race, political theory pertaining to colonialism, and contemporary literature. She is the author of *Desiring Whiteness: A Lacanian Analysis of Race* (Routledge, 2000) and co-editor of *The Pre-occupation of Post-Colonial Studies* (Duke University Press, 2000). Professor Seshadri has also just completed *HumAnimal: Between Law and Language*, which deals with the weak power of forgotten lives.

James Taylor is a teaching fellow and PhD candidate in philosophy at Boston College. His primary research interests are in twentieth-century Continental philosophy and religion, specifically the hermeneutics of religious experience and the relation between philosophy and spirituality. He has published and presented on Heidegger, Gadamer, Foucault and Ricoeur, and is co-director, with his wife Petra Belkovic Taylor, of an annual international undergraduate seminar on the topic of war and peace in the Balkans.

Swami Tyagananda is a Hindu monk of the Ramakrishna Order and presently the head of the Ramakrishna Vedanta Society in Boston. He also serves as the Hindu chaplain at MIT and Harvard. Swami Tyagananda has translated and edited ten books, including *Monasticism: Ideals and Traditions* (1991), *Values: The Key to a Meaningful Life* (Sri Ramakrishna Math, 1996) and *The Essence of the Gita* (2000) and was the editor of the English language journal *Vedanta Kesari*, based in Chennai, India, for eleven years.

Ana Vieira, *Foreigner/Stranger/Other*, 1966. Painted shaped wood. 51 × 86 × 1.5 cm. Col. gAD - galeria Antiks Design.

Introduction

Richard Kearney and James Taylor

Interreligious hospitality is a primary task of our time. We say task because, like most other universally desirable virtues, we are never done with hospitality. There are always more guests to be hosted, ever new strangers to be welcomed as they arrive at the door bearing gifts or challenges, asking for bread or refuge, questioning, calling, demanding, thanking. And there are many different kinds of strangers, not only those aliens and others who come from afar, but also those strangers who come from within ourselves. We are never done with hospitality because we are never done with hosting strangers.

Hospitality is a central and inaugural event in the world's great wisdom traditions. It marks that moment when the self opens to the stranger and welcomes what is foreign and unfamiliar into its home. Judaism tells of Abraham welcoming the three wanderers in the desert. Christianity speaks of the Annunciation as a moment of receptivity to a Word becoming flesh, Islam teaches hospitality to the stranger as a core principle of the Koran, Hinduism recognizes the guest as a manifestation of the divine—*Atithi Devo Bhava* (God is not manifested through the guest; rather the guest by being a guest manifests God), while Buddhism cherishes a radical hospitality of "interbeing" as a way of overcoming illusory antagonisms between friend and enemy.

Most major wisdom traditions, as this volume hopes to show, share a sacred commitment to hosting the stranger. One might even say this is a principle common to almost all religions. But along with this sense of overlapping consensus at the confluence of these spiritual rivers, it is important to acknowledge that traditions of hospitality come from very different sources and travel in their own unique directions. Hospitality can never be hostile to difference if it is to remain hospitable. The common root of hospitality and hostility—*hostis*—carries this sense of primary wager between welcome or exclusion. And this ensures that hosting the stranger is always a risk, never a fait accompli. It is an act of daring and trust, of bold compassion and justice, never a matter of cheap grace or easy virtue.[1]

In this volume we have invited a number of world scholars from diverse cultures and continents to reflect upon the crucial stakes involved in religious responses to the stranger. At a time when many of the world's most bitter wars—the Middle East, the Balkans, South East Asia—have a disturbingly religious character, it seems urgent to seek an ethic of healing at the very heart of interreligious dialogue. If religion is capable of the worst, it is also capable of the best. Where the poison is one finds the cure. That is why interreligious hospitality is not a luxury but an imperative. The refusal to enter into dialogue with other religions itself speaks a violence of exclusion. And many of the worst wars have, history reminds us, been fuelled by perverted religious atavisms. One rarely fights for a constitution or contract; one fights for faith and father-land, myth and motherland, the sacred nation or tribe. So many bloody battles have been waged in the name of God. Interreligious empathy, imagination and compassion are, this volume suggests, essential antidotes to the most egregious excesses of blind fideism and fundamentalism. Exchanging sacred stories bet-ween religions can foster tolerance and healing. This volume is an invitation to traverse the multiple narratives of five major religions.

We have been obliged to confine our comparative analysis to these five wisdom traditions for reasons of limited space. But we intend no implication of hierarchy or supersession in our selection or sequence. This volume, we readily admit, needs to be supplemented by other studies on the practices of hospitality in the great spiritual cultures of Taoism and Confucianism or the rich tradi-tions of Native American, African and Astral-Asian spiritualities. Interreligious hospitality demands no less. One cannot truly welcome strangers in one's own tradition if one is not prepared to welcome strangers from others.

Here we chose as our model of dialogue a hermeneutics of translation. Just as the translator mediates between a host and guest language so must the participants in interreligious dialogue translate and transit between their own religion and those of others. There is double duty here—to remain faithful to one's own language while remaining open to the call of another. The dual fidelity is in constant tension with two temptations: 1) to reduce the foreign to the familiar by an act of appropriation or 2) to surrender one's own language completely to that of the other. In the first instance the guest ceases to be guest; in the second, the host ceases to be host. That is why translation, like genuine religious dialogue, requires a delicate balance between reducing the guest to the host or the host to the guest. The paradigm of linguistic hospitality may thus serve as a template for interconfessional hospitality. As Paul Ricoeur puts it:

> Translation sets us not only intellectual work, theoretical or practical, but also an ethical problem. Bringing the reader to the author, bringing the author to the reader, at the risk of serving and of betraying two masters: this is to practice what I like to call linguistic hospitality. It is this which serves as a model for other forms of hospit-ality that I think resemble it: confessions, religions, are they not like languages that are foreign to one another, with their lexicon, their grammar, their rhetoric, their stylistics which we must learn in order to make our way into them? And is Eucharistic hospitality not to be taken up with the same risks of translation-betrayal, but also with the same renunciation of the perfect translation?[2]

This is not simply a book *about* religions, it is a book *between* religions. It aims to investigate the fragile but crucial hyphen that both conjoins and differentiates the great wisdom traditions. As such it invigilates the two-way liaison of proximity and distance that marks the core ethic of radical hospitality. Interreligious dialogue must be prepared to fully engage with what Antoine

Berman called '*l'épreuve de l'étanger*'—the trial of the strange that faces every translator seeking to respond to the challenge of new meanings, new calls, new responsibilities, new promises.

* * *

We have divided our studies into two sections. In the first we include five studies on the methodology and history of interreligious dialogue as a means to secure reconciliation and understanding between diverse faith traditions. In the second we feature contributions to a discussion of radical hospitality in each of our chosen religions: Judaism, Christianity, Islam, Buddhism, Hinduism.

James Taylor's essay, which opens the volume, wrestles with the challenges involved in the difficult task of bringing different selves, cultures and beliefs into a conciliatory and enriching encounter. He begins by examining the problem of "hospitality to the other" as it is taken up by recent thinkers like Emmanuel Levinas, Jacques Derrida, and most prominently Paul Ricoeur, who (as mentioned above) compares the task of hosting the stranger to the act of translating. Taylor uses Ricoeur's philosophy of translation to show that hospitality is best understood not as an effortless exchange of ideas but as the ongoing task of opening oneself to the stranger by working to make room within one's life, home, language and culture. That is, the task of translating one world into another disrupts the hosts' settled existence and requires us to engage in what Ricoeur calls a "work of mourning" whereby we relinquish the illusory attachments and ideals that prevent us from welcoming the stranger into our lives. Taylor draws upon the "translator's task of surrendering his desire for a perfect translation" to show the way in which we must relinquish our desire for complete agreement with the guest. He concludes by considering the consequences of this transformative encounter for the especially challenging task of interreligious hospitality.

In the next chapter, Joseph O'Leary takes up the problem of interreligious hospitality, and particularly the tangled history of East-West religious dialogue, by examining a number of the more prominent historical and philosophical attempts to engage the other on its own terms. Emphasizing the difficulties, and often outright failures of these approaches, O'Leary also notes the ways in which certain Western thinkers like Kant, Schopenhauer, Hegel, Heidegger and Rahner also succeeded, each in their own way, in opening a door to a conversation with Eastern thought and religion that still needs to take place. O'Leary suggests that if such a conversation is to happen, we must find a balance between refusing to engage the mysterious or inscrutable other and plunging indiscriminately into each other's texts and traditions without any concern for their cultural and linguistic difference. While praising the work of the Second Vatican Council for its intrepid call to interreligious openness and dialogue, he also calls for Western religion to unlearn its habit of creating rigid paradigms that cannot help but exclude all that is alien, and finally for the development of a sensitive and flexible methodology that will look for new and creative possibilities of encounter "as multifarious as those of our everyday lives and relationships."

Catherine Cornille's chapter explores some of the challenges involved in the concrete practice of interreligious hospitality as it takes place in the sharing of a meal, practicing of a ritual or in embracing the other's way of thinking, all of which, she suggests, are likely to generate numerous tensions and experiences of discomfort. Cornille candidly acknowledges that these experiences may convince the participants that their attempts at interreligious hospitality are more harmful than beneficial and lead them to abandon their efforts. But she insists these impasses may also lead to a deeper understanding of the true meaning of religious hospitality and to a greater recognition of and respect for the other as other. The fact that a full realization of interreligious hospitality remains an eschatological rather than a present reality, may also, Cornille tells us, shed a forgiving and hopeful light on and beyond such limitations.

In the next chapter Kalpana Seshadri examines the hospitality of rituals by looking at two practices common to most world traditions, that of leave-taking, i.e. of saluting a departing guest, and of offering food. Speaking from within the Indian context, Seshadri finds that these two acts, which are each as central to the practice of hospitality as the welcoming of a guest, are both present in the pageantry of the funeral ritual. Through close attention to the scene of "the last departure," Seshadri develops this connection between leave-taking and offering food, and suggests that this allows us to conceive of hospitality as an open-ended, never completed form of mediation.

The first section comes to a close with Jacob Meskin's reflections on religious-secular hospitality. While the first four chapters investigate various aspects of hospitality between religions—the necessary attitudes (Taylor), historical exigencies (O'Leary), concrete practices (Cornille), and specific rituals (Seshadri)—the fifth chapter examines the complex relation between religious and secular perspectives. Meskin argues that much can be learned through the hospitable exchange of ideas and affirms that each side is deeply indebted to the other—secular thought to religious traditions and recent religious thought to secular developments and ideals. But he also cautions that this is only half the story, and that too often this rapprochement results in a facile assimilation of one tradition to the other. With this warning in mind, Meskin takes up the question of Derrida's highly influential work on hospitality and asks to what extent the accepted story of its deep indebtedness to Jewish thought and tradition generally, and to Levinas in particular, is accurate. He finds that although Derrida appropriates many Jewish and Levinasian elements, he lacks a distinctively Jewish sense of home, which keeps him from understanding the great value of the Jewish account of home for hospitality.

The second section opens with two essays on Jewish hospitality, both of which confirm the importance of the connection between a home and hosting the stranger in the Jewish tradition. Ed Kaplan offers a spiritual exegesis of hospitality through an exploration of relevant biblical and talmudic passages and Jewish holidays—Sukkot and Passover—and shows the way the experience of home (whether as absent or present) affects the Jewish approach to hospitality. Both holidays teach Israel to treat the stranger with respect and to offer the stranger hospitality by reminding the Jews that they too were strangers in a foreign land. Kaplan notes that this pedagogy of the stranger has extended to modern day secular Jews that find here a calling to universal responsibility and solidarity with the oppressed. Kaplan concludes with a spiritual reflection on prayer as a practice of experiencing God's hospitality. Drawing from a speech by Rabbi Heschel, Kaplan suggests that it is this experience—of "infinite hospitality"—that can allow us to turn our exile on the earth into a pilgrimage toward God.

Hugh Cummins develops the connection between the Jewish holiday of the cabins, Sukkot, and Emmanuel Levinas's reflections on dwelling in a home and hospitality to the stranger as they are found in *Totality and Infinity* and *Otherwise than Being*. Cummins finds in the Jewish festival, as well as in both of Levinas's major works, a way of understanding the home, not as an enclosure for keeping the familiar in and the unfamiliar out, but as a site already exposed to both host and stranger. More specifically, he develops the link between Levinas's reflections on ethical subjectivity as opened to the other, and therefore as already broken open to the exterior, and the sukkah—a temporary shelter, partially open to God and the elements (the sky, the wind, strangers on the road). Both the subject and the sukkah, on Cummins's reading, are determined in advance by the anterior other, which means that the temporary dwelling they inhabit is already a site of hospitality to the stranger. This reflection on the anteriority of the other leads Cummins to a thoughtful consideration of the demands and difficulties of hospitality for Israel today.

Next are the two chapters on Christian hospitality. Patrick Hederman tells us that a true understanding of hospitality requires that we recognize the hospitality shown to us by God as he draws us out of our petty preoccupations and destructive ambitions by adopting us as sons and daughters, and therefore as members of the divine family. This process, Hederman insists, involves liberating us from those natural racist and xenophobic habits—by which we attempt to protect and secure ourselves against the dangers of enemies and strangers—and transforming us into genuinely altruistic selves, capable of showing hospitality to our enemies. According to Hederman this transformative hospitality is the gift of Judaism and Christianity to the world.

Moyaert develops a notion of Christian hospitality—drawn, we will see, from the same Abrahamic well that waters the Jewish and Islamic traditions—as a responsibility to the other that takes precedence over concern for oneself. She proposes Abraham as a preeminent example of this other-oriented hospitality, pointing out that when he hosted the strangers at the Mamre tree, he boldly, or perhaps foolhardily, allowed God to wait until the others were provided for. This illustrates, Moyaert tells us, that at the heart of the Abrahamic faiths is the priority of the universal—the well-being of others, of the world—over the particular—the narrow attempt to preserve one's own life and satisfy one's own desires. With this inaugural example of hospitality in the background, Moyaert turns to the challenges of contemporary interreligious hospitality. She appeals to Ricoeur's work on narrative identity to illustrate the inter-dependence of self and other and to warn against the constant temptation to xenophobic isolation that threatens to derail interreligious dialogue and degenerate into hatred and violence. Following Ricoeur, Moyaert proposes as a counter-measure to these destructive identity games the sharing and interpretation of our sacred narratives, which she suggests will allow us to learn from each other to see in our old stories and traditions new possibilities for a more peaceful and hospitable future.

John Makransky opens the Buddhist hospitality section by drawing upon the Buddhist epistemological insight that our mind's process of grasping onto an isolated, autonomous sense of self alienates us from others by reducing them to self-referential value labels ("my friend," "my enemy," "stranger to me," etc.). Makransky notes that through this conceptualizing process, all persons are rendered strangers in the sense that they are cognitively mistaken for our own limiting thoughts of them. These artificial barriers can be dissolved, according to Makransky, through the experience of the emptiness of self and other—a groundless intimacy in which no one can be sensed as a stranger.

Andy Rotman offers an examination of hospitality in Indian Buddhist literature, which, he points out, provides insight into the central questions of Buddhist ethics. These ancient accounts, Rotman tells us, illustrate the Buddhist category of unplanned giving, by focusing on how one treats a guest who arrives unexpectedly and at an inopportune time. By looking at the component parts of these interactions—the intention of the donor, the value of the gift, and the qualities of the recipient—he sheds light on the ways that Buddhists tried to increase their stockpiles of merit by transforming chance encounters into moments of efficacious giving. Rotman's reflections show us the way in which these interactions help form an important template for Buddhist conceptions of right action.

From Buddhist hospitality we move to two essays on Islamic hospitality. Dana Sajdi approaches hospitality not through the usual route of returning to the canonical Islamic texts or to the intellectual tradition, but through a sociological investigation into the theory and practice of inter-Muslim hospitality in the early modern Levant. By traversing the social and discursive practices of Muslim scholars and mystics that denote social hierarchy—such as appellation, seating arrangements, and burial habits—Sajdi illustrates the contradictions in the acts by which one would make the stranger more familiar or the neighbor more strange. Rather than offering a fixed description of a particular form of inter-Islamic hospitality, Sajdi raises the question whether the refusal to become familiar to others may actually be a willed act. Thus, by viewing hospitality sociologically and historically, Sajdi is able to suggest that being a stranger may itself have been a desired performance. This surprising conclusion allows us to view the task of hospitality to the stranger in a new light.

Joseph Lumbard's essay points out that Muslim custom demands that hospitality be two-directional. Not only does the host have to welcome the guest, but it is imperative that the guest accepts the host's offer as well. Relating a personal story in which he accepted of a cup of water from a stranger that he knew would make him sick, Lumbard emphasizes the costs and blessings of hospitality to and from the stranger. He uses the anecdote to illustrate that Muslim hospitality requires that the person giving or receiving must be more concerned about the other than about himself, even (in ancient practice) to the point that the host would often disregard his own needs and impoverish his family. While such extravagant displays of hospitality are no longer part of Islamic custom, the spirit of selfless giving and receiving remains central to the practice of hospitality. Lumbard notes that this two-way practice serves as a reminder both of one's nothingness before God and of one's potential sanctity, which can be achieved in the many diverse selfless ways of giving and receiving: in sharing a meal with the rich and the poor, in breaking a fast for the sake of another's hospitality, in providing for those in need, and ultimately, in opening one's heart to others.

The Hindu hospitality section begins with Frank Clooney's treatment of the foundations of hospitality as they are expounded in the ancient religious classic, the *Taittiriya Upanishad*. According to Clooney, the teaching of the *Upanishad* is clear: human reality is comprised of spiritual realities grounded in material things; the inner self is deeply interconnected with the body; spiritual flourishing is inseparable from well-being in the actual world. Clooney points out that this ancient emphasis on the vital connection between spirit and body can help us to understand why it is that food—its production, consumption, and sharing—is a key sacrament of the fullness of human life. Clooney's account reminds us that while the *Upanishad* is more than 2,500 years old, its principles remain pertinent and influential today.

The volume comes to a close with Swami Tyagananda's poignant reflection on Hindu hospitality as an act of worship. He points out that worship means giving from man to God and that this can be done inside or outside of a temple, through selfless acts of work and giving. He writes that "life offers infinite opportunities to extend hospitality in one form or another," and draws on the words of Vivekananda to show that even the apparently unreligious person who practices selfless acts can arrive to the same place as the religious person who prays or the philosopher who reflects. Tyagananda also points out that all religions will recognize a human being "who is ready to sacrifice himself for others." These claims, he notes, are grounded in the idea that the only possible guest is God, even if at times it takes us a while to recognize this fact. Tyagananda ends with two stories from India—one mythological and the other contemporary—that testify to the presence of this divine guest who turns up in unexpected places and brings blessings in unforeseen ways.

* * *

Most of the essays in this volume were originally delivered as papers at seminars and conferences organized by the International Guestbook Project. This project was inaugurated by Richard Kearney at Boston College in 2009 and has since seen the organization of a number of interreligious events, performances, conferences and documentaries throughout the world, including Ireland, France, Kosovo, Jerusalem and Bangalore. This volume is one of several publications resulting from the ongoing Guestbook Project, whose aim is to create a "global classroom without walls" on the subject of host and guest, self and stranger, hostility and hospitality. Other publications include two companion volumes, *Phenomenologies of the Stranger*, edited by Richard Kearney and Kascha Semonovitch (Fordham University Press, 2011) and *Journeys of the Heart: Essays in Interreligious Imagination*, edited by Richard Kearney and Eileen Rizo Patron (Brill, 2010), as well as "Hospitality: Imagining the Stranger," special issue of *Religion and the Arts* (Fall 2010), edited by Christopher Yates and James Najarian, and a special section of essays from the "Hosting the Stranger" Guestbook Seminar, Boston College, 2009, in *New Arcadia Review* (2011), edited by Thomas Epstein and Kascha Semonovitch. These and related Guestbook seminars and conferences on the theme of hospitality/hostility toward the other are archived on guestbookproject.com.

* * *

Finally, we wish to acknowledge the generous support of the Institute of Liberal Arts and the Jesuit Institute at Boston College, Glorianna Davenport of MIT, Frank Clooney of the Centre for World Religions at Harvard University, Siddartha at the Pipal Tree Institute for Intercultural and Interreligious dialogue at Bangalore, and The Forum for Cities in Transition project at the University of Massachusetts, directed by Padraig O'Malley. We also wish to thank the following for their invaluable support in the conception and preparation of this volume: Joseph O'Leary of Sophia University, Tokyo; Nóirín ní Riain and the Monks of Glenstal Abbey, Ireland; Larry Friedlander (Stanford University); Petra Taylor (Harvard University) and Anne Kearney (Boston College).

PART ONE
HOSTING STRANGERS

CHAPTER 1

HOSPITALITY AS TRANSLATION

James Taylor

It is not good for man to be alone.

—*Genesis 2:18*

Hosting the stranger is a formidable task. To open our lives to any guest is to allow our comfortable patterns of behavior to be interrupted, at least for a time, as we attempt to provide a welcoming place for the other to dwell. But when it comes to hosting the stranger, who by definition is unfamiliar, enigmatic, and often a little disconcerting, we may wonder whether hospitality is possible at all. Is it possible to welcome the stranger into my life, world, culture and tradition without misinterpreting or offending her? If so, what would such hospitality involve? How might host and stranger enter into a relationship that isn't fraught with misunderstanding, resentment and discord, and that doesn't result in more suffering than it alleviates? Particularly when it comes to the difficult challenge of interreligious hospitality, how might it be possible for the world's religions—Islam, Judaism, Hinduism, Buddhism, Christianity, etc.—to engage in an encounter that would be expansive and enriching rather than coercive and oppressive?

It seems to me that the primary obstacle to hosting the stranger is not that we are ignorant or disrespectful of traditions other than our own, and the main challenge is not to learn to preserve the unique character of those traditions. Rather, I believe our most important and difficult task is to come to terms with our limitations as hosts, and specifically with the fact that we are incapable of offering perfect hospitality to the stranger. We cannot reach a state of perfect justice or harmony that would allow us to relate to our guest without offending him or violating his integrity as a stranger. Nor can we protect ourselves from the suffering that comes with being finite and fallible human beings rather than sovereign or omnipotent hosts. But the challenge is to acknowledge these limitations, to recognize that suffering and strife are inevitable, and to open the door anyway. I will suggest that if we hope to become gracious hosts we must not avoid such suffering but must enter more fully into it by working through the risks and failures involved in hosting the stranger and allowing ourselves to become transformed by the encounter.

Paul Ricoeur proposes that this transformative encounter can be best under-stood through the model of translation. By translating the stranger's world—his symbols, narratives, rituals and practices—into my own world, and by allowing my life to be translated into his foreign idiom, I can learn to understand myself not as an autonomous ego but as one stranger among others. Through this translation process, and specifically through what Ricoeur refers to as a "work of mourning" whereby we surrender our desire for *perfect or ideal hospitality*, we can become capable of *imperfect but real hospitality* to the actual strangers that knock on our doors looking for food or shelter and asking to share our homes, lives, traditions, cultures and religions. Before I examine the translation model of hospitality and show how it can be used to expand and enrich the interreligious encounter, I will offer some general reflections on the demands and difficulties of hosting the stranger.

The Impossibility of Hospitality

Why is hosting the stranger so challenging? What leads certain thinkers to insist that such hospitality is not merely difficult but impossible? As ethical philosophers like Emmanuel Levinas and Jacques Derrida have reminded us, hospitality requires that we respect the stranger as other, which means that we must avoid reducing her to our own preformed categories of meaning. The stranger, in this view, is totally transcendent to us, "wholly other,"[1] and therefore cannot be interpreted according to our familiar meanings and concepts. Derrida remarks that "[hospitality] requires that I open up my home . . . to the absolute, unknown, anonymous other . . . that I let them come, let them arrive . . . without asking of them reciprocity (entering into a pact) or even their names."[2] Hospitality, in other words, must leave the stranger a stranger.

But this creates a problem insofar as in order to treat the stranger with hospitality I need to relate to him, approach him, speak to him and understand him. Indeed, if I am to welcome him into my home and attempt to provide for his needs, I must have some idea of what those needs are, of who he is, where he comes from, what he likes and dislikes, what food he eats and doesn't eat, not to mention what he considers sacred or offensive. And the converse is also true. We must, as Derrida suggests, "ask the foreigner to understand us, to speak our language" as well.[3] It would seem then that I must both understand the stranger and refuse to understand the stranger, relate to her and refuse to relate to her, offer her hospitality and refuse her hospitality.

Derrida gives the sharpest formulation of this paradoxical demand in *Of Hospitality*, where he insists that hospitality, strictly speaking, is impossible.[4] Our attempts to understand the other as other, to do justice to his singularly unique existence, cannot help but violate that singularity by reducing him to our own predetermined categories. We are caught in an inescapable bind. The more we "[make] the other a part of us," the more "the other no longer quite seems to be the other."[5] Hospitality demands that I treat the stranger as a stranger, as other than myself, and yet each of my attempts to do so has the opposite effect and brings the stranger more firmly into my familiar horizons. But if each of our attempts results in the domestication of the stranger then "this hospitality is no longer an absolute hospitality, is no longer graciously offered beyond debt and economy, invented for the singularity of the new arrival, of the unexpected visitor."[6]

This means that despite my best efforts, I can never really treat the stranger with hospitality. In fact, on this reading, I can never truly relate to the stranger at all. Rather than understanding him in his otherness, I am left with an illusion or a figment of imagination, drawn more from my own self-projections and desires than from the stranger himself, who, according to Derrida, continues to recede behind my interpretations, remaining "inaccessible, solitary, transcendent,"[7] and therefore unwelcomed, even as I attempt to open a hospitable place for him to dwell. For Derrida, moreover, what is true of the stranger is true of any other whatsoever: friend, neighbor, family member or God. Each is singular, inscrutable and wholly distinct:

> [W]hat can be said about Abraham's relation to God can be said about my relation without relation to every other (one) as every (bit) other, in particular my relation to my neighbor and my loved ones who are as inaccessible to me, as secret and transcendent as Jahweh. Every other (in the sense of each other) is every bit other (absolutely other).[8]

The closest we can get to the stranger is to catch sight of footprints, "traces" or "cinders" that indicate that the other has passed through but that always fail to tell us fully who she is, where she is going, or even where we may look for her.[9]

The primary difficulty with hosting the stranger therefore is that self and other are incommensurable, "infinitely other in [their] absolute singularity,"[10] which means that any attempt to interpret the other through one's own predetermined categories, no matter how ethical or responsible it may be, will involve violence to the other. Like a secret that if told would cease to be secret, a stranger if made familiar would cease to be a stranger. Thus, no matter how hard we may try to do justice to the other's unique existence, we will fail to reach him, and therefore fail to treat him as other.

We must note, however, that these severe reflections on the nature of otherness do not keep Derrida from insisting that justice must be served, that others must be provided for and that strangers must be hosted. In fact, he finds in the impossibility of hospitality not a license to avoid the task, but a constant provocation to be more hospitable and more generous, to be always more vigilant in our attempts to do justice to the other.[11] That is to say, for Derrida the impossibility of perfect hospitality is precisely what makes possible the limited, imperfect hospitality we are capable of showing the stranger. Accordingly, this impossibility should not dissuade us from our task, but rather incite us further toward the goal of perfect or unconditional hospitality.

Hospitality, then, must be the task of minimizing violence, of being as true as possible to the other's singularity, while recognizing at the same time that these attempts are themselves violations of that singularity. As we intensify our efforts to treat the stranger more justly, we are drawn toward her as to a disappearing zero point that we can never reach. We must continue to approximate that impossible point at which perfect justice would be done, even as we realize that such a hope remains a desire and dream rather than a real possibility.[12]

Perfect hospitality is impossible. This point, it seems to me, is irrefutable. But the question we may want to ask is, "what do we do with this impossibility?" How do we respond to our failure to offer the stranger absolute or unlimited hospitality?

Translation and the Work of Mourning

Ricoeur advocates a different approach to hospitality. He agrees with Derrida that to treat the stranger with perfect hospitality is impossible, and he agrees that we must come to terms with this failure if we hope to become welcoming hosts. But he disagrees that we should therefore continue to strive for such perfection, and that this failure should strengthen our resolve and sharpen our focus, even though we can never accomplish such a goal. Rather, for Ricoeur, we must come to terms with the impossibility of perfect hospitality precisely in order to surrender the desire altogether. We must recognize perfection not as an ideal that would continue to guide our actions, but as a harmful desire that keeps us from relating to each other as finite and fallible human beings, and that ultimately keeps us from recognizing that we too are strangers on the earth.

On this reading, the primary obstacle to hospitality is not simply that we continue to misunderstand each other, and the solution is not to find a way minimize violence. Rather, the real problem is that we are not comfortable with the idea of failure, and specifically with the fact that despite our best efforts we cannot reach perfect accord with one another. There is a deep drive within us, Ricoeur believes, for a perfect meeting of minds, a dream of absolute correspondence and harmony, and this dream keeps us from relating to each other as we are, as limited, fallible human beings rather than omnipotent, sovereign egos capable of lifting ourselves out of our individual contexts and uniting in one universal meta-perspective. Such acts may be possible for the gods but not for us human beings who must continue to misunderstand each other as we muddle along through our halting and fragmented attempts to communicate, and finally learn to accept each other for what we are: disheveled, imperfect, often offensive and unrefined strangers, but capable of genuine acts of grace and kindness nonetheless.

As hosts, our primary task is to engage in what Ricoeur refers to as a "work of mourning," a process he compares to the translator's task of relinquishing his desire for a perfect translation.[13] Just as the host must let go of her desire for perfect agreement with her guest, so must the translator surrender his desire to capture the original text completely in his native language. In fact, the successful translator must remain completely impartial, treating each language as an equally important conversation partner, if she is to allow the original text to speak authentically in a foreign idiom. Paraphrasing Franz Rosenzweig's famous description, Ricoeur writes: "to translate . . . is to serve two masters:

the foreigner in his strangeness, the reader with his desire for appropriation."[14] Through this "dual fidelity," the translator must allow each language to make its specific demands and solicitations and insist upon its peculiar ambiguities, and he must do his best to accommodate their requests. Only if the translator succeeds in maintaining this double devotion to the end, will he be able to render a "good translation" that "does justice" to the original.

An example can help us understand what happens when the translator fails to relinquish his attachment to one of the languages. In Vladimir Nabokov's English translation of Pushkin's *Eugene Onegin* we can see the way in which the translator's devotion to the nuances of the Russian language led to the expansion of a 200-page original into a four-volume work of text and commentary that many would say was more successful as a work of criticism than as a translation. Although Nabokov's keen attention to and admiration for the Russian classic allowed him to preserve much of the cultural, historical, psychological and literary subtlety of the original, this single-mindedness also prevented him from fully embracing the range and resource of English, and from allowing the text to enter unreservedly into a new context. One could say that Nabokov's refusal to let go of the original resulted in a masterful piece of commentary but a less successful work of literature.[15]

This example can help us understand why the translator must refuse the urge to privilege one language over the other; why she must stay on the move between the languages as she navigates between the target text and the original in order to find an equitable solution to her particular semantic problems. And it is here, Ricoeur tells us, in this seemingly never-ending circulation process, and specifically in the frustration the translator will inevitably feel at not being able to find an appropriate word, that he will come to experience each language as inexorably unique, and come to terms with the fact that no one language is capable of capturing the other, or of "saying it all." Ricoeur explains that the more the translator attempts to remain faithful to each language, the more she will find that they are "irreducible to one another":

> Not only are the semantic fields not superimposed on one another, but the syntaxes are not equivalent, the turns of phrase do not serve as a vehicle for the same cultural legacies; and what is to be said about the half-silent connotations, which alter the best defined denotations of the original vocabulary, and which drift, as it were, between the signs, the sentences, the sequences whether short or long? It is to this heterogeneity that the foreign text owes its resistance to translation . . .[16]

The translator will then realize that there is simply too much distance between the linguistic fields—with their different semantic systems, divergent syntactical structures, and incompatible networks of reference—for her to bring them together into one final, all-encompassing translation.

But this recognition is only half the battle, and if the translator decides, despite her frustrations, to press on to the next stage of her journey, she will be faced with the difficult task of choosing inadequate words and settling for an imperfect translation.[17] This translated word is a painful word insofar as it requires the translator to do violence to the original, to choose a phrase or idiom that leaves important things unsaid and fails to express a range of meanings that are essential to a sentence, phrase or passage. She must be willing to inflict this violence on the text, even though her decisions may continue to haunt her even after the translation is completed, reminding her that she failed to accommodate both languages, each of which remains at least partially without voice, stifled or neglected by her particular interpretive choices. This final stage is especially difficult for the translator insofar as to choose a word that doesn't say it all is to "betray" one or both of her linguistic "masters," which is to fail at the task she had set out to accomplish in the first place.

She must fail in order to succeed. We see here the same recurring dynamic whereby in order to gain one must be willing to lose. In this case the loss is the ideal of a perfectly hospitable translation, which would satisfy each partner completely and without reserve. The translator is finding out the hard way that such a dream is impossible. More precisely, she is finding that she cannot finish the translation until she admits failure and relinquishes the ideal, or as Ricoeur puts it, until she "acknowledges and assumes the irreducibility of the pair, the peculiar and the foreign,"[18] and until she recognizes "the impossibility . . . of serving two masters: the author and the reader,"[19] the stranger and the host.

And yet, in spite of these difficulties, the translation does get finished, and the translator finds, to her surprise, that her imperfect or "sufficient translation" is actually better than any perfect translation could be. This is, first, because her translation is real or actual as opposed to imaginary and ideal, and second, because it has a life of its own. The translated text, that is, turns out not to be simply an approximation of the original but a legitimate work in its own right, with its own set of internal dynamics and its own different system of references and allusions, which means that the reader can find there a number of surprising and profound connections, ambiguities and nuances that were not present in the original. In this sense we can understand translation not only as a work of fidelity, but also as what Walter Benjamin refers to as a "stage [of the original's] continued life," and we can see that this translation "manifests a specific significance [already] inherent in the original."[20]

What's more, the translated text itself often comes to provide the original with an expanded life. Precisely by developing new semantic resonances and allusions, it is able to rebound back upon the original to indicate new possibilities and connections that weren't previously visible. In this way, translation sets up a creative exchange between the languages that increases both texts' semantic resources and deepens and expands their referential horizons. Since each text is a linguistic creation in its own right, with its own structural and artistic integrity, and yet since each remains "the same" work, the tension between the two results in more meaning rather than less. Not in the diminishment of the original, as the translator had initially thought as she made her difficult choices, but in the amplification of the original, which now finds itself enlarged and enriched with new semantic possibilities and a whole new set of intriguing readings to explore.

The important point here is that this fecund exchange would be impossible had the translator succeeded in rendering a perfect translation. It is precisely the difference between the two, "an equivalence without identity"[21] as Ricoeur puts it, which is responsible for the distance necessary for this productive interchange of possible meanings. To put it another way, it is the translator's willingness to recognize her inability to reach out and capture the text without remainder that has allowed the two texts to enter into a creative partnership and to share with each other their unique cultural and semantic resources. By surrendering the "fantasy of perfect translation"[22], she finally comes to experience what Ricoeur refers to as the translator's "reward," by which he means the "happiness associated with translating" and the "pleasure" that comes from gaining access to a new and "irreducible" linguistic partner.[23] This translation, moreover, has allowed the translator to experience her own language as well as equally strange and irreducible. Emphasizing the importance of mediation by the foreign language, Ricoeur asks (rhetorically):

> [Without] the test of the foreign, would we be sensitive to the strangeness of our own language? Finally, without that test, would we not be in danger of shutting ourselves away in the sourness of a monologue, alone with our books? [24]

The foreign language has allowed us (translators) to see "our own language as one language among others,"[25] to come to terms with the fact that there are only "peculiar" or specific, concrete languages that each lay claim to a particular, unique way of carving up the world, and which are therefore—through the creative exchange involved in translation—vitally important to the others as well.

It may be helpful, at this point, to reflect briefly on how this translation paradigm relates to our general problem of hospitality to the stranger. It seems to me that Ricoeur's description of the translator's work of mourning can help us understand what is required of any host who hopes to welcome a stranger into his world. Namely, and most importantly, we will have to come to terms with our limits and recognize that we are incapable of facilitating a perfectly harmonious and peaceful encounter. We will have to recognize that we cannot reach a point of pure, unmediated communion or engage in an absolutely hospitable act that would avoid misunderstanding or offense. Such acts, Ricoeur tells us, are "pure fantasy," and stem from a "desperate refusal of the human condition, which is that of multiplicity at all levels of existence."[26] But if we follow Ricoeur rather than Derrida here, this recognition that such pure hospitality is impossible will lead us not to intensify and redouble our efforts to reach this impossible *ideal*, but to relinquish the desire and to opt instead for an imperfect but genuine relationship to another *real* human being. In other words, we must surrender one world in order to gain access to two, and in order to be able, finally, to affirm that two is better than one, and that it is not good for man to be alone.

Translating between Religions

What conclusions might we draw from Ricoeur's hermeneutics of translation for the task of interreligious hospitality? We must keep in mind, of course, that hospitality between religions is a particularly challenging endeavor. Here we are not talking only about cultural difference or personal preference, but about sacred traditions that speak to matters of ultimate importance. Traditions that, through the years, one must admit, have often failed to treat each other hospitably, opting instead for religious persecution, subjugation and colonization. But there are many important and inspiring exceptions to this rule as well, and there is good reason to hope that hospitality will become more and more a defining feature of the world's religions. The brief remarks that follow are attempts to gesture toward what such religious openness may require and how it may be carried out.

It seems to me that two related aspects of interreligious hospitality must be emphasized here: the horizontal dimension, which considers how it may be possible for the world's religions to enter into a hospitable encounter with one another, and the vertical dimension, which asks more specifically about what is involved in our encounter with God. The key to both of these dimensions, in keeping with the theme of this essay, is the stranger, and specifically the ability to relate to the other—whether another religious tradition or God—as a stranger rather than as a projection of one's own desires, prejudices and illusions.

With these two goals in mind, we should note first that it is Ricoeur himself who proposes that the translator's "linguistic hospitality" can serve as a model for other forms of hospitality: interpersonal, intercultural and most notably for us, interreligious hospitality:

> Bringing the reader to the author, bringing the author to the reader, at the risk of serving and of betraying two masters: this is to practice what I like to call linguistic hospitality. It is this which serves as a model for other forms of hospitality that I think resemble it: confessions, religions, are they not like languages that are foreign to one another, with their lexicon, their grammar, their rhetoric, their stylistics which we must learn in order to make our way into them? And is eucharistic hospitality not to be taken up with the same risks of translation-betrayal, but also with the same renunciation of the perfect translation?[27]

Ricoeur follows his own suggestion regarding the connection between linguistic hospitality and religious hospitality up to a point, but he doesn't develop the religious model with anything like the specificity he treats other dimensions and disciplines like psychoanalysis, metaphor, narrative, etc. What he does suggest is that a hospitable interreligious dialogue cannot be a facile, syncretistic exchange in which each religion would remain basically as it was but now more aware of what the others think.[28] Rather, it must be a concerted process of intertranslation between the sacred texts, traditions, symbols and practices that make up each religion. As with the translation process outlined above, this religious exchange too will be costly. It will require each religion to be transformed beyond the immediacy of a dogmatic fundamentalism that assumes that it alone is true and capable of providing the answers to life's manifold problems and complexities.[29] Interreligious translation must convince its participants that religion too is plural, and that each religion has something vital to offer that the others don't.

What might this transformative exchange look like? If we follow the above description of the translator's task we can suggest that any authentic encounter will involve an experience of loss on both sides. Only through the two-fold recognition that one's own religious tradition is incapable of understanding or incorporating the other—which speaks its own religious language and operates according to its own religious rhythms—and that the other tradition therefore says something unique and invaluable about God, can one tradition relate to another with openness and hospitality. Here we confront the same hermeneutic paradox mentioned above, namely loss precedes gain, only through the death of one's illusory prejudices and desires is one rewarded with the life of an expanded perspective made possible by the newly forged relationship to a unique religious partner.

We find a helpful example of such interreligious translation in Richard Kearney's recent reflections on the hermeneutics of the religious stranger.[30] Kearney develops Ricoeur's methodological insights into a fully fledged hermeneutics of interreligious hospitality in which religious traditions are brought into living contact with one another through a hermeneutic "cross-reading" of sacred texts and practices, a task Kearney describes as an "endless and reversible process of translation between one religion and the next . . . whose aim is not some unitary fusion but mutual disclosure and enhancement."[31] One tradition, in other words, confronts, challenges, augments and amplifies another via the collaborative exchange of symbols and narratives. To get some idea of how this might work, we can ask, with Kearney:

> What happens, for instance, if we read the text about Shiva's pillars of fire alongside biblical passages on the Burning Bush or the Christian account of Pentecostal flame? What new sparks of understanding and compassion fly up if we read Hindu texts on the *guha* alongside Buddhist invocations of the "void" (in the Heart Sutra) or biblical references to Elijah or Muhammad in his cave, Jonah in the whale, Jesus in the tomb? What novel possibilities of semantic resonance are generated by juxtaposing the sacred bird (*hamsa*) of Vedanta alongside the dove of Noah's ark or of Christ's baptism in the Jordan?[32]

What is essential here is that interreligious translation is not a superficial exchange that reduces the unique narrative power of each tradition in order create a third more tolerant substitute, but the profound and often disconcerting attempt to allow one's own tradition to be shaken up, made questionable, interrogated and reworked by the other. The engagement is genuine, critical and rigorous, and does not result in a new age "recognition" that "we are all on the same page," but rather raises new questions and generates new challenges as it expands our existing horizons of meaning, and ultimately leads to a new understanding of our own religions, now no longer as "sovereign and omnipotent" but as "one religion among others," and therefore as one stranger among other strangers.

But if the process of interreligious translation results in an experience of one's own religious tradition as itself one stranger among others, how does this process affect our experience of God? Put otherwise, if one's experience of God is mediated through the specific sacred texts, practices, symbols and doctrines of one's own tradition, what does this cross-reading do to such an experience? Does one continue to relate to the same God, and in the same way as before? Or has this translation process resulted in a new, perhaps more confused, religious experience? Or perhaps in a loss of faith altogether?

Of course, the answer to this question will vary from person to person, but it must be admitted that there is no way to avoid the risk that one will lose more than one will gain. Although both Ricoeur and Kearney testify to the productive power of creative interreligious exchange, they make no guarantees regarding outcomes, and in fact remind us that any translation process, religious or otherwise, remains a task and a wager rather than a given. With regard to the experience of God after translation then, we must acknowledge that there is no way to foretell just how one's relation to God will be altered, or whether one will like what he finds.

With these provisos in mind however, we can conclude with the following exploratory remarks. Insofar as the process of interreligious translation involves coming to terms with the finite limits of one's own religious perspective, it will inevitably result in the death of a certain God, i.e. that God understood and experienced through that limited religious lens. But insofar as through the transformation of that perspective one comes to recognize the richness and significance of other religious perspectives, the death of a certain (now limited) God is followed by the birth of a much larger, more capacious and generous God, capable of expressing himself in very different ways, through a variety of sacred narratives, historical epiphanies and personal experiences. On the other side of interreligious translation then, and beyond the death of a monocultural god, is an experience of a multilingual, trans-religious God that exceeds our expectations and continues to surprise us with new invitations, solicitations and visitations, welcoming us again and again into his many homes and asking to be welcomed into ours.

In this sense then, we can say that to allow one's God to be translated, and to translate another's, is to substitute a smaller God for a larger one. But by larger here we do not mean more sovereign or omnipotent, but less bound to our predetermined categories and dogmas and more capable of coming and going as He pleases, across the borders of our religions and through the doors of our churches, mosques, temples, synagogues and ashrams. We can suggest that to engage in interreligious translation is not only to experience oneself as a religious stranger, but to experience God as the religious Stranger par excellence, as one who does not fit, wholly and completely into any one tradition and therefore continues to take new shapes, speak different languages and inhabit different religions. And we can suggest that one way to host the divine Stranger is to take up the task of interreligious translation.

CHAPTER 2

WESTERN HOSPITALITY TO EASTERN THOUGHT

Joseph S. O'Leary

The pursuit of intercultural and interreligious inquiry is now attended by talk of empathy, hospitality and other virtues, which are particularly important in sharing at the social and practical level. This moral emphasis often has a monitory note, and can fuel sermons laced with postcolonial theory in the lineage of Edward Said's *Orientalism*. When the Western philosopher or theologian reaches out to grasp some enticing idea from the cornucopia of Eastern traditions, a warning voice will interrupt: "Not so fast! Respect the other tradition, and refrain from using it for your own opportunistic purposes." There is a danger that just as the discipline of religious studies was overrun at one time by obsessive discussions of methodology, so interreligious ventures could succumb to fraught reflections on the whys and hows of "dialogue" at the expense of a deep plunge into the religious and philosophical traditions of other cultures.

A glance at history suggests, however, that these scruples are more than a paralyzing distraction. The Christian hijacking and allegorization of the Hebrew Bible, masterminded by Origen of Alexandria (ca.185–ca.254), stands as an example of how crushing a generous bear-hug can be, especially when it is inspired by an imperialistic sense of superiority. Showing "hospitality" by welcoming the Hebrew scriptures into the Christian canon, the Church claimed to perceive the true value of these texts, to which the Jews were blind, like people generously taking under their own wing the children of parents perceived as unworthy. An incorrect "ethics of translation" played a role in this process. It is ironic that the two major Hellenizers of scripture—Philo of Alexandria and Origen—had only the scantiest knowledge of Hebrew, though the former was a Jewish leader and the latter spent the last two decades of his life in Palestine. The Septuagint, the Alexandrian Greek translation of what Christians now called the Old Testament, was treated as a perfectly adequate version, equally inspired with the Hebrew text. The idea that texts of classic depth and complexity are fundamentally *untranslatable*, that their horizons are *incommensurable* with the horizons of the translating communities, and that there is in consequence an *irreducible pluralism* written into the history of literary, philosophical and theological tradition, did not occur to Christian readers of the Old Testament. Today scholars are more aware that until they read classics in the original languages they have not really read them at all, and this has bred a very salutary modesty among Christian theologians who want to talk about the Hebrew scriptures.

The Western reception of Eastern religion and philosophy has no doubt been marked by a similar "misappropriation of spiritual property."[1] But an excess of scruple about avoiding such misappropriation, an excessive emphasis on untranslatability and incommensurability, may become a pretext for simply dismissing Indian or Chinese sources as too remote from Western questions. Sanskrit, the chief key to the classics of Indian thought and religion, should not be an insuperable barrier, for its study demands no greater prowess than do Greek or Hebrew, languages that centuries of scholars mastered in order to gain access to the classics and the Bible. But just as the transmission of biblical and classical culture has demanded that teachers and students learn to traffic in translations, so a similar regime of translation forms the major bridge between East and West, making it possible to enter quite deeply into several of the intellectual worlds of India, China, Tibet and Japan on the basis of texts and commentaries in English alone. Philosophers have been slow to appropriate these riches, fearing to rush in where Hegel and Schopenhauer boldly trod.

An ethics of hospitality would encourage philosophers to take in ideas from foreign traditions, as one might welcome an unsettling, sometimes unintelligible guest from a foreign country. Such an ethics purifies the motive of "research," making it a hospitable praxis, in which one opens up to new realms of experience, so that study becomes an exploration rather than a matter of securing tighter control of well-known terrain. In Buddhism, the practice of giving is said to destroy passions of avarice, envy, hypocrisy, dissipation, regret, lack of respect, etc.; in the same way intellectual hospitality, which includes the art of being a gracious and grateful guest, can overcome the passions of imperialist arrogance, romantic projection, greedy misappropriation, idle encyclopedic accumulation. In the Perfection of Wisdom sutras, the virtue of giving is seen as perfect when one realizes that neither giver nor gift nor recipient have any real existence. The giving and receiving between philosophical or religious traditions should be characterized by a similar emptiness. The hospitable researcher puts her received identity on hold as she lets her mind be imbued by the world of thought she explores, and she does not objectify that world of thought as other, but seeks to reach a point where the consciousness of otherness has disappeared. The dialogue takes a new form every day, and the two traditions converge together in their shared task of reflection, no longer putting much weight on their previous separate identities. Such intercultural thinking may cease to fit the reassuring rubrics of standard Western philosophy, but if successful it may realize more fully than a narrowly Western perspective could the basic aspirations of philosophy. Indeed, the closed borders of departments of philosophy are now being broken down as philosophers draw on Eastern sources to shed new light on their questions. I am thinking in particular of the "fusion philosophy" of Mark Siderits and Jay Westerhoff, who pursue questions in analytic philosophy drawing on the insights of classical Madhyamaka thinkers.[2]

Exploration goes beyond mere curiosity when it begins to change the identity and the very body of the explorer. The explorer "goes native" when instead of embracing the culture that is explored he lets himself be embraced and absorbed by it. Unfortunately, explorers have more often been "embedded" in enterprises of conquest. Some enterprising missionaries studied indigenous religions, as one might study tropical diseases, in order to refute and extirpate them.[3] The academic world may regard cross-cultural exploration as a scarcely respectable adventure, one likely to end badly when the explorers find that they lack the essential equipment to continue their quest. Here I should like to look back on the triumphs and failures of some thinkers who attempted to receive the gifts of Asian thought. These stories may leave a sense of unfulfilled promise, but they also confirm that the promise remains real, for if the adventures of the "happy few" who studied Asian thought have had only a dim impact on the philosophical mainstream, it nonetheless lies in the logic of things that this is bound to grow, resulting in far-reaching transformations.

Promising Beginnings

What became of the "Oriental Renaissance," which Jules Michelet, impressed by the labors of Eugène Burnouf, envisaged as reuniting the human race, with Buddhism and Christianity functioning as its two spiritual lungs?[4] Sadly, just as the Renaissance vision embodied in the masterpieces of Raphael, Leonardo and Michelangelo was lost in the bitter, narrow feuds of the Reformation and Counter-Reformation, so the Oriental Renaissance was put on hold, and Europe succumbed to forgetfulness of India, a philosophical amnesia.[5] Instead of a great meeting of minds, a fusing of horizons, we had departments of Indology and Sinology, never visited by philosophers or theologians.

The first great Western thinker to show intellectual hospitality to India was Immanuel Kant, in his courses on geography.[6] Foreign travel was a once-in-a-lifetime experience in those days, an experience missed by Kant, Fichte, Schelling, Hegel and Schleiermacher. It was as armchair voyagers, relying on reports of missionaries and colonists, that the great thinkers of the early nineteenth century opened up to the Orient. While this situation did not favor the overcoming of their Eurocentric horizon, we should admire the reach of their curiosity rather than carp at their blind spots. The tone of denunciation so often adopted by academics today toward great thinkers and writers of the past could itself represent a failure of intellectual hospitality.

The publication of Friedrich Schlegel's *Über die Sprache und Weisheit der Indier* in 1808 is a landmark in the European response to India. Schlegel's intellectual hospitality took the form of serious study of Sanskrit from 1803, which he compared with the linguistic efforts of the Renaissance.[7] He appended to his essay translations from Indian verse, which draw on the English versions of Charles Wilkins and contain a fair number of mistakes, and which can be faulted for imposing a European perspective by resolving in a theistic sense the ambiguities in the *Bhagavad-gītā*.[8] His eldest brother Karl August had died in Calcutta in 1789 in the midst of Indian studies, and another brother, August Wilhelm, was to found the discipline of Indology as holder of the first chair in that subject in Bonn in 1818. Friedrich Schlegel's hospitable outlook is expressed in the following utterance:

As in popular history, the Asians and Europeans form only one great family and Asia and Europe one indivisible body, we ought to contemplate the literature of all civilized peoples as the progressive development of one entire system, or as a single perfect structure. All prejudiced and narrow ideas will then unconsciously disappear, many points will first become intelligible in their general connection, and every feature thus viewed will appear in a new light.[9]

This unitary vision no doubt underestimates the pluralism of historical cultures. The mutual illumination of Indian and European thought is more a mosaic of local affinities and homologies than anything that can be raised to the status of a system.[10]

The Renaissance topos is embraced by Schopenhauer too. He claims in the preface to *Die Welt als Wille und Vorstellung* in 1818 that the influence of Sanskrit literature will be no less profound than that of the rediscovered Greek classics in the fifteenth century—a prophecy that may yet come true. Reading everything available on the Upanishads, Vedantism and Buddhism, he found in them the key to a total transformation of the philosophical and religious landscape; unfortunately he did not study Sanskrit. He called Anquetil Duperron's Latin translation of the Upanishads (from Persian) "the most rewarding and elevating reading" in the world: "It has been the consolation of my life and will be that of my dying."[11] But Buddhists could be embarrassed by Schopenhauer's enthusiasm, for "again and again he explains Buddhist concepts as in direct correspondence with his own teachings," e.g. *upādāna* (attachment) becomes "will to life" and *karman* becomes "empirical character."[12] "Indian philosophy is for him less a source of inspiration or revelation than a mirror and medium of self-presentation and self-confirmation."[13] This may seem a defective hospitality, yet it is the warmest that Indian thought received. The very fact that a major philosopher allowed himself to become excited by Indian thought, to the point of placing his entire work under its patronage, outweighs the errors and misappropriations.

The Romantic poets were intoxicated with the new Orientalism, projecting onto Eastern sources their own longing for paradisal origins. This could be the kiss of death, just as the New Age literature that clogs our bookstores drowns out intelligent reception of Eastern thought. Distaste for Romantic effusions kept leading thinkers from joining in the project of an Oriental Renaissance.

The first reaction against this expansion of the humanistic discourse and its cultural canon was hostile, however, because it appeared to weaken the Greek origins of the Western tradition and its cultural identity. Goethe argued from the point of view of artistic taste and his predilection for the human form against what he considered to be "Calcutta nightmares" of transitions into the subhuman and suprahuman.[14]

Buddhologists are grateful that at a later date Nietzsche replaced the Buddha with Zarathustra as the protagonist of his visionary tract, and that Wagner likewise changed his mind about composing a Buddhist music-drama. Had the

Buddha been misappropriated for Nietzschean and Wagnerian purposes, the Western reception of Buddhism might have been fatally compromised.

Hegel's Role

Hegel (whose friend Schelling had referred knowledgeably to Indian religion as early as 1802)[15] scoffed at the idealism of the Romantics, stressing the non-translatability of Indian thought into European categories. Actually, on that point he shows a sensitivity to the linguistic embeddedness of thought, which could be seen as a kind of hospitality to Indian thought in its otherness, a refusal to reduce it to Western categories. He points out for example that the concept of *yoga*—which he defines, insightfully, as "an absorption (*Vertiefung*) without any content"—has no adequate correlative in our languages.[16] Here he humbly echoes the remarks of Wilhelm von Humboldt.[17] Both Humboldt and Hegel are beginning to understand that linguistic areas, or historical epochs within the same linguistic area, can constitute qualitatively different intellectual worlds such that no immediate and transparent terms of understanding are available, so that conversation must begin with tentative efforts to measure just how different the foreign horizon of thought is. Hegel seeks to "ensure that no Indian text would be admitted to the European 'canon' because of translations that led to 'an (involuntary) mystification of it.'"[18] Hegel acutely notes ontological and moral inconsistencies in the *Gītā* and its adherence to an unquestioned caste-ethic. He is impatient with its repetitions, which might have been more tolerable had he had access to the Sanskrit in a Romanized script that he could have tried to decipher. He notes that what later became the Samkhya philosophy is present in the *Gītā* only in an inchoate form. All in all, his study of this classic text is thorough, respectful, and lucidly critical.

For all his scholarly receptivity, Hegel is impeded by his resistance to any kind of thinking that would put the all-sufficiency of the Concept in question. This resistance is clearest in his account of Neoplatonism, which magnifies the noetic aspect and eliminates the entire dimension of the One that is beyond any conceptual grasp.[19] Whenever Indian thought transcends the conceptual to apprehend ultimate reality in contemplative silence, Hegel reads it as stuck on a level of primitive abstract immediacy and as not yet having attained conceptual definition. India, unlike China, he sees as capable of a certain inwardness: "This idealism is present, but without concept, without reason, ruled by mere imagination, without freedom, a mere dreaming that even though it takes its beginning and material from what exists transforms everything into the imaginary."[20]

Another grave impediment to Hegel's reception of Indian thought is his conviction that India is passive and static, and that it represents a long-surpassed element no longer of value to the West: "Had India transmitted a form of concrete culture, one would have to say that the Western peoples could have done nothing better than to forget this element, for they have raised themselves infinitely beyond what makes up the nature of Indian culture."[21] Ignorant of the thought of Sankara, he declares that Indian pantheism has not—and cannot have—the conceptual power of Spinoza, "rather, the entire stuff is dragged into the universal in a raw and immediate way."[22] For pages on end Hegel exhibits the logic, not of Indian culture or thought, but of a prejudiced Eurocentric view of it, even to the point of accepting the slanders of the East Indian Company as the real truth about Indian culture and character.[23] "The British, or rather the East India Company, are the masters of the land; for it is the necessary fate of Asian realms to be subjected to the Europeans."[24] To understand the grip of Eurocentrism on his mind, we should recall that his entire system seemed to confirm a triple convergence: in the history of philosophy, Greece was the place where philosophy was born and Germany was the land that brought it to fulfillment; in the history of religion, Christianity, especially in its reformed German form, best realized the Concept of religion; in history as such the world-spirit moved from East to West and was now borne by Europe, notably by the British Parliament and the Prussian State. Perhaps philosophers cannot overcome this Eurocentrism, even today, except by letting their thinking be fed by non-European sources.

Hegel was misled by an old missionary anecdote to the effect that at the point of death the Buddha confessed that his entire teaching masked an atheistic nihilism; this was taken up by Joseph de Guignes in his *Histoire générale des Huns, des Mongoles, des Turcs et des autres Tartares occidentaux* (1756–1758), which was republished in 1828–30, influencing the 1830 lectures on the philosophy of religion.[25] An English travel report, published in Leipzig in German translation in 1750, is another source for Hegel's view of Buddhism as the religion of nothing: "From nothing, we are told, did everything proceed; to nothing does everything go back."[26] Here the Mahāyāna doctrine of emptiness is reduced to a crude metaphysics. But Hegel could not know this; Nāgārjuna would not be accessible in German until 1911.[27] This frightening vision of Buddhism greatly dampened European enthusiasm for Indian thought: "Hope gave way to fright, dream to nightmare, India as Paradise to Asia as Hell. The pact that was believed to have been sealed was broken by Buddhism."[28] Hegel introduces the notions of God and pantheism into the Buddhist religion, prompted by polemics of the time (against Schleiermacher in the 1824 lectures, against accusations of pantheism in 1827). Though his principal source, H. T. Colebrook, brought him to see that India had developed real philosophies,[29] this insight was not allowed to destabilize his view of the history of philosophy, nor was it taken up by historians of philosophy, who ritually repeated the declaration that philosophy was unique to the Greeks.[30]

We must give Hegel credit for his desire to know the world empirically and his refusal to make an ivory tower of the Concept.[31] His rewriting and rethinking of his philosophy of religion in the four lecture courses of 1821, 1824, 1827 and 1830 might indicate the beginnings of a breakdown, as the superb machinery of the *Science of Logic* proved increasingly irrelevant to the different logics that he seemed to discern in each exposition of the historical sequence of religions. Hegel's changing estimations of Indian religion and thought "indicate that the essentialization of difference within the Hegelian system of cross-cultural understanding was not as fixed as some have supposed."[32] Had he lived longer he might have found that no arrangement of the religions in logical sequence could accommodate the great plurality of religious perspectives. He might then have come to appreciate the relativist currents in India, which even in Vedic times had harbored the thought that "there cannot be a religious or philosophical doctrine valid for all people and for all times."[33] India maintained six philosophical schools recognized as orthodox despite their incompatibility and their unremitting mutual refutations. Beyond that orthodoxy, the Jains developed a subtle perspectivism, while the Buddhist practice of skillful means implied a considerable tincture of relativism.[34] Helmuth von Glasenapp claims: "This 'dynamic' attitude to the concept of truth made possible for Indian philosophy, already in early times, the insight that all efforts to interpret the world can never have more than a provisional and symbolic value."[35] A philosopher of pluralism will have to argue that this Indian outlook is not the scepticism that Hegel's philosophy has integrated and overcome, but a higher vision that goes beyond Hegel's. The construction of such an argument would be a valuable bulwark, keeping philosophical traditions open to other horizons they cannot fully assimilate, and preventing them from closing back on themselves in conceptual self-sufficiency.

Paul Deussen, Nietzsche's schoolmate and a convinced Schopenhauerian Vedantist, resisted Hegel's dismissal of Indian philosophy not by constructing abstract arguments against it, but by devoting the first half of his "general history of philosophy" to the traditions of Asian thought, examined in thorough detail.[36] Deussen asks us to imagine how exciting it would be to meet Martians and to compare their thoughts about the great issues of being and value, life and death, with our own perspectives as earthlings. He suggests that the comparison of Indian and Western philosophy offers just as fascinating an intellectual adventure. But the flood of insights Deussen promised did not take place. The encyclopedic cast of his work perhaps explains why it failed to waken Europe to a philosophical engagement with India, even if it succeeded in planting the idea that Indian philosophy enjoys parity of status with European philosophy. Deussen's excessive hospitality to religious lore risked making philosophy lose all shape and identity. One of the defining marks of philosophy is that it has cast off the leading strings of religion. A historian of philosophy should attempt to distill the purely philosophical achievements of India and East Asia, disengaging them from their religious matrix when they have not already done so themselves. This will demand even more delicate discriminations than in the case of medieval Christian scholasticism, especially given the close association of Buddhist ontological insight with the practice of meditation. (And of course, even in the West, complete clinical separation of philosophical vision from its religious background is rarely possible.)

Heidegger's Hospitality

Heidegger's reluctance to talk of texts that he could not read in the original language is a mark of academic distinction. He would have seen little point in Karl Jaspers' encyclopedic coverage of the Buddha, Nāgārjuna and Lao-Tse, which seems to rely on a hermeneutically naïve belief in some universal inter-translatability of philosophical systems. Heidegger did find some inspiration or confirmation in D. T. Suzuki and in writers on Taoism, but he made no effort to absorb them imperialistically as "hidden sources."[37]

His one published exercise in dialogue with the East is mainly concerned with explaining his own thought to the Japanese interlocutor; but the latter does have an opportunity to expound some suggestive Japanese notions. Discussing the characters that correspond to "form" and "emptiness" in the Heart Sutra ("Form itself is emptiness; emptiness itself is form"), the Japanese explains: "*Iro* means more than color and everything of that sort that the senses perceive. *Ku*, the open, the emptiness of the sky, means more than the super-sensible."[38] A phenomenology that undercuts the Platonic schema that exalts the supra-sensible over the sensible could not but delight Heidegger, who seems more interested in a Japanese immanentist sense of worldhood than in Buddhist emptiness. He does not know of Zen Master Dōgen's (1200–1253) description of language as "flowers of emptiness," but is pleased by an etymology of *kotoba* (speech) as meaning "petals that come from the thing (*koto*)."[39] He identifies the "thing" as beings and their Being. The brief exposure to Japanese language leads him to conclude: "If humans through their language dwell in the claim of being, then we Europeans probably dwell in a quite different house from the people of East Asia."[40] This would imply that "being" is something more than what the West apprehends and addresses humanity through the key words of other civilizations; or perhaps if pushed further Heidegger might be ready to admit that the word "being," and the scenario of its claim and address are constructions of the West, not necessarily applicable to the concerns of Asian thought.

Given how respectfully Heidegger spoke of the other "great beginnings," we can interpret his stance as a hospitable one, putting the stress not on utterances that suggest a Greco-German chauvinism and echo the received idea that philosophy existed only in Greece, but on the modesty of the way he sites the Greek question of being as just one of these "beginnings." This question, in its particular Greek form, lacks any obvious correlative in Indian or Chinese thought.[41] There is a tendency among Christian thinkers today to see Heidegger's concern with the truth of being as intrinsically pagan and anti-Christian,[42] as if his failure to show how it could be placed under a biblical rubric were somehow inhospitable to Judaism and Christianity. In regard to the biblical world, Heidegger's reserve is again due to linguistic modesty and to the perception that ancient Hebrew thought was not concerned with the question of being as such.

The Heideggerian question of being and the Hegelian Concept could serve as platforms for a powerful philosophical dialogue with Asia, if we built on the hospitable dynamics of both—on their open, interrogative, self-revising character. Hegel challenges us to recognize the power of reason at work in Asian philosophical systems, while Heidegger attunes us to their phenomenological dimension, which may turn out to be very remote from the Greek fascination with being.

Rahner and the Religions

It might be thought that theology would have had greater success than philosophy in overcoming Eurocentric horizons, given the excitement about interreligious dialogue and the awareness that we have entered the age of a "world church." Unfortunately, the vitality of the dialogue has often been sapped by scruples about maintaining the integrity of Christian identity and orthodox teaching. Here again a persuasive ethics of hospitality needs to be brought into play. A hospitable mind is one that enters deeply and sympathetically into ways of thinking with which it is in radical disagreement. Interreligious dialogue can be liberally peppered with expressions of disagreement with the tenets of the other religions, but in generous recognition that further study of those religions and of one's own might reduce the disagreement. Ecumenical dialogue between Christian denominations already provides a tried and tested model for this.

Christians, when they think of the other religions, are tempted to settle into an attitude of comfortable inclusivism. This may take a militantly Eurocentric form, when a theologian insists on the providential centrality of Rome, Mediterranean culture, and Greek metaphysics in God's dealings with humanity. Or it may take a more refined, abstract form, as in Karl Rahner's meditation on the structure of human existence as a fore-grasp (*Vorgriff*) of the divine mystery. One who lives in accord with that structure, opening up to the divine, is an "anonymous Christian," though he or she may live as a Buddhist or even as an atheist or an apostate. This way of thinking roots Christianity in universal values, and opens up Christian discourse to philosophical insights into the depths of human nature. It breaks with one dimension of Hegel's triple convergence in that it prepares the ground for a world Christianity no longer centered on the West and on Rome. But in its structure it is dependent on Western metaphysics, taking no account of Eastern perspectives. Nor does it qualify the centrality of Christianity, which is rather reaffirmed in a skillful apologetic.

Rahner's hospitable gesture toward the entire reach of human experience, including that of other religions, remains abstract. He strove to give phenomenological body to his theory of anonymous Christianity, but did not get beyond very general evocations of the situation of the human being before the divine mystery, which were centered on the consciousness of the isolated individual and were immediately translatable into the terms of a metaphysics of finite and infinite. He did not go on to deal with the broad range of human experience, with specific social and political situations, or with the detailed texture of the arts or of particular religions. His metaphysical or dogmatic framework encumbered his effort to encounter the phenomena, as one may see even in his handling of scripture. The phenomena are explained before the labor of interpretation has been undertaken.

Despite the wide circulation of the notion of anonymous Christianity, it has not lent itself to fertile development. Today it no longer feels or looks generous and hospitable to locate Jews, Muslims and Buddhists on a Christian map. A world peopled with anonymous Christians is a surrealistic world in which no one is what they appear to be. A regime of pseudo hospitality keeps the religions in their place and prevents them from unsettling Christian identity. Rahner's vision became a staple reference in the discipline known as "theology of religions," which is commonly more concerned with finding a satisfactory place for the religions in a Christian scheme of things than with actually studying any given religion at close quarters.

The Second Vatican Council expressed a more vivid awareness than Rahner of the empirical reality of the religions, recognizing elements of truth and grace in them and seeing them as reflecting the light of the divine Word and the power of the Spirit moving in all hearts.[43] Through ongoing exchanges such as the interreligious meeting called by Pope John Paul II in Assisi in 1986, the Catholic Church has advanced toward accepting the religions as the normal channels of grace, revelation, and salvation for their adherents. John Paul II gives religions a more crucial salvific role than Vatican II had done, and avoids the aura of pseudo legitimacy suggested by the idea of anonymous Christianity, when he says that God "does not fail to make himself present in many ways, not only to individuals, but also to entire peoples through their spiritual riches, of which their religions are the main and essential expression."[44] Here it is not only in the depths of their spirit that people are open to the mystery of Christ. Rather, it is above all their religious traditions that foster this openness. There is then no need to imagine that, in addition to their deepest religious wisdom, non-Christians also have some arcane connection with Christ of which they are unaware or which must be sought in the twilight region of their unconscious.

If we view the humanity of Christ empirically, in the concrete texture of the numerous relationships that he lived, culminating in his gift of himself as "a ransom for the many" (Mk 10:45), then in dealing with the human response to Christ we need not resort to invisible metaphysical conjunctions but can see how *in their religions* human beings are positioned either in actual dialogue with the message of Christ or in potential dialogue. The other faiths are not a second-rate *ersatz* for the Gospel, but they are turned to the Gospel in a dialogal posture, implicitly or explicitly. From the Christian vantage point all religious communities are seen as visibly striving, with many setbacks, toward the goal designated by Jesus as "the Kingdom of God." Their mutual enrichment in that process should be thought of in terms of complementarity.

Despite such advances toward a richer, more phenomenological and pluralistic awareness of the religions and their cultures, the Vatican maintains an inclusivist insistence that the religions receive their goodness and grace from the mystery of Christ. A certain theological logic obliges us to see Christ at work in the background of the other religions, and yet it is felt that this solution is more a puzzle for further reflection than a fully satisfying vision. Mulling over the puzzle quickly becomes a futile speculation. There comes a time when such questions and theories must be shelved for later discussion, since they hinder the really fruitful pursuit of interreligious thought and engagement. Suffice it to recognize the blessings abundant in the world's religions and cultures and to bring the values of the Gospel into dialogue with them. The need for a lofty theoretical framework for this activity is perhaps a need that should be unlearnt. By all means let theologians draw on "Christocentric," "theocentric" and "regnocentric" pictures of how the religions relate to the Christian faith.[45] But these paradigms should not become dogmatic straitjackets. Rather they are merely vague ways of thinking to be brought into play only when found useful and illuminating.

The implication of this is that a Christian vision of the religions—as striving along with Christianity toward the future Kingdom of God, for instance—is merely a practical regulative idea, not a speculative Concept that can claim to understand the religions better than they understand themselves. Encyclopedic overviews of the entire history of human intellectual, aesthetic, political or religious activity can no longer be reduced to the unity of a system in which history becomes a logical progression. Rather we are presented with avenues of exploration and possibilities of encounter as multifarious as those of our every-day lives and relationships. Such experience is unified not only by our ideas, which are always only provisional sketches, but also by the ethical principles we bring to bear on it, and notably by the determination to practice the art of intellectual hospitality.

CHAPTER 3

INTERRELIGIOUS HOSPITALITY AND ITS LIMITS

Catherine Cornille

In the discourse on religious pluralism, the notion of interreligious hospitality has become the new motto, upheld as the only way forward toward peaceful and positive religious coexistence. Paul Ricoeur discusses it as one of his pro-grammatic principles for the future of religious relationships,[1] Martin Marty dubs it as the positive rendering of counter-intolerance,[2] I propose it as not only a necessary but a sufficient condition for interreligious dialogue,[3] and Amos Young has developed a veritable theology of hospitality in relation to people of other faiths.[4] There are various reasons for the appeal. The idea of hospitality implies recognition of the other as other, as a stranger who is welcomed in spite of fundamental differences in background, beliefs and way of life. It creates an atmosphere of friendship and trust in which those differences are not only tolerated but engaged in an open and constructive way. Moreover, the virtue of hospitality plays a role in most religious traditions, and extending it to the religious other seems like a relatively small step.

In focusing on only the Christian tradition, it is clear that hospitality to the stranger permeates both scripture and tradition. The Hebrew Bible calls upon the people of Israel to "love the alien as yourself, for you were aliens in the land of Egypt" (Lev. 19:33-34), and in the New Testament Jesus identifies himself directly with the guest in need: "I was a stranger and you welcomed me" (Mt. 25:35). Hospitality thus represents not only a moral injunction, but a spiritual virtue. In welcoming the stranger, one actually receives Christ, which may be seen to blur the roles of host and guest. This approach to hospitality is also at the heart of the later monastic tradition, where, in the Benedictine Rule, hospitality becomes closely tied to humility and to receiving Christ himself. The Christian call to hospitality is unconditional. Whereas the injunction of hospitality in the Hebrew Bible may have at times been restricted by rules of ritual purity,[5] the New Testament places no qualifications on the importance of welcoming and accommodating the stranger. This is evident in Jesus's own attitude toward the Syro-Phoenician woman (Mk 7:24-30), and the centurion (Lk. 7:1-10).[6] Though not belonging to his own ethnic and religious circle, Jesus interacts with these individuals in the most open and receptive way, eventually lifting them up as examples of faith.

It is thus not surprising that the virtue of hospitality has been invoked as the basis for cultivating a more cordial and constructive relationship between Christians and members of other religions. In *Par la foi et l'hospitalité*, the Belgian Benedictine monk and pioneer of intermonastic dialogue, Pierre-François De Béthune, uses the ideal of monastic hospitality as the model for welcoming and recognizing the religious other.[7] He points out that interreligious hospitality involves welcoming the religious other not in spite of, but *in* their difference. It offers the opportunity to shake one out of religious complacency, question one's religious presuppositions, enlarge one's religious understanding, and render one more accountable for one's faith. Viewing the guest belonging to a different religious tradition as an embodiment of Christ moreover stretches the religious imagination to consider the ways in which the Spirit of Christ may be at work in other religious traditions. In addition to this, Martin Marty points to the important critical role of interreligious hospitality.[8] It offers the opportunity to see oneself through the eyes of the other, and to purify the tradition from elements of religious bigotry. It renders one more directly aware of how symbols or rituals may include elements of insult, or how the historical use of those symbols may have left painful scars in the religious memories of others. Rather than removing symbols that may cause offense, Marty suggests moving toward a new interpretation of the stories behind particular symbols.[9] Hospitality thus offers the opportunity to turn the tide of religious suspicion and hatred, of doctrinal antagonism and religious exclusivism. Amos Young, for his part, grounds the notion of interreligious hospitality in the abundant and unconditional hospitality of God and in a "pneumatological theology of guests and hosts." Insofar as God has poured out God's Spirit throughout the world, Christians are invited, nigh required, to become both hosts and guests toward their religious neighbors.[10] While Young's theology of hospitality is developed from a Christian perspective, it does not presume a privileged host position for Christians in relation to other religions. On the contrary, he points to the fact that Christians, even where they are in the majority, must relate to others from a position of vulnerability and marginality which renders them now hosts and then again guests. For Young, the ultimate goal of religious coexistence is one of "mutual hospitality that empowers mutual transformation."[11]

While the virtue of hospitality thus offers a rich and promising resource for reconsidering the relationship between Christians and members of other religions, or more broadly between religious traditions, it also includes risks and challenges that may point to certain limits of interreligious hospitality. These challenges reveal themselves on different levels: in the tensions that may arise when people with firm and divergent religious beliefs attempt to share a meal and negotiate the simple daily ritual requirements of their respective faiths in the home; in the more direct and explicit restrictions of participation in the ritual life of the other; and in the limits to welcoming and affirming religious teachings that may be in direct contradiction to one's own. I will discuss the limits of hospitality across religions in the home, in the sacred space and in the sphere of religious reflection not in order to debunk or minimize the importance of interreligious hospitality, but rather to acknowledge challenges that may otherwise threaten the ideal.

Hospitality at Home

The act of welcoming and receiving members of other religions into one's home represents a privileged occasion for developing and expressing friendship across religious traditions. It is through sharing a meal and the space of a home that a basic attitude of trust is created and a more intimate understanding of the life of faith of the other. As such, interreligious hospitality in the home plays an indispensable role in fostering interreligious friendship and understanding. However, it is undeniable that such hospitality also includes challenges. Marty already pointed to the challenge of confronting symbols that cause offense. His own response to this is not one of timidity or embarrassment:

> If you are invited to my house and accept, or if you knock on my door and are welcomed, I, as a Christian will not remove the crucifix, icons, or other Christian symbolic art from my wall . . . As I risk hospitality with you, I will not ignore or cancel all observations of the holy seasons, integral to the rhythm of the year and my life as these may be.[12]

True hospitality involves openness and transparency and a willingness of both host and guest to reveal themselves. On the other hand, one cannot deny that such honesty also involves confrontation, and at times discomfort. While one may attempt to explain and reinterpret symbols to cause less offense to the other, it is impossible to erase painful memories, or to ignore the fact that religious symbols divide religious groups. At its best, interreligious hospitality may include recognition of this fact while also moving beyond it to the deeper spiritual meaning of the other's symbols. A second challenge of interreligious hospitality in the home is that of accommodating the dietary needs of the other. Here, one may assume that the host will make every effort not to serve foods that would be forbidden for the guest. But for some religions, dietary restrictions go beyond merely what is eaten to include how and by whom the food is prepared. This very quickly limits the possibility of interreligious hospitality. Some may also offer up the food to their god or gods before serving it, thereby changing the status of the food as consecrated. To eat such food might be considered sacrilegious for the guest, while not sharing in this food might be considered an insult by the host. There are no easy or ready solutions for these types of conflicting intentions. To verbalize the reasons for one's actions and feelings seems to be the only way to mitigate the situation. In addition to the meal itself, there are also questions about the prayers offered at the beginning and/or at the end of the meal. In order to avoid discomfort or confrontation, a more generic prayer may be offered. But this may be seen to obfuscate the religious life and practice of all.

Interreligious hospitality in the home thus raises the question of who is to adapt to whom? Is the guest expected to respect the religious ethos of the host and participate as much as possible in the religious habits that traditionally inform the home? Or is the host to adapt to the guest and make as many allowances as possible for him or her to observe their religious practices? While the host may exercise unlimited generosity with the guest in sharing his or her religious identity and way of life with the guest, there may be certain views or practices that the guest cannot in all conscience embrace or accept. In participating in the religious life of the host, the guest may feel a certain sense of betrayal with regard to their own tradition, and hypocrisy with regard to the tradition of the host. Conversely, while the host may genuinely wish the guest to be at ease and true to their own tradition, the latter may be shy to engage in certain practices that cause a sense of unease to the host. Is a Christian to provide room for a Muslim to pray *salaat* in their home? Or is a Muslim to forego that religious obligation out of deference to the host? In many cases, religious practices of one tradition do not cause immediate offense to those of another, and there will be little resistance to allowing for the other to remain as faithful as possible to their tradition. However, as is the case with symbols, prayers may be experienced as not only different but also divisive. All forms of interreligious hospitality in the home thus require some degree of compromise. This may be regarded as a stumbling block, and as a reason to avoid commensality with members of other religions. But it may also be seen as a fruitful tension that opens the way to deeper mutual understanding and solidarity in and beyond differences.

Ritual Hospitality

A more formal and collective expression of interreligious hospitality may be found in the welcoming of the religious other into one's sacred space or place of worship. Whereas participation in the ritual life of the other may be incidental in the home, here hospitality involves sharing one's religious rituals with members of another religion. This type of hospitality is an expression of genuine benevolence on the part of both guest and host. On the part of the guest, it demonstrates real interest in the host religion, and on the part of the host a desire to share the most intimate dimensions of the life of that faith. While textual study of other religions may yield solid historical and intellectual understanding, it is through participation in the ritual life that one may gain a more direct comprehension of the affective or inner dimension of a religion and of the way in which religious beliefs become embodied within a particular tradition. This is why anthropological research into religion stresses the importance of participant observation, and why students of a particular religion are encouraged to visit the place of worship and, if possible, participate in ritual life.[13]

Religious institutions are on the whole welcoming toward visitors from other religions. Whether out of a desire to be known or to convert, individuals are usually allowed entry into temples, mosques, shrines or churches, regardless of their religious identity. At times, they may also be invited to participate in religious acts and rituals. However, this is where the limits of interreligious hospitality become more evident. While strangers may be allowed participation in some rituals, others may be off limits for those not belonging to that religion. Rites of initiation and passage are evidently only accessible to individuals who are members of a religion. But even some of the more cyclical ritual acts may be reserved only for those fully initiated into the religion. Religions marked by strong conceptions of purity and pollution may moreover regard the act of mixing with members of other religions or transgression of ritual boundaries as an act of pollution. Some Hindu temples do not allow outsiders into their most sacred spaces and the Eucharist is reserved for Christians who are baptized and in good standing in the Roman Catholic Church. Members of other religions are thus barred access to that which is considered the height of ritual life and religious experience. There are of course important variations with religious traditions with regard to ritual hospitality to members of other religions. Many Hindu temples are welcoming toward non-Hindus, and some Christian churches are more lenient than others with respect to sharing the Eucharist. Some theologians have also developed new or renewed conceptions of the Eucharist that would allow for greater liturgical hospitality. Amos Young, for example, turns to the Wesleyan notion of an "open table" combined with a return to early Christian practices, where outsiders were invited to share in the Eucharistic celebration.[14]

For the guest, participation in the religious rituals of another religion poses its own set of challenges. Such ritual crossing-over may be experienced as a betrayal of one's own religious tradition, and as pretense with regard to the other religion. Since one does not actually share the faith of the other, empty mimicry of ritual gestures of another religion may not be seen as the most genuine expression of respect for the other. Refusal to participate in the rituals of another religion is thus not always a sign of animosity, aversion or disrespect.

One area in which interreligious hospitality is pushed to its extreme is that of the actual sharing of sacred spaces or the taking over of the sacred space of one religion by another. This change of religious designation of sacred spaces is of course far from new in the history of religions, as the dominant religion tends to control the meaning and purpose of sacred. Throughout the world, Christian churches have thus been built over pagan sites, mosques over temples, and churches converted into mosques. There is of course a certain spiritual and practical logic to this. Since religious places of worship and practice tend to be built in locations that exude a natural sense of sacredness, one religion may find such location as appealing as another. And since religious spaces serve distinctive functions, it is not surprising that they may be used to serve analogical functions in different religious contexts. However, the intense emotional reactions involved in switching the religious designation of religious spaces points to the difficulty of this type of hospitality. Any idea of past or present transference of religious space from one religion to another seems to have the power to awaken a strong sense of religious identity. This has been handily exploited by Hindu fundamentalists, whose campaign to "restore" the mosque in Ayodhya to its original Hindu dedication as a temple commemorating the birthplace of the god Rama, has ignited militant religious nationalism. But even the threat of dedicating deserted religious spaces for use by a different religion may suddenly awaken a strong sense of religious identity. The very thought that churches might become the place for Muslim prayer and practice has generated a new religious fervor and commitment among otherwise completely secularized European Catholics. When in 2006–2007 Belgian bishops allowed squatters who were mostly Muslim to stay in Catholic churches to protest government immigration policies, Belgian citizens (less than 10 percent of whom are practicing Catholics) became very concerned that this was turning churches into Muslim places of worship and that Christians were "selling out" to Muslims. And when in 2007 a deserted Methodist church in Clitheroe, England, became a mosque, the transformation was preceded by a bitter fight and many years of painstaking negotiations. The recent vote in Switzerland against the building of minarets may be regarded as another sign of the threat felt when a different religion is perceived to establish itself within one's own traditional sphere of religious expression. Of course, interreligious hospitality does not usually entail taking over the space and the role of the host. And the rededication of religious places of worship undoubtedly awakens historical memories of religious triumphalism and colonization. But the very anxiety about this issue also illustrates the limits of interreligious hospitality when it regards the sharing of ritual life and sacred spaces.

Doctrinal Hospitality

The third form of interreligious hospitality that merits reflection is that of welcoming the religious beliefs of the other into one's own process of religious reflection. This theological or doctrinal hospitality involves an act of openness and receptivity toward the religious worldview and teachings of another religion. This may be seen to stretch the meaning of the term hospitality. It does not occur between individuals, but rather between religious systems of belief and practice, and it does not necessarily involve time spent with actual believers of another religion. However, it does require an attitude of openness and receptivity toward the other akin to hospitality. This type of hospitality places one in the role of the guest as much as in that of the host. It involves moving out of one's area of comfort and predictability, entering the religious world of the other, and, as a guest, learning from the religious beliefs and practices of the other. And the guest becomes again the host when the teachings or practices of the other religion are welcomed within one's own religious universe and allowed to enrich one's own religious beliefs and practices.

While the challenges to the previous types of hospitality were mainly personal and institutional, the possibility of doctrinal hospitality places considerable strain on the theological or theoretical self-understanding of most religions. Most religions regard themselves as full, final and self-sufficient repositories of truth. And the very idea that there may be truth, let alone distinctive truth, outside of one's own religious framework threatens that very self-understanding. Religions may thus be regarded as fundamentally inhospitable toward the teachings of other religions. While exclusivism (the denial of the presence of any truth outside of one's own religious framework) has been generally condemned and banned from the discourse on religious pluralism, it remains the implicit religious paradigm against which other paradigms need to wrestle.[15] Doctrinal hospitality thus presupposes a shift in the traditional religious conceptions of truth. It requires both humility about one's own grasp of ultimate truth, and generosity about the possible presence of truth in other religions. In *The Im-Possibility of Interreligious Dialogue*, I attempt to demonstrate how both these attitudes of doctrinal humility and doctrinal generosity may be and have been cultivated within the Christian tradition. Resources for doctrinal humility may be found in the apophatic tradition of Christian mysticism, in the modern historical-critical and dynamic understanding of truth, as well as in the eschatological orientation of the tradition as a whole, while most Christian theologians have focused on the Trinity, and in particular on the Holy Spirit as the basis for acknowledging the presence of truth beyond Christian revelation and tradition.

A first step toward doctrinal hospitality lies in the recognition of similarities across religious traditions. It is indeed often through the discovery of a common language, common questions and at times also common answers that a real conversation may ensue between different religious systems. The act of hospitality toward truth in similarity does not immediately threaten the truth of one's own religious tradition. On the contrary, it may be seen to confirm the truth of one's own beliefs. And it creates a basic familiarity or recognition from which to move into the area of differences. The question of hospitality toward teachings and practices that are different from one's own cannot be treated in a general way. It is of course impossible for any religion to accept and welcome any and all alien teachings. Some teachings will be in direct contradiction to one's own while others may be insignificant from within one's own religious perspective. Hospitality, when true to the differences between religions, may moreover in time reach a limit when the teachings of one religion become disagreeable, even reprehensible to the other. Speaking from within a Christian framework, Amos Young warns that "there will be occasions when the protocols of hospitality are deemed broken by our guests and hosts of other faiths, but only because of the scandal of the gospel."[16] One might indeed imagine situations where the beliefs of one religion would directly affront those of another. But apart from the inevitable contradictions between religious systems, religious teachings and practices may also complement one another, each focusing on different dimensions of the divine, human and social realities. In that case, interreligious hospitality may become a source of genuine religious enrichment and transformation. It is indeed the possibility that one might discover excess or distinctive truth in other religions that moves a religion beyond tolerance to a genuine welcoming of the other, not in spite of, but in their particularity and distinctiveness.

In this area of doctrinal hospitality, the host religion will ultimately set the stage for what may or may not be welcomed within a particular religious system. But this is the inevitable result of the specificity of every home religion. And different religions function alternately as the host and the guest in this process of doctrinal hospitality.

Conclusion

The notion of hospitality is particularly apt to describe or rather prescribe the ideal relationship between religions. It goes beyond mere tolerance in fostering actual reciprocity and cordial rapport between members of different religions. And it establishes friendships without erasing differences. It may be conceived of on an interpersonal, a community, or a national level and it captures the promise of a future of peace and harmonious coexistence between different religions. Interreligious hospitality may moreover be regarded as a spiritual discipline. The hospitality called for by most religious traditions refers not so much toward the welcoming of family and friends (which is effortless), but toward the stranger. In a world of religious plurality, the stranger par excellence is the person whose beliefs and principles are radically different from our own. Interreligious hospitality thus offers the opportunity to deepen one's own religious practice while also reaching out to the religious other.

Each of the types of hospitality discussed above may be practiced irrespective of the others. But combined, they may be seen to reinforce one another. Hospitality in the home is often the first step to visiting the place of worship of the other and to a greater interest in and appreciation of the particular teachings and practices of the other religion. Conversely, a greater receptivity to and recognition of the teachings of the other religion may be seen to pave the way to a more comfortable relationship in the home and in the place of worship. A deeper knowledge of the tradition of the other, and respect for its teachings and practices renders the interaction between guest and host more familiar and predictable, and offers the chance for genuine dialogue and exchange.

However, as pointed out, the practice of hospitality across religious tradition is not without its challenges and limits, both for the host and for the guest, and both on the level of ritual practice—whether in the home or in the sacred space—and on the level of doctrinal openness and accommodation. On the part of the guest, it requires a willingness to leave one's level of comfort and familiarity and venture into a world of unfamiliar and at times threatening views and practices. It involves a genuine risk: how far can one go in accepting the other's hospitality without losing one's own identity? To which extent can one participate in the ritual life of the other without betraying one's own religious tradition (or that of the other)? On the part of the host, the challenge of hospitality consists of generously sharing one's own life and identity without imposing oneself on the religious other or causing embarrassment and discomfort. If hospitality is understood as a complete, unqualified and unconditional sharing of oneself and one's life with the other, then interreligious hospitality is nigh impossible. There will always be rituals in which one cannot participate (either through one's own sense of propriety or through limits imposed by the tradition), practices one cannot tolerate, and beliefs one cannot accept. Young himself admits that "absolute hospitality, gift giving, and forgiveness are impossible: because they are all bound up within an economy of exchange, scarcity and reciprocity."[17] He thus proposes distinguishing the *how* from the *what* of interreligious hospitality.[18] Whereas the latter may be disagreeable to the religious other, this should not compromise the way in which one reaches out and welcomes the other into one's country, church or home. Even though the ultimate goal of interreligious hospitality may be that of welcoming the other *in* their religious identity, the need at times to do so *in spite of* their religious particularity and difference does not necessarily invalidate the gesture. On the contrary, it may be regarded as a measure of the unconditionality of one's hospitality.

While perfect hospitality and harmonious exchange between members of different religions may be difficult to attain as a historical reality, it is critically important to remain focused on the idea and the possibility of its ultimate realization. Theologians such as Amos Young in fact approach interreligious hospitality from an eschatological perspective, from the realization that "absolute hospitality remains an eschatological ideal and norm even as we adjudicate historical situations in anticipation of the redemptive hospitality of God."[19] Young points out that Christians themselves do not know who will ultimately be at the table and that we might be "surprised both by seeing those around the table who we did not think would be there, and missing the presence of others whom we presumed we'd see."[20] The image of the eschatological banquet at which God will be the ultimate host may thus relieve some of the worries or concerns about the limits of interreligious hospitality while also impressing on us the need and urgency to work toward its fuller realization.

CHAPTER 4

DEPARTURES

HOSPITALITY AS MEDIATION

Kalpana Seshadri

The term "hospitality," derived from the Latin *hostis* and *hospes*,[1] is best trans-lated into the (Hindu) Sanskritic tradition as *atithitva*—or a state of guesthood. A related term is *satkāra*, literally truth (*sat*) doing (*kara*), which refers to acts of consideration toward the other, and *satkriya* (truth actions), which extends the concept of hospitality to ceremonies as in "*vivāha-satkar*, the celebration of a wedding" or "'*para-loka-satkar*' honouring in regard to the other world . . . funeral ceremonies any purificatory ceremony" (Monier-Williams). Any attempt to trace the intellectual history of the concept, to decipher the ground-ing of the rules of *atithi dharma* would entail grappling with the formidable archive of *Dharmashāstra* literature, and their explication of *ācara* or norms and traditional customs[2] as one of the foundations of Hindu deontology known as *dharma*. However, hospitality as a practice prevails in a sphere that is largely indifferent though never opposed to such scriptural exegesis. There is the level of *anubhava* or a form of insight and knowledge derived from lived experience that may derive from *ācara* as a way of life, but may or may not be oriented toward *dharmic* ends. While scriptural exegesis is a mode of exercising moral authority and authenticity, experiential knowledge as *anubhava* can be only historical, foundationless, and resolutely impure.

As a non-theologian whose knowledge of scripture is entirely culled from the domestic and customary, the following reflection on hospitality is founded on my *anubhava*—the impure plane where norms and lived experiences com-bine to produce a thoughtful practice. First of all, we must acknowledge that hospitality in India is always plural, non-secular, and singular because of the sheer heterogeneity of beliefs and practices. The old joke that in any discussion four Indians will produce ten opinions could not be more accurate than in this instance. Such multiplicity and singularity of views attests to hospitality as a praxis, rather than pure norm, that develops out of the contingency of the unknown neighbor, who may be, given the mixed neighborhoods of any Indian city, of a different "community"[3] (for example, Aggarwal, Reddy, Yadav), or religion (Sikh, Muslim, Christian, Zoroastrian, Jain, etc.).

Reflecting then on my lived experiences, and the scenarios in which the customary and practical concepts of hospitality were transmitted, I recall on the following pages three learning moments, events of *anubhava*, which will serve as scaffolding for my inquiry.

I believe I learned my first lesson in hospitality as a child when I happened to ask our newly arrived guests how long they would be staying. For this, I was later admonished. Never ask guests when they will leave. My mother explained that a guest *Atithi* means the one without a proper date (*a-tithi*) and that he or she must always be honored as a god—*Atithi Devo Bhava*. She asked me: Would you ask a god when he arrives the date of his departure? Would I? Listen: *Atithi Devo Bhava*: God is not manifested through the guest; rather the guest by being a guest manifests God. (*Bhava* is usually translated as "being," but is more precisely the taking place of being, a coming into being. The aphorism is found in the *Taittirya Upanishad*.[4]) In other words, it is the guest who brings the gift of hospitality to the host, which the host receives.

And yet, with the distance of decades, I notice now that in this particular linguistic and ethical context, the question even from a child could only have been "how long are you staying?" and not "when are you leaving?" or "when do you go back?" At some point, a child learns, even before other rules of speech and conduct are mastered, two things: never to say goodbye without mentioning return, and never to deny passage to one who is taking leave, i.e. to not say at the hour of departure "do not go." "*Athithi Devo Bhava*" is a fundamental "yes" in the sense that it not only implies an unconditional welcome, but more importantly it is the hope for the return of the guest, multiple returns. It is a "yes," an unconscious silent "yes," that implies that between the present coming and the future perfect of the return, one affirms a departure, a safe departure.

The second lesson I imbibed, with no memory of a time when I did so, has to do with the responsibility of offering food before eating. In the morning, when the rice was cooked and consecrated, my grandmother would go out to the broad mango tree in the back courtyard with a spoonful in her hand, place it at the foot of the tree, and call the crows. And always even before I rose, my mother, grandmother or one of the maids had drawn at the threshold of our house intricate geometric patterns or *kolam* with rice flour. The patterns were decorative signs of welcome, but why were they not simply painted on permanently? "The flour is to feed the little invisible creatures," my mother said, "the ants, the insects, the squirrels, all the forgotten little lives." It is the other then that must eat first—its life honored and nourished, before we nourish ourselves.

The third is not so much a lesson as an enigma—which on reflection seems to bring the first two lessons together. It was the great yearly memorial ritual, when the kitchen would go into a different rhythm, and the priests and their assistants arrived one by one, and my father performed the *śrāddha* ceremony. This was the grand ceremony that topped the fortnightly one he practiced when he honored the ancestors with prayers and sacrificial offerings of rice. As children, we were sent upstairs with board games and books and told to be quiet. And as the somber Sanskrit verses floated up from below mixed with the smell of burning sacrificial fire, it would seem to us that even the birds had stopped singing to listen. Afterwards, the numerous priests were honored with a specially prepared feast—an ostensibly austere though perfectly delicious and elaborate meal—that we children looked forward to. This yearly ritual had always been an enigma so different from community holidays such as

Diwali (the festival of lights when we played with firecrackers) or *Sankranti* (the harvest festival honoring the sun when we flew kites) when once again feasting and eating was central. The difference was that the day of *śrāddha* was unmistakably a singular day of hospitality—but to whom? How can one be hospitable toward the dead? What would that mean?

Perhaps it is time to confront if not solve that enigma by asking: is there a relation, albeit an unwritten one, between the hope for the safe departure of the *atithi*, our responsibility to welcome and offer food to the invisible and the forgotten, and the sacrifice for the dead? When these disparate *ācaras* are brought into relation with each other, what kind of a praxis of hospitality can we derive from such a juxtaposition? That it won't be a *dharmic* injunction is evident, for nothing in this relational thought experiment can claim authenticity or authority. But so long as it offers a singular praxis, we are perhaps justified in not discounting it. Thus, it is not to any of the *Dharmashāstras* I shall turn but once again to the *Taittiriya Upanishad*[5] in the hopes of discovering a praxis and ethic of hospitality in relation to the sacrificial logic of food and departure, but now in the context of the absolute departure of death.[6] In other words, can there be a praxis of hospitality that is founded on a relation between offering food to the invisible and honoring the departing guest and the departed dead? What connects the triangular points at which hospitality meets departure (either of the guest or of the departed) and food (nurturing the visible and the invisible guest?). In the following I suggest that in the host's dual responsibility for the guest's safe departure, even as she recedes from vision, and in the duty is to welcome and offer food first to the minute and the imperceptible, an ethic of hospitality is disclosed as an always unfinished act because it is directed toward the unapparent.

The Metaphysics of Food

In order to pursue the interrelation between food and departure, let us turn to the way in which the *Upanishad* speaks of food. The verse in which the aphorism quoted earlier (*Athiti Devo Bhava*) appears, in fact begins thus:

> Neglect not the funerary works due to the Gods (and) Ancestors
> Let the Mother be (as) God
> Let the Father be (as) God
> Let the Teacher be (as) God
> Let the Guest be (as) God[7]

What is interesting here is the metonymic arrangement of the verse: "works," *pitṛkārya* or post funeral rites (or *śrāddha*), i.e. the works due to the ancestors/progenitors is mentioned first, alongside the veneration toward the mother (who nourished one with her own body), the father (who engendered), the teacher (who gives the word) and the guest (who brings the gift). What constitutes the equivalence of these elements, of post-funeral rites to the guest as God? One could of course simply read the verse as a list of ethical injunctions, but that would be to neglect the main and repeated thrust of the *Upanishad*, which is to speak of ontological union—*samhita*, and also the essential function of the nutritive. In other words, the *Upanishad* as a whole can be said to offer a "metaphysics" of food or a food metaphysic. (The word here that is being translated as food is "*annam*," which possesses the connotation of sanctified substance.) A dominant reading of the text turns on II.8.5, in which "individual" being (*puruṣa*) is said to be identical with *Brahman* (universal being), the former being composed of *anna* (matter or food), *prāna* (life breath), *manas* (thought, imagination, reflection, intention, mood), *vignyāna* (understanding, intellect) and *ānanda* (bliss). The text not only urges the necessity to respect and venerate food by acquiring and sharing it, it also insists on the materiality of being, or being as food, the being of food. Verse II.1.1 offers a cosmology that posits Self or *Brahman* as the origin of *akasa* (space), from which springs *vāyu* (air), from *vāyu*—*agni* (fire), from *agni*—*āpa* (water), from *āpa*—*priṭvi* (earth), from prithvi—*aushada* (herbs), from *aushada*—*annam* (food) from *annam*—*puruṣa* (being of man). It then concludes (*purushoannamrasamyah*) that *puruṣa* (being) is the (*rasa*) essence of *annam* (food). What does it mean that food's essence is the being of man? This ambiguous line is usually interpreted by the *Advaitins* to mean that man's essence (in this case his form) is constituted by food.[8] The second *Anuvāka* (verse) goes on to say:

> From food are produced all creatures which dwell on earth. Then they live by food, and in the end they return to food. For food is the oldest of all beings and therefore it is called panacea . . . They who worship food as Brahman, obtain all food. For food is the oldest of all beings . . . Different from this, which consists of the essence of food, is the other, the inner Self [*ātma*], which consists of life breath. The former is filled by this. II.2.1-3

The entire chapter proceeds in this manner—food is original, and it is "filled" by being, which is "filled" by *prāna* (breath/life), which is "filled" by *manas* (mind), which is "filled" by *vignyāna* (understanding), which is "filled" by *ānanda* (bliss). This cosmology is not easy to diagram, for it does not in fact function as a chain of being based on causal relations. Instead there is an inside/out and outside/in movement that proceeds from universal being or bliss to individual being or bliss and back again. This movement of the verse that mimics the in/out pattern of inspiration and respiration refers then to organic matter, food, the digestive process (assimilation of the good and separation of dross) as the origin. But food here is not simply that which sustains the body—permitting breathing to occur, thereby housing being or *purusha* sometimes translated as "inner self."[9] Rather there is something like a topology of a vortex that is better expressed by the word "*purnah*," translated as "filled" but also meaning to be completed, supplemented (*tenaisa purnah* is the repeated phrase). The *Upanishad* does not appear to recognize a strict opposition between body and inner self or "soul," or even food and body.[10] The body as such is not mentioned in this chapter—there is only the form of matter. Form-matter (whether called food or body) is not inert—mere corporeality—but is itself life. At best, it can be said that the body that is food, the food-body nourishes (sustains, harbors) the inner self or soul. We can infer (and this is a completely heterodox inference) that the soul in a sense feeds off the body, as the growing embryo feeds off the mother's body, or more properly the life she sustains is sustained by the food that sustains her life. The relation of such a metaphysics of food to hospitality can be clarified by extending the metaphor of pregnancy to serve as the supreme instantiation of hospitality toward the imperceptible.[11] The offering of food then (like the mother's offering of her body) is always an offering to a body that is itself food for the soul. Hospitality is always incomplete because in a sense it is only a mediation of giving to what cannot be seen.[12]

From this underlying notion of the body as food for the soul derives perhaps the general injunction in all schools of Hindu thought to develop technologies for the "care of the self," i.e. to only eat in great moderation substances that are nourishing for the soul—food that is considered to have properties of truth, "*sāttvik*," and the counsel to realize the body's potentiality through practices of discipline and austerity—*raja yoga* and *tapas*. Where does this leave our embodied selves? It appears that the logic of the *Upanishad* posits that the body is food for the soul; it is that which both eats and is eaten. (The sacrificial logic here is troubled by its own circularity, which is perhaps a consequence of a fundamental non-dualism, rather than monism per se, that posits the absolute immanence of being.)[13]

Ultimately it is food that is body for the soul. The soul does not live in the body; the soul has a body that is made of food. And this food takes the form of body. In other words, the body is the form of food. And this form is one that is actualized in historical time and is subject to death. (Matter without soul is the disappearance of form.)

Feeding the Dead

Given the salience of food in grounding an ethic of hospitality (as mediation toward the imperceptible soul), how should we situate the significance of food in the funeral ritual when the body can no longer nourish the soul? The *Upanishad*, as is well known, urges hospitality and the necessity to acquire and offer food. The plenitude of food and the offering of it is bliss itself. But the same text associates such hospitality with duties toward the ancestors—post-funeral rites. In other words, there is a sense in which the ultimate hospitality is the rites that follow the funeral rite, wherein for over a period of eleven days the living aid the soul of the dead to depart, to ensure it safe passage to the world of ancestors, and to alleviate its suffering (for the spirit—the *preta*, which is not the same as *purusha*, the soul—is bereft without matter) as much as possible by anticipating and fulfilling its needs. It is the hospitality for the dead—the *preta* or the disembodied for its departure, to part once and for all fulfilled and safe.[14] Related to this sentiment is perhaps the above-mentioned *ācara* (custom) in traditional households to always place a small offering (*annam*) at the foot of a tree for the birds, especially crows, to be the very first to eat, before serving food to the family. David Knipe says that "the crow [has] widespread folkloric associations with the souls of the dead. Not only the collective remote ancestors but perhaps also the *preta* may be personified by the crow." (I cite this piece of folklore if only because not only food but also stories seem to insist themselves on hosts and guests alike in every scene of hospitality.)

The importance of funeral rites and monthly rituals for the ancestors within Hinduism is perhaps unsurprising given that in the absence of physical monuments, the ashes of the dead are buried in the river. More properly, it is language alone that offers a place for the dead. However, as David Knipe writes, these rituals are nevertheless "the least studied aspects of Hinduism." Though the performance of the rituals is no doubt meant to aid the grieving to mourn and cope with the loss, the rituals are for the other, for the dead. In other words, the rituals are fundamentally a crossing of borders, thresholds and limits between "this side" of mortality and the "other side" of immortality.[15] Insofar as they are primarily designed to assist the spirit of the departed, the disembodied *preta*, to enter the world of the ancestors or *pitṛloka*, by providing it with a "temporary body," the rituals are considered profoundly inauspicious. As Knipe writes: "So inauspicious are the cremation and the *pre-sapindikarana* rites that many ritual texts covering the rites of passage (*samskaras*) omit funeral ceremonies altogether. Others, like the *Prayogaratna*, append a separate manual on the subject."[16] In other words, the rites are "inauspicious" because they constitute a crossing of thresholds rather than a separation as is proper to making sacred.[17]

The rites focus on the departed's need for a body or nourishment. This body is the *pinda* offering consisting of boiled rice (*annam*) without salt or spices. This plain rice is formed into a "lump," which is the literal translation of *pinda*—a form clearly without aspect, thereby honoring its invisibility—that is the offering of a food-body for the *preta*, which suffers (popularly described as hunger and thirst) without a body. The rituals surrounding the *pindas*—their number, significance and ritual function—are incredibly complex, and the accompanying liturgy is equally so. As David Knipe and Jonathan Perry in their separate studies show,[18] the rituals vary in detail among the heterogeneous communities according to their class and caste status.[19] But as Knipe rightly observes, there is a broad uniformity in some of the basic assumptions about what happens to the soul after it has separated itself from the food-body, and the necessary implication of the three preceding generations of deceased ancestors who are also invoked and are to be nourished with separate offerings. As Knipe puts it: "These three paternal generations are the recently deceased, the powerful immigrants to the three worlds who exist in symbiotic connections with their living descendants. They require sustenance for their continuing journey to the unmanifest, the ocean of dissolution that lies beyond these three worlds. And the living have need of these celestial intermediaries for health and long life, for wealth and progeny" (118). The instrumental view of the rites notwithstanding, we can still derive that it is the host—in this case the main "sacrificer"—who gets more than he can ever give.

While the power and significance of offering food in any scene of hospitality cannot be overstated, my sense is that the metaphysics of food as articulated by the *Upanishad* gives us a way to think of hospitality as mediation and attunement toward the imperceptible and the unknown. Thus even more than the arrival, when the guest makes an appearance, it is the scene of departure that enjoins an exigent responsibility. Hospitality in this context is not only the welcoming of the guest who appears at our door, it is a responsibility that continues beyond departure to his or her disappearance. The food that is offered in hospitality is that which ultimately nourishes and honors what is imperceptible or absent.

A famous story of hospitality in the Hindu context is that of Krishna and Sudama, also known as Kuchela (a surname or epithet). It appears in the Bhaghavata Purāna, Book 10, cantos 80–81. It is a surprisingly simple story, enigmatic in its lack of didacticism and moral allegorization, but it is relevant here for it engages many of the themes (especially the gift of the soul's hunger) touched on above. Sudama or Kuchela is a learned but impoverished Brahman. His good and long-suffering wife suggests that he visit his old school friend Krishna, who is now the king of Dwāraka and married to Rukmini, known as the incarnation of Lakshmi, the goddess of fortune. Sudama agrees, and takes a heap of puffed rice borrowed from a neighbor as a gift for Krishna. Sudama arrives at Krishna's glittering palace, and surprisingly no one bars his way. When Krishna sees Sudama, he embraces him warmly, reminisces about their school days and eagerly partakes of the puffed rice that Sudama is too ashamed to offer. When Sudama returns to his village, he finds that his humble hut has been transformed into a luxurious palace and that he and his family have been provided with every material necessity. The text says he was liberated from labor. Sudama dedicates his life to living happily, teaching, practicing austerity and humility, and eventually he attains salvation.

It was not until I was reminded of other meaning contexts—such as the tale of the poor fisherman and his greedy wife, or the parable of Lazarus and the rich man—that I discovered the strangeness of this tale. How should one understand this story, which seems uncritical of the complaining wife, the luxury of the rich, and even equates reward with material wealth? Let us try again by contemplating the story as it unfolds:

This time I shall call the story "Eating the Nothing."

I see this:

Despair, a pathless future, a deep poverty, an unquantifiable crisis of body and soul grips the young scholar. His wife offers a solution: try to remember—only recall, she says, for all knowledge and all having are wrought by the power of memory.

Reflecting quietly, under the shade of a Bodhi tree, the scholar recalls the time of a friendship. A friend during the days of learning, and that friend was he who could eat the nothing. The scholar smiles as he realizes that this time of friendship is neither the past nor the future. It comes about, it merely comes about around nothing. Thus called to a time within time, the poor scholar gathers together, in a piece of clean sari torn from his wife's shoulder, a heap of puffed rice, itself borrowed from a kindly neighbor—emptiness itself, rice with kernels removed, with nothing inside. And this he sets out to give to him, the friend who had the great capacity to receive.

A long and arduous journey, a pilgrimage, a prayer later, the poor scholar arrives at the gates of the friend. No questions are asked as one magnificent door leads to another. The doors stand wide open within the dazzling palace, no one bars his way, no questions are asked of him. The scholar's path brings him to the innermost sanctum, where the friend dallies with fortune herself. Spying the scholar hesitating at the doorway, the friend hastens, embraces him with delight. There is no hesitation, no uncertainty, no surprise. Only delight, sheer delight. No questions are asked: how are you, when did you come, why did you come, how long has it been, but have you not changed? etc. Just delight, sheer delight. The poor scholar finds his tired feet washed by the friend, as she, the brilliant one who bestows fortune, fans him, offers him fresh fruit, nuts and honey. Nevertheless, the friend is ashamed—*vriditta, avan mukah* (literally, a face without words). For Kuchela is bare, emaciated, unkempt, "*ku-cailaṁ malinaṁ kṣāmaṁ; dvijaṁ dhamani-santatam*" (10.80). He cannot escape himself, he stands exposed in an "ultimate intimacy," a nakedness that is not only his bare body, his empty belly, but the nakedness of his very being. He cannot cover himself before his friend. The friend only smiles. He speaks of their school days and the time when they lost their way together in a dark forest during a rainstorm. Remember—the crack of lightening, the thunder, the tall dark trees, the whistling storm, the flood. Discovering them at dawn, the teacher had blessed them. For what? For having lost their way together. The friend and the scholar reflect in silence on the words of that blessing from Sāndipani, their teacher. Then the friend smiles, and asks a question: did you bring me anything from home, dear one? Hospitality confounds giving and receiving, host and guest, agent and patient. But Kuchela is *avan mukah*—a face bereft of words, he hangs his head in shame. What must he do? The friend spies the poor bundle of puffed rice; he gamely grabs it from the naked and emaciated scholar—he who has come to give because he has nothing. Is it audacity, or is it love this giving nothing, giving what he does not have? The friend sinks his palm in the heap of rice and opening his mouth wide eats a fistful with sheer delight, of the emptiness and the nothing, and reaches for more, and yet more, until Fortune gently stays his hand. It is enough, she says, it is more than enough, for he is already liberated: "*karma-bandhād vimucyate*" (10:81.41), freed from the bondage of material work.

And as the friend empties the emptiness within the puffed rice, the scholar feels himself filling up. His satisfaction is immeasurable. Incalculable happiness and fortune accrue to him, the more he gives of what he does not have, the more he finds himself receiving what he could not imagine. Can something come out of nothing? Is it possible to give, eat, and be full of the nothing? Is this the meaning of grace?

And is this also the time of hospitality? Is hospitality a time, a fortunate time, rather than a something that is given or received? Does hospitality simply happen when, or rather because, we lose our way together?

Later, Sudama recalls that he had asked nothing, indeed he needs nothing. And once again, he loses his way—his hut has disappeared, his bare belongings have disappeared, nothing has disappeared, and for this he is again blessed.

CHAPTER 5

MISGIVINGS ABOUT MISGIVINGS
AND THE NATURE OF A HOME

SOME REFLECTIONS ON THE ROLE OF JEWISH TRADITION
IN DERRIDA'S ACCOUNT OF HOSPITALITY

Jacob Meskin

If we accept the verdict of the popular media, the contemporary conversation about religion belongs in large part to the raging debate initiated by "the four horsemen of the new atheism."[1] Be that as it may, many thoughtful people today mourn the acrimony and accusations that mar discussions between those who speak on behalf of various religious traditions, and those who speak for the modern secular world of science, government and academia. On the one hand religious believers who participate actively in the modern world often feel that their ancient traditions offer great benefit, not only to themselves but also to their non-religious contemporaries. From the perspective of such an adherent, who usually embraces some form of pluralism, his or her tradition contains an untapped wealth of wisdom that can ennoble contemporary systems of thought, invigorate bio-ethical deliberations, and help modern folk to navigate the complexities of personal and social life amidst rapidly changing circumstances. On the other hand many secular people who lament the all too widespread hostility between religious tradition and modernity maintain a parallel conviction. They are willing to accept the validity and value of many forms of traditional religious life, and yet maintain passionately that their modern secular texts, ideas and disciplines offer great benefit, not only to themselves but also to their religious contemporaries.

Against the view popular media tends to advance, I concur with this consensus of the thoughtful: we all have much to gain from a fruitful exchange between religion and secularity. That being the case, however, the argument I present here will come as something of a surprise.

Much current philosophical and theological interest in the phenomenon of hospitality, and in the related phenomena of friendship, national identity and so on, stems from the work of Jacques Derrida. As is fairly well known, Derrida's work owes a certain intellectual debt both to Emmanuel Levinas and, more generally, to Jewish tradition, that is, to the variety of texts, rituals and practices through which Judaism has articulated and continues to articulate its many-sided understanding of hospitality. Thus we have here an impressive effort in contemporary thought that for the most part implicitly, and sometimes explicitly, might seem to conform to the irenic consensus articulated above. Nonetheless, something vital has been lost or overlooked in the admittedly complex process whereby Derrida derived his understanding of hospitality from Jewish tradition. As one who shares the pacific sentiments outlined above, I would much prefer to applaud such an effort and encourage others to emulate it. Nonetheless, it remains incomplete and one-sided, omitting from view several features of the phenomenon of hospitality that attain great prominence and urgency within that background context of Jewish tradition from which Derrida can be said to have abstracted his own, contemporary conception.

Here we encounter Derrida's misgivings about just these features of the Jewish tradition's understanding of hospitality, misgivings that undoubtedly caused him to elide them from his discussion of hospitality. Yet in what follows I want to voice meta-level misgivings; that is, I want to express misgivings about these misgivings of Derrida's. The themes Derrida *omits* from his discussion of hospitality—themes of central importance in at least one of Derrida's original sources—may well be *just as vital for nurturing hospitality* as those he includes in that discussion. These omitted themes revolve around the Jewish tradition's approach to both *the nature and the necessity of a home*. I will not of course be able here to offer a thorough account of the many issues this claim raises, but I do hope at least to sketch the general shape of a few of them, and to begin a conversation about their relationship to how we think about hospitality today.

I

In addition to his best-known and still vigorously debated works that first developed the ideas of deconstruction and post-structuralism, Jacques Derrida left an impressive legacy of sustained meditations on some of the "conceptual flash-points" central to modernity and modern thought. Each of Derrida's investigations focused on a discrete conceptual nexus crucial to understanding a particular area of and set of institutions in contemporary life, including religion, economics, politics, gender, history and art, to name a few.[2] Provocative and fecund, these investigations have in turn generated many new explorations by others. So it should come as no surprise that Derrida's acute, searching reflections on the phenomenon of hospitality[3] recently inspired—inter alia—an ongoing, multi-media conversation and set of meetings among scholars, artists and representatives of different religious traditions on the meaning of hospitality within and across their disparate ways of life. Including academic presentations, freewheeling discussions and artistic compositions and performances, this event, held in different locations internationally, was called the "Guestbook Project."[4]

Religious traditions offer an intriguing context in which to explore Derrida's meditations on hospitality, one that must almost immediately generate certain urgent questions. In a great many places (though in some more than others) religions play an important role in shaping the quotidian social atmosphere within which questions of hospitality constantly arise. Speaking even more generally, religious traditions have contributed (and continue to contribute) in a deep way to the set of common associations, shared narratives and so on, that shape the pre-theoretical and affective background out of which basic sentiments of and attitudes toward hospitality emerge. This does furnish an impressive variety of important material for philosophical reflection on hospitality. At the same time, the sheer number and diversity of religious traditions might occasion worry as to whether any one historically and culturally specific philosophical discussion, even one as essentially multivocalic as Derrida's, could help us to gain an understanding of the reality of hospitality as it takes on concrete shape in so many different and unrelated religious and cultural contexts. However, the Guestbook Project's open and polyphonal format helped to assuage this worry. Asking self-identified representatives of different religious traditions, who are also trained scholars, to speak on behalf of their own ways of life reduced well-known risks of homogenization and projection, and catalyzed unfettered interchange. With these impediments, which have all too often dogged similar efforts in the past, minimized, it becomes easier to focus on whether one can fruitfully apply Derrida's understanding of hospitality to a variety of religious and cultural worlds, even those seemingly far removed from what was, after all, the expansive ambit of Derrida's thought. Indeed this paper began life as a panel presentation therein.

Thinking about hospitality in the context of religion also raises another, basic question. It is a question that, in a slightly different form, lies close to the heart of Derrida's meditations on hospitality. On the one hand, religious traditions travel across vast expanses of time and space. Such traditions organically encode both these extensive historical and geographical journeys, and the life experiences and wisdom of those who succeeded in passing them down. Leaving to one side for the moment normative matters of theology, belief or doctrine, this organic encoding makes it likely that a religious tradition can serve as a source of valuable insight into the basic realities of human life. One such reality is the phenomenon of hospitality, in which cultures and individuals must find ways to navigate the crucial, yet delicate set of relations among home, house, host, guest, traveler, native and foreigner. It stands to reason that religious traditions encode paradigms, narratives, rules, ceremonies and rituals, inter alia, through which such navigation can and should be accomplished.

Simultaneously however, religious traditions also make possible that thematic, goal-directed marshalling of resources through which varying forms of organized collectivity arise. With such forms comes the necessary capacity to exercise power, a power intrinsically connected in each case with the furtherance of a particular theological and ideological content, and with the need to maintain the social order embodying this content. Yet this same power has also sometimes been exercised in savage attempts to impose this content on others outside that social order, as well as on dissenters within that order. In this way, as has been pointed out, leaders and representatives of religious traditions end up violating distinctive teachings concerning the hospitality owed to others that *their own* traditions and ways of life have generated. What then is the relationship between a religious tradition's "enacted code" enjoining hospitality toward others, and that same tradition's potential capacity for inciting varying degrees of violence against others? Here we arrive at what is perhaps the central misgiving that drives Derrida's analysis of hospitality.

II

Derrida introduces us to this founding worry by exploring the simultaneous possibility and impossibility of hospitality, the self-possession and dispossession it requires all at once. To grasp this worry we will need first to get clear on Derrida's account of the interminable dialectic of hospitality.

Derrida articulates what he calls "an insoluble antinomy, a non-dialectizable antinomy" between "the hyperbolic law of hospitality" on the one hand, and "concrete laws of hospitality" enacted as practical measures, on the other. The former hyperbolic law demands an absolute openness to the other, the stranger, the foreigner, to the point of self-sacrificiality on his or her behalf. It is unconditional, and beyond particularities of time, place and so on. Yet this unconditional law would evaporate into nothing more than fine sentiment and utopian hand-wringing were it not for the reality of specific legislation and enjoined patterns of behavior, through which hospitality is made to occur concretely in the world. Thus it is thanks to such concrete laws of hospitality that the absolute law of hospitality enters the world. However these concrete laws come into existence only in particular contexts, cultures, countries, patriotisms, homes, etc. Yet just such utterly specific locatedness must, at the same time, produce a profound tension with the unconditionality and independence of time and place of the absolute law of hospitality. For Derrida hospitality is an aporia, an endlessly and irresolvable paradoxical relationship.[5]

Absolute hospitality will require that the home be opened up to the other, to the point of the giving up, the abandonment of this home. It requires that a host exchange his status as host for the guest, for the stranger. Indeed, Derrida goes so far as to say that unconditional hospitality implies that the guest becomes the host and the host the guest.[6] Of course, these exorbitant demands gain a foothold in reality only through concrete gestures, thoughts, and programs of hospitality in day-to-day life. Yet what ultimately lies behind mundane hospitality or, to put it another way, the truth that mundane hospitality in fact expresses, far exceeds the normal parameters of the world. We thus encounter here a set of two mutually exclusive and yet interdependent perspectives, seemingly stuck in an endless oscillation. 1) Seen from the perspective of the quotidian, the unattainable requirements of absolute hospitality would seem to make real hospitality in the world impossible. However, one might say that only the hyperbolic urgency of absolute hospitality can counteract human inertia and competing interests, thus making it possible that actual hospitality may "break through" and emerge in the real world. 2) Seen from the perspective of absolute hospitality, the usual, worldly subordination of unconditional claims to commonplace necessities of politics, culture, power and so on, would seem to make hospitality impossible. However, one might say that it is precisely and only this all too real concreteness through which absolute hospitality may find a way to become a real possibility!

Derrida holds on to both the possibility and the impossibility of hospitality, keeping the paradoxical simultaneity of self-possession and dispossession it requires in full view. This means, to follow out the implications of this impossible possibility, that hospitality in our world must always walk a knife's edge. It is always in danger, from both the limitless supernal demands and from the limiting natural conditions and tendencies that dwell together uneasily in its core, of turning into something else, of "falling" into some other state.

Derrida's founding worry mentioned above now becomes clear. In his view, hospitality in our world will always be a touch and go affair. In particular, as we have seen, there must be homes and hosts, localities and concrete laws for there to be hospitality at all. Yet Derrida worries that all of the various types of home, and the processes through which they get constituted, will always tend at the same time to create a distinct, bounded community—one that will inevitably include some and exclude others. Derrida sees this process of the creation of home as posing great danger to the possibility of hospitality. In one of his essays on hospitality he asserts powerfully that "[h]ospitality is the deconstruction of the at-home; deconstruction is hospitality to the other."[7] To say this in a different way, for Derrida "at-homeness" is a threat and must be the subject of the work of deconstruction in order to minimize and contain this threat. This is also connected with Derrida's well-known meditations on the politics of friendship. One can forge a friendship with anyone; yet friendship in all its apparently unlimited openness will inevitably become fraternity or brotherhood, a collective identity defined by specific traits that function to draw a boundary between "us" and "them." Derrida worries about this, and sees deconstruction as an attempt to exert constant critical scrutiny and vigilance about the "taken-for-grantedness" of such boundaries.[8]

Now in all of this Derrida is, as he says, working with Levinasian ideas—for example, the notion of subjectivity as always already subjected to the demands of the other, indebtedness as a precondition for selfhood, the core of selfhood arising from the self as a substitution for the other, and so on.[9] Yet, and this is the central point, Derrida, in all his eloquent admiration for Levinas, also makes it clear that he worries about Levinas's apparent lack of complete and utter vigilance about the ongoing effects of constituted communities, identities, religious groups, states and so on. This is hardly to say that Levinas was some sort of apologist or advocate for existing religious institutions and doctrinal beliefs. On the contrary, Levinas is always clear that he is a philosopher, and as such keeps his distance from apologetic claims lacking rigorous argument, and from the often philosophically undeveloped views that generally characterize existing religious institutions. And yet Derrida worries that Levinas's careful appropriation of Jewish texts and ideas, his philosophically critical and complex embrace of Jewish identity, and his admittedly qualified and ethically demanding form of Zionism—Derrida worries that in all these aspects of Levinas's thought, Levinas may have still failed to be vigilant enough. That is, Derrida

worries that at times Levinas comes too close to solidifying permeable and dia-
lectically unstable notions, such as "identity," "community," "nation" and so
on, in just the sort of way that can set up exclusions, chauvinisms and the like.[10]

Derrida's worry would certainly seem to be valid. It even has, among other
things, a solid philosophical pedigree. For even Derrida's worry about Levinas's
lack of sufficient vigilance has roots in Levinas's original notion of my unchosen
ethical responsibility before the face of the other. The other in effect chooses me,
making me a self, and charging that self with an infinite ethical responsibility
for other. I am never able, for Levinas, to discharge fully this ethical charge.
Ethically, for Levinas one is always and forever on the job. Whence one source
for Derrida's invitation to endless vigilance.

III

Yet I have misgivings about these misgivings. In its zeal for being vigilant at
the very second that positive community formation and identity formation
show up, Derrida's worry perhaps forgets or loses sight of what has in this case
made such a disposition to worry possible in the first place, namely, a certain
kind of experience, that of the Jews and Judaism historically and religiously.
Levinas in many ways and at many times admits that his philosophy owes a
debt to this experience, especially as it is set out in and shaped by the texts
of the Jewish tradition. Thus Derrida too, in working with and transforming
Levinasian notions in his own discussions of ideas like friendship, brotherhood,
community, democracy and hospitality, also stands in a line of debtors to this
experience. Yet Levinas constantly keeps this debt in view, apparently taking the
view that it is—beneficially—one that cannot ultimately be repaid and so done
with, once and for all. I am not always certain that Derrida agrees. This may
not be a problem in itself. But it does, perhaps, lead Derrida to pay insufficient
attention to certain necessary factors that lie behind the phenomenon and virtue
of hospitality in the Jewish tradition.

I want in particular to draw attention to two such factors that emerge from
Jewish experience. Professor Edward Kaplan in his paper on the nature of
hospitality in the Jewish tradition has already spoken eloquently of the first
of them.[11] This is the overwhelming sense of obligation and responsibility that
Jewish texts and practices invoke in their promulgation of the duty of showing
hospitality. I would add to this only a point that Edith Wyschogrod has made,
namely that Judaism itself is an experience of the weight of law, that is, of the
weight of obligation and responsibility. This surrounding ethos of religious
and ethical weight is clearly one central factor in Levinas's and Derrida's
philosophy, and most certainly in Derrida's insistence on the demanding and
uprooting responsibility, up until or even beyond the point of dispossession,
that hospitality requires.

However the second factor in the Judaic conception of hospitality to which
we must attend is the unique nature of the home as it is constituted in Jewish

tradition. As is well known, one of the innovations of the rabbis in the times after the destruction of the Second Temple was the working out of a series of legal and symbolic equivalencies, through which the Jewish home came to stand in for the Temple, while the table of such a home and the family eating its meal upon it became a substitution for the altar on which sacrifices had been offered.[12] The institution of Jewish law itself, whose commandments and rituals can be performed anywhere at any time, thus making Judaism a transferable and mobile religion, specifically reapplies many of the laws once germane to the Temple to the Jewish home. If the table becomes the altar, then the householders become the *kohanim* or priests. The side of a Jewish home facing east, or the direction in which the temple once stood, is often marked with a special sign, and when building a new home, the classic code of Jewish law instructed faithful Jews to leave at least some small part of the house unfinished to remind them, in their homes, of the loss of the Temple, and the unfinished character of the world until God brought about the final redemption.

In an intriguing article entitled "Exile And Expulsion in Jewish History," the historian Yosef Yerushalmi explores the myriad of cultural and religious practices through which Jews managed to build up for themselves a sense of home and of being at home, even as they dwelt in various lands of exile.[13] Once again, a process of analogy and patterning comes into play, one through which countries, regions, neighborhoods and streets all received specific ancient Hebrew names and designations reminiscent of Jerusalem and the ancient Land of Israel. Yerushalmi terms this the dialectic of "Exile and Domicile," the transformation of a powerless and exilic existence into one in which the displaced could nonetheless achieve a state of being at home. Yerushalmi pays special attention to the case of Jews reflecting on having being expelled from one country and forced to relocate to another. In these cases, he notes wryly, the writings of Jewish intellectuals and poets reveals a formal longing for return to Jerusalem and the Land of Israel, and yet a far more intense desire to return to the former country of residence. Nonetheless, Yerushalmi maintains that just this apparent preference for remaining "at home" in a strange and ultimately exilic land was in fact accomplished through what one might call the individual and collective work of "imaginative transfer," whereby features of the lost Jewish homeland were rediscovered as present in the new location, thus making it into a new home.

Through a myriad of these sorts of creative religious and cultural practices, the Jewish people "worked up" not only what came to be real homes, but also and at the same time their own unique, religiously and socially constituted sense of "being at home." With this sort of background in place, the responsibility assigned to the virtue of hospitality in Judaism begins to take on its real weight. For that which one presides over, that is, one's own home, is *also* one microcosmic realization of the temporarily missing macrocosmic home of God, namely, the Temple. Even more powerfully, one's own home is also located in a land which itself has been rendered in some way akin to and referentially connected with the ancient land that is temporarily missing. It is *this* home, located in this land, that one must open to the guest, the stranger, the wanderer. According to Jewish law, the value of hospitality is inestimably and immeasurably great. Perhaps if I may speculate, this is in part because what one is opening up to the stranger in hospitality has been achieved only through so much personal, religious and cultural work. To push this line of thought further, one might point out as well that this religiously fashioned home (and sense of home) was, for most of Jewish history, situated in a land that, at best, regarded the Jew as a perpetual foreigner and only tolerated his or her presence.

No doubt, the Jewish sense of home contributed to Jewish survival amidst immensely adverse circumstances. As even the brief sketch provided here makes plain, this stems in part from the considerable "religious and social capital" invested over time in crafting this sense. Yet we need to keep in mind the considerable challenge that elicited this response. The challenge was to survive and, if possible, to flourish in exile in another's land, that is to say, without a native homeland to which one belonged in the present moment and to which one might return. Given this extremely steep gradient, the extensive symbolic, religious and legal resources expended in this project of cultural and religious creation make much more sense.

IV

Perhaps now misgivings about Derrida's misgivings may begin to swim into view. It is certainly not an easy thing to insist, perhaps rightly and importantly, on the dangers that the concrete home may pose to hospitality, and to commend relentless vigilance in the face of hospitality's fragility in any and all particular settings. Ironically though, without minimizing Derrida's always sobering and enlightening work, the Jewish experience reminds us of the unending labor, over centuries, on the part of a religious and cultural system, that it takes to create a home. It also underlines the vital role such a home and sense of home play. In short, while it may not be easy to attend to aporetic phenomena such as hospitality and to issue monitory exhortations regarding them, is it not far harder yet to build up homes and a sense of being at home within them? Do not philosophical formulations of, and worries about hospitality presuppose homes?

Derridean vigilance, upon which all honor, neither builds nor maintains a home, nor does it create and shape land on which the home rests. Perhaps even more tellingly, it plays no role in the psychological, cultural, religious, symbolic and political work through which a human being comes to see him- or herself as belonging to, and being seamlessly and pre-theoretically located—"at home"—within such a home. Perhaps then sober consideration of the Jewish tradition, which itself inspired Derrida's own worry, allows us the perspective to add yet one more worry. One must have a home—and presumably perform all the many kinds of work having a home requires—in order to be hospitable. Home, community, identity, may each be, in Derrida's famous way of putting it, a *pharmakon*—a remedy that at once may cure or kill. But perhaps you also have to *be somewhere* in order to have a discussion about this apparent and fascinating undecidability? And will endless invocations of undecidability, and vigilance about the ontological and socio-political lability they indicate, help to build up "this somewhere" you must be in order to have these discussions? Vigilance is not enough. Vigilance must remain vigilant about what makes it possible.

Of course there need be no "either/or" here. The work of building the home, and of cultivating the capacity to be at home are, it seems to me, perfectly compatible with an additional vigilance about the potential problems that can result from the home. Yet I find little if any recognition of this in Derrida, for whom, it often seems, the overabundance of "sheer positivity" and belonging involved in any sort of tangible identity constitute *nothing more than* overwhelming dangers calling out for immediate deconstruction. With a home and a sense of being at home, one can and indeed must attend to the other, for one's self *is* for the other. Yet without a home and thus also, in a sense, without a self, such attending seems impossible. Perhaps this is one among many lessons Jewish history continues to teach.[14]

PART TWO

INTERRELIGIOUS HOSPITALITY

I

Jewish Perspectives

CHAPTER 6

THE OPEN TENT

ANGELS AND STRANGERS

Edward K. Kaplan

To welcome guests we need to have a home. One way to examine the Jewish tradition of hospitality is to view it as part and parcel of the Jewish condition, which has been one of homelessness, instability, even exile—at least until the recent establishment of the State of Israel in 1948. From the expulsion of humankind's mythic ancestors from the Garden of Eden, through the enslavement of the ancient Israelites in Egypt, the Babylonian exile (586 BCE), and the destruction of the Second Temple in Jerusalem by the Romans in 70 CE, Jews have yearned for a homeland.

My reflections today, however, are not primarily historical or ideological, but, hopefully, spiritual. Spiritual as rooted in historical and daily realities. Jewish tradition has canonized at least three major affirmations of hospitality toward the stranger.

First, the biblical paradigm of hospitality in the book of Genesis (B'reishit, 18:1-33): the story of Abraham and his wife Sarah, the original patriarch and matriarch of the Jewish people. And I shall begin with that text. The opening is intriguingly elliptical:

> The Lord appeared to him [Abraham] by the terebinths of Mamre; he was sitting at the entrance of the tent as the day grew hot. Looking up, he saw three men standing near him. As soon as he saw them, he ran from the entrance of the tent to greet them and, bowing to the ground, he said, "My lords, if it please you, do not go on past your servant. Let a little water be brought; bathe your feet and recline under the tree. (Gen. 18:1-5)[1]

Abraham's response is characterized by extraordinary zeal: "He ran from the entrance of the tent to greet them." Bowing to the ground, he treated his guests with utmost respect, even with reverence.

Abraham then prepared the next stage of hospitality, food, again on the run:

> Abraham hastened into the tent to Sarah, and said, "Quick, three *seahs* of choice flour! and make cakes! Then Abraham ran to the herd, took a calf, tender and choice,

and gave it to a servant boy who hastened to prepare it. He took curds and milk and the calf that had been prepared and set these before them; and he waited on them under the tree as they ate. (Gen. 18:6-8)

The three men enjoy a special meal, a feast. (The repast of curds and milk, along with beef, is not kosher, at least according to the subsequent Divine Revelation at Mount Sinai.) In any case, the three men reward Abraham and Sarah's hospitality by announcing that Sarah, already 90 years old and well past menopause, would become pregnant with a son, thus fulfilling God's promise to Abraham to be the father of a numerous nation (see Gen. 17:1).

Who are these strangers? These wanderers? The lack of transition from line one, "The Lord appeared to him by the terebinths of Mamre," with the ambiguous definition of the three strangers as men, suggests that these are angels from God. And yet the text repeatedly states that Abraham had welcomed and recognized ordinary human beings. Here the status of "stranger" is imbued with sacred mystery.

This story is the biblical paradigm of Jewish hospitality. Some commentators have emphasized Abraham and Sarah's extraordinary hospitality even beyond what is indicated in the biblical text, claiming that their tent was open on four sides to welcome wayfarers.

The next episode in Genesis confirms Abraham's status as a moral model. God tells Abraham that He will destroy Sodom and Gomorrah for their sins. And Abraham has the nerve to challenge God, arguing and convincing God to save the Cities of the Plain if ten righteous persons could be found. God changed the divine Mind: "When the Lord finished speaking to Abraham, He [God] departed; and Abraham returned to his place" (Gen. 18:33).

Biblical paradigm number two. We fast forward to the book of Exodus (Sh'mot) and the captivity of the Israelites in Egypt. Abraham and Sarah's son Isaac had continued his parents' covenant with God. By the end of the book of Genesis, Isaac's son Joseph had successfully saved Egypt from famine. But after Joseph's death, "a new king arose over Egypt who did not know Joseph" (Exod. 1:8). According to the famous phrase, the Israelites were "strangers in a strange land," slaves and aliens. Thus begins the story of Moses and the liberation of the Israelites from Egypt.

The Passover festivity commemorates this second biblical model of Jewish hospitality. The ceremonial dinner, the *Seder*—the highly symbolic (as well as tasty) Passover meal—is probably the most observed by Jews around the world, and by Christians too, especially if we include the Last Supper of Jesus and his disciples and its re-enactment in the Eucharist.

For Jewish families, the Seder is a pedagogical tool as well as a holy celebration. At the beginning, well before the actual meal, a child asks "the four questions," the first of which is "Why is this night different from all other nights?" The answer begins: "Because we were slaves unto Pharaoh in Egypt, and the Eternal, our God, brought us forth from there with a mighty hand and an outstretched arm."[2]

It is an obligation for all Jews to transmit this story from generation to generation. The Passover story is an essential part of Jewish identity as it nurtures a sense of social responsibility, of which hospitality to the stranger is a keynote (see Exod. 12:23-27; 13:3-4). To remember that we were once "strangers in a strange land" not only constitutes an act of solidarity with Jews around the world, it also, and especially, establishes solidarity with all oppressed people. Even secularized Jews celebrate the Passover as a call to universal responsibility.

So the liberation of Exodus is not the endpoint. One major lesson for us (as for the ancient Israelites) is the significance of 40 years of wandering in the desert before entering the Promised Land. During those 40 years the people Israel struggled with God and God's commandments. Numerous times, such as the incident of the golden calf, God had to punish the Israelites, to remind them of their subordination to Divine values.

In fact, it is in the desert itself that Moses commands the Israelites to celebrate the Passover: "throughout the ages; you shall celebrate it as an institution for all time. Seven days you shall eat unleavened bread; on the very first day you shall remove leaven from your houses, for whoever eats leavened bread from the first day to the seventh day, that person shall be cut off from Israel" (Exod. 12:14-15).

The integrity of the Jewish home becomes a precondition for hospitality. Later in the same discourse, Moses repeats, with a significant addition, the basic rule of "kosher for Passover." "No leaven shall be found in your houses for seven days. For whoever eats what is leavened, that person shall be cut off from the community of Israel, whether he is a stranger or a citizen of the country" (Exod. 12:20).

A new category of human social being has been established, the *ger* or "stranger" in Hebrew, or "resident alien," who dwells among or even with the Israelites. The *ger* is subject to the same regulations, privileges and prohibitions—or almost the same. Only the Israelites, however, are required to eat matzah.

Further distinctions apply to the *ger*: "If a stranger who dwells with you would offer the Passover to the Lord, all his males must be circumcised; then shall he be admitted to offer it; he shall then be as a citizen of the country. But no uncircumcised person may eat of it. There shall be one law for the citizen and for the stranger who dwells among you" (Exod. 12: 48-49).[3]

The stranger receives even more attention later on, in the book of Leviticus (Va'yikra), as God establishes laws of justice in the city. The order and context are essential—notice how God reasserts divine authority as a foundation of human, social values:

You shall rise before the aged and show deference to the old; you shall fear your God: I am the Lord.

When a stranger resides with you in your land, you shall not wrong him. The stranger who resides with you shall be to you as one of your citizens; you shall love him as yourself, for you were strangers in the land of Egypt: I am the Lord your God.

And you shall not falsify measures of length, weight, or capacity. You shall have an honest balance, honest weights, an honest *ephah*, and an honest *hin*.

I the Lord am your God who freed you from the land of Egypt. You shall faithfully observe all My laws and all My rules: I am the Lord (Lev. 19:32-37).

God cares about details. Every act of dishonesty is a major crime. In addition, this is a universal morality; the stranger must be treated with as much deference as any other citizen.

(The converse is also true: "Anyone among the Israelites, or among the strangers residing in Israel, who gives any of his offspring to Moloch, shall be put to death," Lev. 20:2.)

The Jewish festival of Sukkot marks the third and most explicit reference point for Jewish hospitality. Apart from the Passover Seder, to which many non-Jews are invited, perhaps to advance interfaith relations, Sukkot—the harvest festival of booths—provides a systematic space for hospitality, which has become an actual divine commandment, a *mitzvah*.[4]

We are enjoined to construct an impermanent room-like booth, whose roof is covered with greens but open to the sky—often subjected to the cold and rain. Traditional Jews strive to obey the commandment to sleep in the sukkah for seven nights; at the very least, we are commanded to invite guests for dinner. It is an obligation of Jewish law. There is a commandment (*mitzvah*) to eat in the sukkah, the booth, and a *mitzvah* to welcome guests.

It is true that most culturally assimilated Jews do not actually build a sukkah. But all synagogues have a sukkah for their members and the commandment to welcome guests for a festive meal is widely practiced in our synagogues and in homes.

Guests are welcomed in such a way as to canonize the *mitzvah* of hospitality, that is, hospitality as a response to God's will. Upon entering the sukkah, special prayers are said to welcome the guests, who are called *ushpizin* in Hebrew. I read the English translation of the first Hebrew prayer:

> Enter, exalted holy guests, enter, exalted holy Patriarchs, to be seated in the shade of exalted faithfulness in the shade of the Holy One. Enter, Abraham the beloved one, Moses the faithful shepherd, Aaron the Holy Kohen (Priest), Joseph the righteous one, and David the anointed king. In succos you shall dwell, be seated, exalted guests, be seated; be seated, guests of faithfulness, be seated.[5]

These are no ordinary guests, of course, but the seven patriarchs of the Jewish people: Abraham, Isaac, Jacob, Moses, Aaron, Joseph and David. The Jewish mystical tradition in the Zohar explains that when guests enter the sukkah in faithfulness, the wings of God's presence, the *Shekhinah*, are spread over them.

Without entering into more details of this complicated Kabbalistic tradition, one more interpretation fills out the sacred significance of this act of hospitality. The order of the *ushpizin* (guests) is like a summary of God's attributes or emanations, as evoked in the Zohar:

Abraham is loving kindness or hesed
Isaac, power or gevurah
Jacob, splendor or tiferet
Moses is eternality or netzakh
Aaron is Glory or hod
Joseph is foundation or yesod
and David is kingship or malkhut[6]

Such is the spiritual significance of hospitality. The mystical Zohar becomes concrete as it embodies God's emanations in the patriarchs of the Jewish people. And yet, are not all finite human beings an image of God, according to the story in Genesis? And every human being a messenger from God? That is why Abraham and Sarah keep their tent open on all four sides. A radically open tent. Metaphorically speaking, we must keep our hearts open.

In the Jewish world after the Bible, and after the talmudic discussions, religious law (*halakah*) has encoded these rituals in a general principle of hospitality/*hakhnasat orkhim*, "a serious legal obligation" to welcome the stranger.[7] We have thus traversed the books of Genesis, Exodus and Leviticus, from the spiritual to the ethical, which were indeed never separated.

* * *

Finally, I want to share with you a more metaphorical—but no less concrete—approach, an approach to the ideal of hospitality, one which is perhaps even more universal than the open tent or the sukkah. I am speaking about Abraham Joshua Heschel's understanding of prayer. Rabbi Heschel was a direct descendent of the founders of Hasidism, the pietistic movement that began in eighteenth-century Poland, whose main purpose was to bring all Jews closer to the living God through prayer and celebration.

Rabbi Heschel spoke these eloquent words about prayer at a Christian conference on Liturgy, held in Milwaukee, Wisconsin in 1969. The metaphor of home represents the enveloping power of prayer to welcome seekers of God and of spiritual integrity. Here, God is the host and we are the guests. Prayer can become our spiritual dwelling place:

> All things have a home: the bird has a nest, the fox has a hole, the bee has a hive. A soul without prayer is a soul without a home. Weary, sobbing, the soul, after roaming through a world festered with aimlessness, falsehoods, and absurdities, [the soul] seeks a moment in which to gather up its scattered life, in which to divest itself of enforced pretensions and camouflage, in which to simplify complexities, in which to call for help without being a coward. Such a home is prayer. Continuity, permanence, intimacy, authenticity, earnestness are its attributes. For the soul, home is where prayer is.[8]

Yes, we are in exile in the world, Heschel suggests. One task of religion is to transform exile into a pilgrimage, a lonely journey energized by a goal. For God's hospitality is infinite, always available to the pilgrim, to the stranger:

> What is a soul without prayer? A soul runaway or a soul evicted from its own home. To those who have abandoned their home: The road may be hard and dark and far, yet do not be afraid to steer back. If you prize grace and eternal meaning, you will discover them upon arrival.[9]

Heschel goes on to evoke the transformative power of hospitality, for the stranger, the *ger*—and are not all of us "resident aliens"? The guest is indeed liberated:

> How marvelous is my home. I enter as a suppliant and emerge as a witness; I enter as a stranger and emerge as next of kin. I enter spiritually shapeless, inwardly disfigured, and emerge wholly changed. It is in moments of prayer that my image is forged, that my striving is fashioned. To understand the world I must love my home. It is difficult to perceive luminosity anywhere if there is no light in my own home. It is in light of prayer's radiance that I find my way even in the dark.[10]

Thank you for this opportunity to join our Jewish journeys to yours.

CHAPTER 7

SUKKOT

LEVINAS AND THE FESTIVAL OF THE CABINS

Hugh Cummins

Emmanuel Levinas became an adopted French citizen in 1931, eight years after leaving his native Lithuania to study philosophy in Strasbourg. In the last decade or so of his life, he gave numerous interviews that shed a late, retrospective light on his thought and also, to some extent, on his biography. In a 1982 interview he recalled being asked if, as a Jew, he didn't still feel like an outsider in France. He had replied, he told his interviewer, that "wherever I am I feel I am in the way," embellishing this answer with a much-quoted verse from Psalm 119: "I am a stranger on the earth."[1] For Levinas this is not the maxim of a Romantic outsider but the very basis of sociality. Thus he has often pointed to its inseparability from the verse that succeeds it: "Give me your law."[2] Strangers require a law, the law that binds us to responsibility for the other and enjoins us to welcome the stranger we all are.

Levinas's two major philosophical works, *Totality and Infinity* and *Otherwise than Being*, reflect numerous shifts of perspective on the theme of the stranger and the neighbor, and on their relation to the "host" and the "hostage." Arguably both works employ what one commentator has called "two logics"[3] that are not easily, if at all, reconcilable. Dominant in both works, of course, is the ethical relation to the other, a "relation without relation" that is presented as pacific and pedagogical, on the one hand, and persecutory and obsessional on the other. In the following I will explore the linked themes of home, homelessness and hospitality as they are figured and refigured in the two major works. However, I wish to pursue these themes via a somewhat circuitous and perhaps speculative route, in relation to the annual Jewish Sukkot festival, briefly referred to by Levinas as "the festival of the cabins." Involved here will be a double movement, on the one hand seeking out resonances of the "sukkah command" in Levinas's texts, and on the other hand reading into the command some of Levinas's key concerns, tropes and concepts. This double movement, it is argued, will illuminate not only central aspects of Levinas's ethical philosophy but a crucial feature of the Jewish tradition that informs it.

At the outset it must be noted that explicit references to the Sukkot festival are scarcely to be found in either Levinas's philosophical or religious writings. I will discuss what to my knowledge is the single exception I have already mentioned, but also what is undoubtedly his most significant explicit reference, in the form of a verbal contribution to a discussion at the first Colloquium of French Speaking Jewish Intellectuals in 1957.[4] However, I also wish to examine how an implicit awareness of the biblical command to build a sukkah can be seen to inform Levinas's reflections on "the dwelling" in *Totality and Infinity*.

Whether the sukkah command can be discerned in the significantly different analysis of ethical subjectivity in *Otherwise than Being* must also be considered. Here the question arises whether an ethics of radical homelessness, where ethical subjectivity involves "an openness of self without a world, without a place, utopia,"[5] can be in any sense an ethics of hospitality, as Derrida has claimed of the ethical relation in *Totality and Infinity*.[6] To put the question another way: does an ethics of radical homelessness not in fact involve, to use an expression from a talmudic text to be discussed below, "kicking down the sukkah"? But first it is necessary to say something about the Sukkot festival itself and the command that inaugurates it.

Sukkot

Sukkot, which lasts for seven days in autumn, is the last of the three Jewish pilgrim festivals, following Passover or *Pesach* (commemorating the exodus from Egypt) and *Shavuot* (commemorating the reception of the ten commandments by Moses on Mount Sinai). As a harvest festival, it is celebratory and joyful and according to some is the origin of the Puritans' Thanksgiving festival in America. The word itself is the Hebrew plural of "sukkah," variously translated as tabernacle, booth, hut, cabin. The festival recalls the biblical commandment to "live in booths for seven days" (Lev. 23:42), "keeping holiday again and making good cheer, with son and daughter, serving man and serving maid, Levite and wanderer, orphan and widow that are thy neighbors" (Deut. 16:13-14). When observed nowadays it is with great variation depending on levels of orthodoxy and geographical climate, but in one form or another it reflects the command to forsake the security and stability of one's normal dwelling and live in a temporary shelter for a period of time. The sukkah itself is loosely constructed, sometimes as an annex to the house, its roof composed of detachable organic matter such as tree branches, wooden boards, reeds, thatching, etc. Thus Jews are summoned to remember the 40 years of homeless wandering after the exodus, when they lived in desert-tents. As such, the festival is a symbolic recreation of past conditions and an attempt to integrate them into present experience.

The movement from house to sukkah symbolizes a movement from security to dependence and interdependence—on God and on other people. Hospitality is thus an essential feature of the festival, the obligation to entertain guests both familiar and strange. Recalled also therefore is an exemplary instance of biblical hospitality when Abraham welcomes three strangers into his tent (Gen. 18:4-5) and thus the divine Stranger who predicts new life. Here one might also mention a contemporary and humorous depiction of the Sukkot festival and the law of hospitality it enjoins, explored in Gidi Dar's 2005 Israeli movie *Ushpizin*. This Aramaic word for "holy guests" points to another aspect of the festival for Orthodox Jews, who welcome in prayer spiritual ancestors from Abraham onwards into the sukkah as *ushpizin*. In the movie Moshe and Malli, a childless couple and modern-day equivalent of Abraham and Sarah, play host in their sukkah to two escaped criminals. To the bemused and not very holy guests, who nevertheless have a transforming effect on their hosts, Moshe explains the meaning of the Sukkot festival thus: "Why has the Lord commanded us to stay in the sukkah? Not only stay in it, but eat, drink, sleep in it? Why is that? God wanted us to feel that just as a sukkah is a temporary dwelling, so is the world temporary, fleeting, where we are merely guests." The notion that guests might be unruly or otherwise difficult to welcome, explored in this humorous fable, will be relevant when considering later the way the notion of hospitality is transformed in *Otherwise than Being*.

Levinas and Sukkot

In the essay "A Religion for Adults" from *Difficult Freedom*, Levinas's brief allusion to "The festival of the cabins" (*La fête des cabanes*) is noteworthy both for itself and the context in which it appears. It occurs during the course of the following reflection:

> The Jewish man discovers man before discovering landscapes and towns. He is at home in a society before being so in a house. He understands the world on the basis of the Other rather than the whole of being functioning in relation to the earth. He is in a sense exiled on this earth, as the psalmist says, and he finds a meaning to the earth on the basis of a human society . . . Man begins in the desert where he dwells in tents, and adores God in a transportable temple.[7]

The memory of this existence—"free with regard to landscapes and architectures, all those heavy and sedentary things that one is tempted to prefer to man"—has as its liturgical form "the festival of the cabins," announced by the prophet Zechariah, Levinas notes, "as though it were a festival of all the nations."[8]

The significance of its extension to "all the nations" becomes apparent in Levinas's only other reference to the Sukkot festival or the "sukkah command." As indicated already, this comes not from his published writings or interviews but from a recorded contribution to a discussion at the first Colloquium of French Speaking Jewish Intellectuals in 1957. Levinas helped to organize this first colloquium but he did not present a paper.[9] His contribution to a round-table discussion, however, is especially noteworthy in the context of this essay. This follows a paper by Edmond Flegg on "The Meaning of Jewish History," and at issue is the role of the state or politics, on the one hand, and on the other hand religion, which for Levinas pertains to the ethical or the interpersonal. Talmudic literature acknowledges the necessity of the state—"without it men would eat each other alive"[10]—but also a limit to the state that otherwise "announces oppression." This reflection is followed by the observation that the biblical tension between the Jews and other nations is universalized by the

Talmud into a conflict between ethics and politics. Levinas then illustrates by way of allusion to a particular talmudic text, a tractate on idolatry, in this case *political* idolatry, and its transformation by the religious or the ethical.

Robert Gibbs has reproduced the talmudic passages that Levinas draws on in his contribution to the discussion. To give only the immediate context: on Judgment Day the nations seek finally to be part of the covenant, to accept the commandments of the Torah and thus obtain a "second chance." Levinas's summary is as follows:

> In the treatise on idolatry a passage is found which dealt with a sense of history [i.e. the subject of the paper to which he is responding]: different people are presented before the Eternal in order to claim their place in history . . . Let us affirm in passing that there is no racial superiority for the Jews. A pagan who fulfils the Torah is as great as a high priest. But everything gets its meaning from the Torah . . . There exists a simple to fulfil commandment: the Sukkah. Everyone is put to build a Sukkah. But God sends a torrid heat. Everyone abandons the sheds and demolishes them by kicking them apart. They cannot withstand the test. Here Levinas quotes directly from the tractate: ". . . but the Jews, would they always stay in the torrid heat?" "No they also would leave, but they would not destroy the temporary dwelling."[11]

To obtain a "second chance," then, the nations are commanded to build a sukkah. God sends a torrid heat that makes their sukkot uninhabitable. Forced to leave, the nations destroy the sukkot whereas the Jews, although they would also leave in such circumstances, would not destroy the temporary dwelling. What, therefore, does the sukkah ultimately represent or symbolize here? What is the significance of the heat God sends and of the decision to kick down the sukkah on the one hand (the nations) and to preserve the sukkah on the other (the Jews) after it becomes necessary to leave it?

Gibbs offers a reading of the talmudic text before turning to Levinas's account. When the nations kick their sukkot in, he suggests, "they are rejecting Jewish religion, not the Jewish theocracy or kings." But what does Jewish religion mean here, and why is it linked to the sukkah? Levinas's interpretation of the text he has summarized will give an answer that is anticipated when Gibbs notes: "God requires a series of practices that disrupt the rule of politics but do not revolt against them."

Another reading focuses on the Jews rather than the nations. Here again the sukkah represents Jewish religion and the Jews are enjoined to maintain it in a time of instability, "without the priests and temple, without the state and its control of power." When Gibbs turns to Levinas's account he notes that the latter reveals another dimension when he affirms that "there is no racial superiority for the Jews" and that "a pagan who fulfills the Torah is as great as a high priest."[12] The Torah commandment in this case is the building of a sukkah, and it is extended to all the nations. Thus Levinas's allusion to Zechariah above is an affirmation of universality, at once a universal command and invitation, so that the festival of the cabins will become a festival of all the nations. In his conclusion, however, Levinas returns to the import of the sukkah command for the Jews:

> To retain the possibility of remaining outside the solid dwellings of the sedentary and historic peoples is the privilege of the Jewish people. The essential arises in interpersonal relations and not in the splendors of architecture. The Jews also protect themselves from the heat and set themselves up in a house (the State) but without forgetting the Sukkah because of it. The Jew does not situate his humanity in rootedness.[13]

This recalls in similar terms the context of Levinas's first reference to "the festival of the cabins" above, where he also stresses the interpersonal relation over all forms of enrootedness. Of particular interest here, however, is Levinas's comparison of the house to the state, and in turn the contrast between the house-state and the sukkah. The Jews do not reject the ontological order of the state, which has a legitimate protective function. But they do not forget the sukkah, which signals the interruption of the political but not the rejection of the political. To kick down the sukkah, on the other hand, is to reject Jewish religion, which is to say the interpersonal relation to the other which is beyond ontology and disrupts the self-possession of the ego at home in itself and its world. It is to reject that that is fragile and exposed to the "heat" of the unpredictable and fall prey to the illusion that the political is enough, or that one can set oneself up in a fortress state.

But I wish now to take a step back from the political, from the house as state to the house as dwelling or home, and to explore to what extent the sukkah command may be relevant here also.

Sojourning in a Home

Totality and Infinity, its subtitle attests, is "an essay on exteriority." Metaphysics, transcendence, infinity, the Other, the Stranger—all indicate an exteriority that calls into question the sovereignty of an ego at home in itself and its world. This calling into question of the subject by the Other, however, is also a "welcoming" of the Other by the subject. Thus in his preface Levinas announces: "This book will present subjectivity as welcoming the Other, as hospitality . . ."[14] At issue, then, is not only an essay on exteriority but "the welcoming of the other by the same" (TI, 43) and therefore an exploration of the conditions that make this welcoming possible. Levinas's willingness from the outset to link the ethical relation to the notion of welcoming justifies Derrida's claim that "*Totality and Infinity* bequeaths to us an immense treatise of hospitality."[15]

Central among the conditions that make hospitality possible are "Interiority and Economy," the title of section two of this work, and for our purposes explored most significantly in Levinas's chapter on "The Dwelling." Levinas begins this chapter by invoking Heidegger's notion of habitation as the utilization of an implement, where the home would be, like the "room" in *Being and Time*, "equipment for residing."[16] For Levinas, in contrast, "The privileged role of the home does not consist in being the end of human activity but in being its condition, and in this sense its commencement" (TI, 152). It is because I can withdraw to a home where I can recollect myself that the world of objects is made possible through representation, labor and possession. Similarly, it is because I can withdraw from the elemental world that I can give myself over to it in immediate and spontaneous enjoyment. To bathe thus in the element "is to be in an inside-out world" (TI, 132), but it is the event of dwelling that has made this exposure possible. The anteriority of the dwelling is concretized when enjoyment becomes inverted into "care for the morrow" (TI, 150) and allows for the suspension or deferral of an uncertain future. In the interiority and hiddenness of my home I am, like Gyges in Plato's *Republic*, able to view and plan my engagement with a world from which I have withdrawn into invisibility.

Thus far in Levinas's analysis of the dwelling there seems little to discern of the fragility of the sukkah; on the contrary, the home is more akin to a secure house, a place of retreat and fortification against the world that also enables engagement with the world. It is when Levinas asks what makes this withdrawal and recollection possible that the dwelling first reveals an aspect associated with the sukkah command. "Recollection refers to a welcome," Levinas observes (TI, 155). My home welcomes me and as such presupposes a welcoming Other. Problematically, Levinas names this welcoming Other the "Woman" or the "Feminine," designations whose difficulties are not quite overcome by his insistence that he is not assuming in every home "a person of the 'feminine sex'" (TI, 158). Suffice to say that for Levinas the home, even the home of the solitary occupant it may be assumed although he does not explicitly say so, does presuppose the "discreet" presence of an Other that welcomes its proprietor. The crucial point, as Derrida has noted, is that "The head of the household, the master of the house, is already a . . . guest in his own home."[17] Derrida relates this condition to the "divine law" recalled by Franz Rosenzweig in *The Star of Redemption*, which disallows the eternal people, the Jews, full possession of the home. The eternal people are already strangers in their own land, guests of a divine hospitality. For Levinas too the home is possessed only in the qualified sense that "it already and henceforth is hospitable for its proprietor" (TI, 157). Here, I would argue, Levinas demonstrates an implicit awareness of the sukkah command that recalls the Jews to a state of primordial dependence as guests, a dependence that precedes and interrupts the sovereign possession of the home.

For Levinas, however, even a withdrawal and recollection that refers to a welcoming Other does not constitute the essence of the home. The possession that I enjoy by virtue of the dwelling, even if it be the possession of a guest, must be contested by an Other who not only welcomes me but puts me and what I possess in question. In short, as Levinas puts it, "I must be able to give what I possess." It is the "face" of the Other that calls me into question and "paralyzes possession" (TI, 171).

Moreover, the "epiphany" of the face that contests possession of the home calls forth "a certain mode of sojourning in a home" and "a certain form of economic life" (TI, 172). What mode or form? Levinas's earliest references in *Totality and Infinity* to a "sojourn in the world" and to "sojourning" indicate the way the ego maintains its identity by gathering its alterations to itself and representing them to itself, thus establishing itself at home with itself. This "presence at home with oneself—sojourning in a dwelling" (TI, 37), has an essentially nomadic structure, a movement of endless Odyssean return and thus, as Levinas put it in an interview from 1982, "Nothing is more enrooted than the nomad." In contrast to the Greek Odysseus, what is exemplary about the Hebrew Abraham for Levinas is that he is an *emigrant* who does not return to familiar sites or places. Therefore to the above statement Levinas adds: "But he or she who emigrates is fully human."[18] Ultimately for Levinas, the wanderings of the nomad pertain to Heidegger's "ontological adventure," where Dasein always returns to itself from its ecstatic sojourning, gathering its projections and recollections to itself. The ethical relation, in contrast, involves a "departure without return," a movement that is exodic rather than nomadic.

But is it possible to be an emigrant in Levinas's sense and "sojourn in a home"? Levinas's reference to *a certain mode* of sojourning in a home is intended to indicate precisely this possibility. This is confirmed when he writes:

> The chosen home is the opposite of a root. It indicates a disengagement, a wandering [errance] which has made it possible, which is not a less with respect to installation, but the surplus of the relation with the Other, metaphysics. (TI, 172)

To disengage and wander in this sense is not an aimless drifting, or a nomadic revisiting of familiar sites, but a response to the call of the Other, the paradigmatic instance being Abraham's obedience to the command that inaugurates the three monotheisms: "Go. Leave thy country behind thee, thy kinsfolk, and thy father's home, and come away into a land I will show thee" (Gen. 12:1). In the biblical account, this involves a geographical leave-taking, a literal "departure without return." What is essential for Levinas, however, is the *ethical* import of this departure or disengagement, where the ego is set to wandering like the needle of a compass that can never predict in advance the location of the Other. Crucially therefore, at least in *Totality and Infinity*, the Other is welcomed from a home, albeit a transfigured home. Thus: "The relation with infinity remains another possibility of the being recollected in its dwelling. The possibility of the home to open to the Other is as essential to the home as closed doors or windows" (TI, 173). What is entailed, finally, in Levinas's analysis of the dwelling, and of sojourning in a home, is not an ontological movement from "here" to "there" qua Heidegger's Dasein, although this too is made possible by the dwelling, but the ethical transformation of an enrooted "here" into a wandering "here I am."

* * *

I have pointed out one important resonance of the sukkah command in the above analysis—being recalled from the status of a proprietor to that of a guest—but of course it has been my intention to imply others. Let me state now more explicitly what I take these to be.

The command to build a sukkah and live in it for a time each year reminds the Jews not only of their dependence on God and their status as guests but also of the obligation to extend the hospitality they have received to others, including strangers. The movement from possession to being welcomed by what I possess, and in turn to giving what I possess by way of hospitality, is clearly discernible in Levinas's analysis of the dwelling. The sukkah command also recalls a time of homelessness and wandering in the desert, a constitutive experience for the Jews. However, the biblical command to build a sukkah is directed toward Jews who have acquired secure homes. Moreover, the command to move from the house to the sukkah during the Sukkot festival is not a command to permanently forsake the house. In fact, pious insistence on remaining in the sukkah during a time of rain or extreme heat or cold, for example, is frowned upon as a form of pride. "From affliction one is exempt from the sukkah . . . 'but who would kick it down'"[19] says/quotes one of the rabbis in the talmudic passages discussed above. The sukkah command is animated by the necessity to transform the house rather than abandon it, or to interrupt the habitual manner of dwelling in a way that continues to be experienced when one has returned to it. The talmudic insistence that the sukkah not be kicked down applies also to the house, whether the latter be the state whose laws protect me or the dwelling that welcomes me. To sojourn in a home, in Levinas's sense, is also to transform the house into a sukkah without forsaking either.

Levinas's treatment of the dwelling is not only implicitly informed by the sukkah command but reveals, arguably, something essential about the sukkah itself. The sukkah, that is to say, is not a *less* with regard to installation in a house but a surplus, open to others in way that exceeds the house, a *more* symbolized by the loosely or partially constructed roof open to the infinite. In this sense, the sukkah is anterior to the house, even if it is discovered or recalled "after the event" of dwelling in a house. The tent where Abraham welcomed the three divine strangers, it could be said, is anterior to the house he left in Harran.

Levinas's dwelling, like the sukkah or the sukkah-house, both welcomes and questions its proprietor. What is possessed by virtue of a welcoming Other who enables recollection can be given to "the Stranger who disturbs the being at home with oneself" (TI, 39), calling me out of my place in my place to sojourn in a home. Here it is worth citing at length a figure deemed by Levinas too often present in *Totality and Infinity* to be cited, Franz Rosenzweig:

Sukkot is at the same time the festival of wandering and rest; for the memory of the erstwhile long wandering which finally led to the rest there, the inhabitants of the house do not join together for the meal in the usual rooms of the house, but under a light quickly built roof that allows the sky to show through it. Here the people can remember also that the house of today's day at any given time, may it be ever so alluring for rest and a secure dwelling, yet is only a tent that permits temporary rest during the long wandering through the desert of the centuries . . .[20]

Rosenzweig, like Levinas as I have been arguing, is revealing the house in the sukkah and the sukkah in the house. It is a case of wandering *and* rest. Whether this analysis can be sustained, or whether the sukkah command is in any sense applicable, must now be explored in relation to Levinas's very different treatment of these themes in *Otherwise than Being*.

A Shelter Exposed to all the Winds

Totality and Infinity seems to presuppose a separated subject at home in its world and subsequently put in question by an Other who is also welcomed. The impression remains despite the fact that for Levinas a separated subject is possible only because of a relation to the Other. In *Otherwise than Being* the focus shifts from the intentionality of consciousness, however interrupted, to the radical passivity of a subject already subject to the Other or, more precisely, "the other in the same" (OB, 111). As hostage to and substitute for the Other, I am assigned to the Other's place and therefore expelled from my own. The persecuting proximity of the neighbor, already "under one's skin" as it were, causes the subject "to lose his place radically, or his shelter in being" (OB, 185).

The notion of hospitality as that which an active subject extends from a place, site or home is clearly problematized here. If, to recall Derrida, *Totality and Infinity* offers us a vast treatise on hospitality that leans on the word "welcome," *Otherwise than Being* presents us with what appears to be a stark contrast:

> As a subject that approaches, I am not in the approach called to play the role of a perceiver that reflects or welcomes . . . Proximity is not a state, a repose, but a restlessness, null-site, outside of the place of rest. (OB, 82)

The radical passivity of the ethical subject precludes any initiative in relation to the proximity of the neighbor, whether of perception or welcome. Moreover, there is no "place" from which such an initiative would arise, or the repose necessary to realize it. Hence the question posed in my introduction: does Levinas, in *Otherwise than Being*, "kick down the *sukkah*" as a place of hospitality? To do so would in this case be in the name not of a political security that rejects the fragility of the ethical but of a nihilist, ethical utopia. The following would also appear to confirm this possibility: "[T]he openness of space signifies the outside where nothing covers anything, non-protection, the reverse of a retreat, homelessness, non-world, non-inhabitation, layout without security." Crucially, however, he adds: "These significations are not only privative; they signify the end, or the hither side, of the dark designs of inwardness . . ." (OB, 179). What is surpassed in the above significations, I would suggest, making them "not only privative," is the inwardness or interiority of Gyges, who is "the very condition of man," according to Levinas in *Totality and Infinity* (173). Gyges enacts his "dark designs" from a concealed position, accepting the rules of the game only to cheat. Levinas posits another kind of interiority, not of concealment but, paradoxically, exposure. Inwardness in this sense "is not a secret place somewhere inside me; it is that reverting in which the eminently exterior concerns me and orders me in my own voice" (OB, 147).

It is in the very intimacy of the I, then, that responsibility for the Other is rediscovered as that that is anterior to all encounters with others and how I might respond to them. It is significant that Levinas speaks of a "reverting," given that elsewhere, as noted above, he has referred to ethical subjectivity as a "departure without return." Yet if some kind of return is in question, or what he also calls "recurrence," it cannot be to the sheltered ego at home in itself and its world. The nominative ego (*moi*) departs so that the self (*soi*) may return as subject to the Other, an Other who "concerns me and orders me by my own voice." This return or reverting or recurrence is to a state of exile and homelessness, on the hither side of the ego. But again these terms are not merely privative; they indicate a state of exposure and restlessness that is the no-hiding-place of conscience.

But how does this analysis bear on the question of hospitality, or the sukkah as a place of hospitality? Bernasconi has observed how in the 1970 essay "Without Identity" Levinas seems to abandon the word to Heidegger when he writes of the latter's thought: "The process of being, or being's essence, is from the first manifestation, expansion onto a site, hospitality."[21] Here Levinas is associating hospitality with Heideggerian notions of place, site and world. His own use of the term in *Totality and Infinity* was justified, according to Bernasconi, because "Levinas introduces another sense of dwelling to counter Heidegger's."[22] I have explored above the sense of dwelling that for Levinas justifies the term hospitality—"the chosen home is the opposite of a root" and calls for disengagement, wandering, "paralyzed possession"—and must leave aside to what extent it is counter to Heidegger's.[23] Levinas cedes the word to Heidegger, as Bernasconi puts it, "because his account is now directed, not to the Other putting me in question, but to the passivity of a self more passive than the receptivity of welcome of an active ego."[24] In *Otherwise than Being*, the subject is also a stranger, exiled from any kind of identity that would enable it to coincide with itself. But it is precisely this condition of shared strangerhood that allows Levinas to reclaim the word "hospitality" in the following passage:

> In the subject, it is precisely not an assembling, but an incessant alienation of the ego (isolated as inwardness) by the guest entrusted to it. Hospitality, the One-for-the-Other in the ego, delivers it more passively than any passivity from links in a causal chain. Being torn from oneself for another in giving to the Other the bread from one's mouth is being able to give up one's soul for another. (OB, 79)

Thus for Levinas hospitality is inseparable from the logic of substitution. It is possible only because I have been rendered a stranger to myself by the proximity of the Other as neighbor in me, incessantly alienating me but in a way that animates rather than deprives.

* * *

I would like to return to the theme of "conscience" in light of the above for here, I believe, it will be come apparent how the sukkah command continues to resonate in Levinas's treatment of hospitality as substitution. In the "recurrence" of ethical subjectivity, where the active ego (*moi*) reverts to the passivity of a self (*soi*), consciousness reverts to conscience. Conscience as such strips away the ego's shelter in being; it is an extreme exposure to the Other, an inability to hide from the Other. This condition—Levinas would say "incondition"—is precisely that enjoined by the command to build a sukkah and welcome guests, who include widows and strangers. But is the sukkah not a shelter, if only a makeshift shelter, partially if not entirely walled and covered over? This is true, yet for Levinas too conscience is a shelter of sorts. Thus he writes, in the 1966 essay "Nameless":

> When the temples are standing, the flags flying atop the palaces and the magistrates donning their sashes, the tempests raging in individual heads do not pose the threat of shipwreck. They are perhaps but the waves stirred by the winds of the world around well-anchored souls within their harbors. The true inner life is not a pious or revolutionary thought that comes to us in a stable world, but the obligation to lodge the whole of humanity in the shelter - exposed to all the winds - of conscience.[25]

Conscience, then, is an exposed shelter that may have no recourse to a stable world whose institutions would underwrite it. Thus "Judaism," as Levinas puts it in the same essay, "is humanity on the brink of morality without institutions."[26] Institutions, however, are not to be kicked down on that account. Neither the house nor the sukkah are to be kicked down.

On the other hand, conscience is that to which the Other has recourse, a shelter or sukkah for the Other. But, if the analogy is stretched this far, does this not make of the sukkah a place of persecution? Here it may be instructive to recall again the Israeli movie *Ushpizin*. In this movie the two guests do in a sense persecute their hosts, by their unruly behavior and incessant demands. Thus Moshe is led to practice a deception to get rid of them, telling them he is about to travel with his wife Malli to another city to visit her parents. When the guests leave on this account, the couple continue to occupy the sukkah and eat in it, but their meal is overshadowed by feelings of guilt. Malli believes she has failed the test of hospitality to her guests, even when Moshe assures her: "You treated them just fine. They weren't too nice themselves." She replies: "It's clear as day it was a test. Some test it would have been if they were nice guests." And later she adds: "We blew it Moshe. We blew it big time."

For Levinas, to be responsible for the Other is already to be too late to actively respond to the Other, to have "blown it" in a sense. In his elaboration on a theme in Ionesco's *The Bald Soprano*, the stranger who rings my door-bell has already departed by the time I open the door, and may not even have been there in the first place.[27] So why bother to open the door? Because ethical subjectivity is precisely this persecuting uncertainty, which I cannot avoid but which calls me to act even if belatedly. This is also what might be called the "Levinasian moment" in the Song of Songs as cited in *Otherwise than Being*, when after the love-sick bride hears a knock on the door and her lover's voice pleading to be admitted, she opens the door to discover him gone. "I opened . . . he had disappeared" (Song of Songs 5:6). As Levinas puts it, "The delay is irrecuperable" (OB, 88). The proximity of the stranger and the lover at the door in each case "does not enter into the common time of clocks, which makes meetings possible. It is a disturbance" (OB, 89).

Proximity as disturbance and persecution, obsession and belatedness, also involves, as we have seen, "the incessant alienation of the ego by the guest entrusted to it" (OB, 79). But Levinas also indicates that alienation is not only privative. Thus he can ask, in "Without Identity": "Is it certain that in the deportation or drift of identity perceived through the reversal of human projects the subject does not signify with all its youthful radiance?"[28]

To live in the sukkah is also to undergo a reversal of sorts. But it is also to be recalled to the radiance of hospitality. The sukkah as conscience, as a shelter for the Other, "exposed to all the winds," may therefore also signify something youthful and joyous celebrated in the festival of the cabins.

Conclusion

I have attempted to show how, despite only two explicit references elsewhere, the sukkah command can be seen to resonate in Levinas's two major philosophical works. In *Totality and Infinity,* the dwelling, like the sukkah, is hospitable for its proprietor who is therefore also a guest. This involves a movement from possession to being welcomed by what I possess, and in turn to a "paralyzed possession" that enables me to give what I possess. Here the home reverts to a place of wandering or "sojourning" in response to the call of the Other. This analysis, I have argued, also reveals the sukkah to be anterior to the house and to be that which exceeds the house, the possibility of the house to open to the Other.

In *Otherwise than Being*, the radical homelessness of the ethical subject invites the question of whether Levinas kicks down the sukkah as a place of hospitality. But "homelessness" here is not to be understood in a merely privative sense. Consciousness reverted to conscience becomes a shelter for the Other. Obviously the degree of exposure here is more radical than that of the dwelling in *Totality and Infinity* and far exceeds that of an actual sukkah. But conscience, I would suggest, like Levinas's "utopia," does not so much abandon the notion of place as reveal it to be exposed or "inside-out." This is what Miguel Abensour has called "the paradox of utopia." It is, as he has said, "as if utopia had to learn to make *fragility* its home."[29]

The reverting to ethical subjectivity as conscience also reveals a fundamental aspect of the sukkah command recently recalled by Richard Kearney. The Sukkot festival, Kearney notes, "serves to remind the followers of Abraham that they are forever tent dwellers, strangers on the earth committed to the hosting of strangers." Moreover, "This is a reminder that has to be made again and again, year after year."[30] The reminder is necessary, according to Kearney, because the alternative to hospitality, hostility toward and rejection of the stranger, is also an ineradicable aspect of the human revealed by the biblical religions. Thus the Abraham who welcomed the three strangers into his tent (Gen. 18:1-8) is also the Abraham who drove Hagar, his mistress-slave, and their son Ishmael into the wilderness (Gen. 21:14-15).

* * *

Levinas, to recall again his contribution to the 1957 colloquium, observes in relation to the talmudic passage on which he comments: "The Jews also protect themselves from the heat and set themselves up in a house (the State) but without forgetting the sukkah because of it." Here it is reasonable to ask: have extreme elements in modern Israel forgotten the sukkah or kicked it down?

This would be to retreat into a fortress state, to seek to eliminate the risk of hospitality to strangers and enemies, in this case Palestinians. It would also be, to repeat what Robert Gibbs notes above, to reject Jewish religion as that which interrupts and suspends the rule of politics without revolting against it. But to pose the question in this way is also to indicate that a solution can only come from within, animated by the retrieval of something precious in the Jewish tradition itself, and not by the critiques of "beautiful souls" from without.

At issue here as well, of course, is Levinas's complex relation to Zionism. In a controversial 1982 interview, after the massacre of Palestinians by Christian Phalangists in the camps of Sabra and Chatilla in Lebanon, and in which complicity by the Israeli Defence Forces continues to be disputed, Levinas defined "the essence of Zionism," no less, as "that which signifies a state in the fullest possible sense of the term, a state with an army and arms, an army which can have a deterrent and, if necessary, a defensive significance."[31] Does Levinas forget the sukkah here? "There is," he goes on, "an ethical limit to this ethically necessary existence." He does not specify the precise nature of this limit, and his definition of the Other who might set this limit has aroused much controversy and misunderstanding that it is not possible to explore here.[32] He does however, insist that both ethics and politics have a limit, the one by the other, and that "the place where everything is interrupted, where everything is disrupted, where everyone's moral responsibility comes into play, a responsibility that concerns innocence, unbearably so, that place is Sabra and Chatilla."[33] The appeal to innocence here is perhaps disingenuous so soon after the events in question. But the appeal to conscience as that that comes into play via interruption and disruption indicates that Levinas has not forgotten the sukkah. Rejecting any confusion between Zionism and "some sort of commonplace mystique of the earth as native soil," he invokes a talmudic text and concludes: "A person is more holy than a land, even a holy land, since, faced with an affront made to a person, this holy land appears in its nakedness to be but stone and wood."[34]

* * *

The Jews, as Gibbs observes, also link Sukkot to peace, a concept that Levinas has suggested "goes beyond purely political thought."[35] Let me end, then, with an image of peace, albeit prefaced, as I began, with some biographical details.

In 1939 Levinas became an officer in the French army, his rank protecting him from deportation to a concentration camp when taken prisoner in 1940. Instead, he was sent to a prisoner of war camp in Northern Germany where, with a segregated Jewish unit, he did forced labor in the forest. Liberated in 1945, Levinas returned to Paris with his wife and daughter, who had escaped the Nazis with the help of friends. Most of his family in Lithuania, including his parents and brothers, had been murdered in 1940.

When Levinas returned to Paris, he became Director of the École Normale Israélite Orientale (ENIO), a Jewish school originally founded to train teachers. He held this position until 1980, even though this period coincided with his growing reputation as a philosopher, and Professorships from 1964. In Salomon Malka's biography, a former pupil of Levinas at the ENIO recalled "his joyous mood during the festivals in contrast to his seriousness in study: 'Pesach is a wonderful festival . . . Sukkot also. We would build the booth together. I would see Levinas across from me, beaming, very happy.'"[36]

Don't kick down the sukkah.

II

Christian Perspectives

CHAPTER 8

HOSPITABLE BY CALLING, INHOSPITABLE BY NATURE

Mark Patrick Hederman

I cannot imagine any great religion that does not proclaim hospitality as a fundamental precept and obligation. Hospitality has been a mark of civilized living in most societies and one that often determines the global reputation of religions, countries and peoples. The Greeks had one word—*xenos*—for enemy/stranger and guest. In Latin, the experts see an etymological relationship between "*hostis*" and "*hospes*." Our romantic account of ourselves is that civilization took a gigantic step forward when enemies became guests.

Sometimes hospitality is for reasons of enlightened self-interest: "Do not neglect to show hospitality to strangers, for by doing that some have entertained angels without knowing it."[1] Sometimes hospitality is your ticket to everlasting life, as when the sheep are being divided from the goats in the final round-up of Christianity: "Depart from me ye accursed into everlasting burnings!" Why? "Because I was a stranger and you did not welcome me." Those who did welcome the stranger, even if they did not realize it, are forever blessed: "I was a stranger and you took me in . . . When did I take you in, Lord? . . . Whenever you did it to the least of these, you did it to me."[2] Even at its most unselfish, hospitality is still somewhat tribal; our welcome is for fellow aboriginals: "We are all citizens of the world," as Epictetus said some years before Christianity was founded, "nowhere will one find a stranger."

Christianity itself is based on the difficult premise that we should love our enemies, even those that hate us.[3] That is the theory. It is simple, and I am sure universal. However, it remains at the level of wishful thinking. What is the reality on the ground? Most of the great religious traditions decry xenophobia and prescribe love of the stranger. However, as we all know, it is not what is advertised on the brochure that matters, it is what happens in the hostel when you get there.

I come from a Christian country where at least one local politician is getting elected on the grounds that, I quote, "86% of the Irish people do not want to meet a foreigner." This statement is not wacky and eccentric incongruity; it is what appeals to his constituents and gets him elected. In another part of our Christian country, seven-year-old children will not stand beside each other because one is Protestant and the other Catholic.

In 2002 Mr David Trimble, then leader of the Ulster Unionist Party and first minister in Northern Ireland, presumably in an attempt to advance the so-called Peace Process and improve cross-border relations between the two parts of our Christian country, described the Republic of Ireland as "monoethnic, monocultural, pathetic and sectarian." Mr Bertie Ahern, Taoiseach of the Republic of Ireland, countered: "No one would identify that description with this State." He went on to smirk: "We don't have any Drumcree or Garvahy Road down South." This was to show where true sectarianism was to be found.

These two politicians presumably saw themselves as trading insults. However the proposition I want to explore is that every person who arrives on this planet is by nature and biology "monoethnic, monocultural, pathetic and sectarian." Is this not the way we are born? Is this not the way we are by nature? If we were not, might we ever have survived as a species? We are selfish, short-sighted, and antisocial by definition, otherwise we might have been eliminated. Whatever our hopes about progress in terms of history and civilization, is it not true, in Herbert Butterfield's phrase, that each one of us is born "equidistant from barbarity"?

We belong to a biological species that is, for better or for worse, now definitively in charge on this planet. *Homo sapiens*, as we have been taught to label ourselves, have been on earth perhaps 50,000 years. It was not a foregone conclusion that our unlikely species out of the millions of others would eventually gain hegemony. Dinosaurs, gorillas, cheetahs and pterodactyls must surely have been favourites before us.

Those who have seen films such as *Jurassic Park* will be aware of what it must have been like to live in a world where other species were in charge and where we were like irrelevant insects being crushed between their claws and toes. It took us, with a great deal of evolutionary effort, several thousand years, they tell us, to produce the first billion of our species; whereas, now, in this blessed twenty-first century, we are producing a billion every ten to fifteen years. We have subjugated the other species and are not just in charge, but here to stay.

It is only through education, through art, and through religion, worthy of the name, that we can prize ourselves out of this natural cocoon. We are racist by birth, xenophobic by nature; we become cosmopolitan by education, altruistic by imagination, hospitable to our enemies by religious conversion. We love what we know and we fear what is foreign. Hatred is a self-protecting mechanism, an instinct of self-preservation.

If we begin from the basis that we are all racist to start with and that it is only through education and imagination that we can learn to be multicultural, ecumenical, and hospitable, it takes the guilt and the high moral ground out of the indictment.

Culture is a thing we weave ourselves. We are "unfinished" animals who complete ourselves through culture. Otherwise we remain "natural." The forces of nature want to grow a roof over our heads where none was intended and raise thick walls around our homes. Our automatic response to complexity and danger is construction of an indestructible labyrinth around our deepest, most vulnerable and fragile selves. We are all aware of this force of gravity in ourselves.

There is a difference between the evolutionary process that unfolded the animal, vegetable and mineral world and the world that is now in place, since humanity established itself as the dominant species on the planet. Animals are determined by nature. They do nothing more than instinctively fulfill the pattern inscribed in their genes and chromosomes. They are DNA docile. Our DNA also provides us with a Lego set to build our own completion. Ours is not a blueprint encoded in our genes, it is the basic score for an unfinished symphony. We complete or finish ourselves through culture. We are what Clifford Geertz has called "cultural artifacts." We become who we are "under the guidance of cultural patterns, historically created systems of meaning in terms of which we give form, order, point and direction to our lives."[4] Culture is universal. Every one of us comes wrapped inside it. It is also particular and local. It is different for every part of the planet and at every time a child is born. There can be no definitive antidote. Each manifestation of it requires the particular genius of the particular place to provide its own pioneering trailblazers who can lead the people out of its bondage.

And there is a natural religion that comes with this package and which is the one we live by if we haven't been taught anything else. Religion like art can paint the walls of the prison and decorate the bars. It can be a natural biological phenomenon instead of being a call to go beyond the black tents of the tribe. In fact it nearly always is such a deadening restrictive straitjacket unless it is led out of such slavery and bondage through an exodus to an alternative viewpoint.

Denominational religion is nearly always such a cultural artifact. We can label this cultural religious growth around us: Catholic or Protestant, Mohammedan or Hindu, depending upon the tribe into which we happen to be born. Every tribal religion believes itself to have been planted where it is by God Almighty and to have the right to remove from its territory those who believe otherwise. The fundamental principle of such natural religion is the sacrifice of the alien on the altar of the incumbent.[5]

We need imagination and genuine religious leadership to get us out of the prison we are in; we have to imagine what it is like to be outside, to be looking at the world from a different point of view.

Art and genuine religion can help us to see differently and to move ourselves outside tribal religion and politics. But we have to access authentic art and revealed religion. Emmanuel Levinas seemed to be of the opinion that before Judaism all religions were "natural": they were both a worship of nature and a natural worship. The basis for all of them was fear. Fear, that fragile human beings, the least likely species to survive on the planet, would be thwarted, starved, suppressed, by the power or "powers" of Nature. Religion was a strategy devised to appease, seduce, captivate, harness, delude, distract, disarm the overriding thraldom of these gods of the natural world, on which human beings depended for the air they breathed, the food they ate, the water they drank, the crops they cultivated, the herds they kept, the prey they hunted, and the health that allowed them to undertake and enjoy all of the above.[6]

Judaism was, thus, the first atheism. It cut the roots of that sacral connection with the earth that tied humankind into a slavery of service to greater and lesser gods. Judaism's fulmination against every form of idolatry was an attempt to free humanity from slavery to divinity at whatever level. Every time primitive human beings heard a clap of thunder or a flash of lightning they fell to the ground in terror. They imagined powerful gods behind each manifestation of elemental fury. They had gods of fire, of water, of earth and of air. It was the genius of Judaism that released them from such fealty.[7] The Jewish religion was built from an experience of liberation.

The essential movement of this religion is to remove the deity away from the earth and place it in a realm beyond, which is untouchable, unreachable. The account of creation is to show that God created everything in heaven and on earth. In other words that everything in the world we inhabit is the same as ourselves, a created object, a thing. God is essentially "other" than such created stuff. Primitive humanity thought there were descending orders of divinities that inhabited the heavens, the stars, for instance; that there were gods of the ocean and gods lurking in every bush and tree in the countryside. Judaism swept away all those deities and squarely determined the essential difference between the created world and the "other" world where the glory of the Lord dwelt in inaccessible splendour.

God put human beings in charge of this universe as his representatives, as his "image and likeness." This was not to give them license to destroy or diminish the rest of creation but to ensure that they realized their own full potential and nobility as sons and daughters of God. They should be free from all inferiority complexes, calling no one or no thing "master." Judaism also changed the relationship with the divinity into a relationship of love between equals. This monotheistic God was not a whimsical tyrant who slaughtered and punished at will. He had entered a covenant with his partners on earth and this was embodied in the law. The great intuition of the Jews was that the law in this sense was greater than God. That God was in fact subject to the law, which was what established the equality of all of us, including God. The law, the Torah, was that great invention of an omnipotent God, which allowed God to abdicate sovereignty and allowed us to establish our independence. It was the mortising conduit, like a lock in a river or canal, which allowed two levels to align with each other. Later, according to Christianity, which always remains a branch of Judaism, the law became hardened into a barrier and was replaced by the flesh and blood of Jesus Christ, who carried in his person the ever-abiding link between God and us.

The Jewish religion not only established a new relationship of responsible stewardship with nature and the created world, but it also changed the relationship of each of us as human beings with each other. Each one of us became a unique infinity, in short, a God. We were all placed on that pedestal and became Gods by adoption, which means equality with God and with each other, because there is no greater or lesser in the category of "unique." It is like zero, it is unmatched and equal to itself. Our hospitality is to ourselves as Gods. We welcome each other as royal personages.

Love your enemy, welcome the stranger, treat everyone as your equal; treat them as you would treat yourself. All this ran contrary to the "natural" order where most tribes thought of themselves as the chosen people, the place where the world began, and every other tribe as lesser and less favored by the Gods. All human evaluation was hierarchical. Such is the basis of most sacral religions, which for the most part condoned human sacrifice and found aliens and strangers the least troublesome of these necessary propitiatory offerings. Religions of sacral power are sedentary, nationalistic, partisan, racist and earthbound. Better no religion at all, Judaism would proclaim, than a "natural" religion.

There is a tendency today, both in ecologically sensitive observers, and anthropologists, to demonize the Judaeo-Christian religious insight as having led to the domination and destruction of the planet, and to idolize the aboriginal and indigenous religions of the world as having had more respect for nature. This is like every heresy (a word that comes from the Greek, meaning to select or to choose) an exaggeration of one half of a truth to the exclusion of the other half. Because truth is always complex and comprehensive, it contains the correct elements in both sides. Most primitive religions were indeed "respectful" of nature, but at what price? It was mostly a dehumanizing fear that caused it. So, the step forward toward freedom, the exodus from the slavery of Egypt, led by Moses and accomplished by the Jews, was essential and definitive. Humanity was different from that time forward. It was certainly taken too far, and became totalitarian technological rape of the planet. But this eventuality must not blind us to the truth that made the option possible. We could have used that freedom more beneficently, and could still do so, but the ultimate value is that freedom.

Now such arguments might seem somewhat academic if it were not for the fact that these realities still exist today. There are still tribes, peoples, nations who have not been liberated by the cutting of the umbilical cord with the earth. They are still living in sub-human fear of some deity, some principality or power, which reduces them to trembling non-entities when they should be walking tall and taking their place as equals. Having lived in Nigeria for some years I am aware of what one Nigerian leader has said:

> Nigeria is the one true giant of Africa. Her peoples constitute nearly one half of the black people of the continent and two in five of all black people in the world. The resources concentrated within her borders would be the envy of most countries in Europe and the Americas, her landmass is huge, her climate largely benign. All this should have made her not only the most powerful country in the Black world, but among the dozen most powerful nations on the globe.

This is the view of the former leader of the Biafran war of secession, Emeka Odumegwu-Ojukwu, communicated to the BBC correspondent covering that terrible war, which Biafra lost. The BBC correspondent, who was Frederick

Forsythe, said he had rarely met a more gifted human being. He wrote a book about him.

Obviously Emeka's analysis of Nigerian failure to measure up to its potential includes bad government:

> Without organization a society is destined to seize up, choke and eventually die. A state where the services do not function, where the citizenry is not disciplined, where crime at every level runs unchecked, where leaders are not accountable to the led, and where justice is available to the highest bidder—such a state cannot inspire in others outside that confidence needed for leadership abroad.

But there is more than that, he thinks, and this is where his argument touches the need for the revolution at the heart of every person's liberated humanity. Emeka sees himself as a black man inheriting a religion of another kind:

> Being black means having a certain concept of life, of which the major strain is of being close to nature. But this also has a concomitant weakness in lack of technology and fear of the supernatural . . . The black man's God is a God of retribution; awe-some, unapproachable and merciless. The white man's God is a God of love, mercy and forgiveness . . . Faced with a strange mountain . . . the black man turns his back on this terrifying monster, seeks out a calf from his miserable herd and begins the regular sacrifice to the god of the mountain. Very soon the mountain has become sacred and therefore impenetrable.[8]

The possibility is that Judeo-Christianity has had a benign influence on planet earth. Although this influence has led to unspeakable crimes and inexcusable exploitation, such aberrations were not necessary, were not "Judaeo-Christian" in essence; they resulted from the dangerous freedom that these specific religions instituted. And that freedom alone can liberate an otherwise irretrievably cowed and terror-stricken human race.

It took several centuries for humankind to work out the mind-blowing extent of this freedom. In Christianity, it was the Council of Chalcedon (451 CE) that defined it most accurately. The key verb here was the Greek *sozein*, meaning to save. This word defined an incredible awareness that God had come on earth not just to "save" us from ourselves but, more importantly, to save us from God's self. The scope and extent of this freedom accomplished by Judeo-Christianity has only become apparent in the past century when we developed it sufficiently to allow ourselves to destroy the whole planet.

The fact that we have used this freedom to become genocidal monsters, technological murderers, planetarian devastators, is certainly attributable to Judaism and Christianity, but only because these were the instruments of our liberation, the teachers of our autonomy, the midwives of our freedom. Nothing must prevent us from recognizing the irreplaceable and incalculable value of that freedom. Judaism and Christianity snapped our chains; what we used our hands for after that liberation is a different story.

There are at least three kinds of religion, as there are at least three kinds of art: there is an art of propaganda, which tries to persuade you of a particular point of view; there is an art of entertainment, which can be high-brow or low-brow, depending upon your taste and on what is available; and there is an art of excavation and exploration, seeking meaning where ordinary human discourse can no longer be trusted to register the subtlety of what is being experienced. And similarly for religion: there is a religion that is propaganda, a religion that is sentimental and self-serving, and there is a religion that calls us to move beyond our comfort zone to the space of otherness.

> Institutional religion, and certainly Christianity the religion, is always a human construct. It is itself a work of human hands and manned [sic] by ordinary men and women who are no more gifted by the grace of God than the rest of us. Nor are they any more than the rest of us ring-fenced from the incursions of the original temptation and the weakness of the race . . . Christians must recognize the fact that they have regularly distorted the truth of the faith of Jesus, in various ways and to varying degrees over virtually the whole history of their religion.[9]

The human machine, wherever it exists, functions normally according to a predetermined program: "maximum pleasure at minimum cost." To bless those that curse you is a miracle from the point of view of the "normal and natural" functioning of the human machine. Hospitality at this level does not just happen, it has to be done. It is like an artwork—it is a truth that enters the world through human being. Christianity is as much a kind of "doing" as a way of being. "*Do* this in memory of me,"[10] Christ tells us at the crucial moment of his life on earth. Such doing is similar to what Heidegger describes as "poetry," from the Greek word to do or to make. Everything that happens in our world is part of automatic functioning unless we perform the miracle of changing our human nature into the body and blood of Christ, turning water into wine, turning "natural" reaction into supernatural action. Such "doing" is always a miracle in the sense that it goes beyond nature as we know and understand it. In this sense one only *does* miracles, and anything that is done in such a way is always a miracle, and nothing can be done in this way without it being a miracle. So much so that whatever occurs normally is not a miracle, is not really *done*—it simply happens. Hospitality is the miracle that we do.

In other words there is no such reality as Christianity in itself; there are only Christians who are moved by the Spirit to be like Christ. Which means that Christians are quite likely to be unbearable unless they are crucified. And crucifixion in this sense does not mean the literal fact, as is sometimes carried out on Good Friday in certain parts of the world with gruesome and wrong-headed imitation. It means the sacramental and symbolic reality. Christianity can only prevent itself from reverting to the horrors of a natural religion by renewing the stigma of crucifixion. It is only though the pentagram of the five wounds that we are prevented from congealing or reverting to type. Under this sign, benediction flows. Each of the wounds of Christ are effective against the five dark currents of human motivation: the desire to be great, the desire to take (the prerogative of the right hand), the desire to keep (the prerogative of the left hand), the desire to advance at the expense of others (prerogative of the right foot), the desire to hold on to, at the expense of others (prerogative of the left foot). The twentieth century made us more than ever aware of the currents of natural energy that normally motivate us and spur us to action. Three philosophers each suggested one of these instincts as the primary motivation for everything we do or say: Freud nominated sex, Neitzsche suggested the will to power, Marx thought money made the world go round. The five wounds of Christ were a five-sense breakthrough into our world of greedy senses and covetous limbs. *Vulnus* is the Latin word for a wound; vulnerability is the hallmark of a Christian.

A wound is a door. The eye, for instance, is a wound covered by a mobile skin that we call an eyelid. Our eyes are open wounds. So are our other senses. They are wounds through which the world impresses itself on us. These five senses are organs of perception, not of action. They are passive receptors.

The five organs of action, on the other hand, are our two legs, our two arms, and our head. These must develop analogous wounds, which will become the stigmata of our alignment to the cross of the divine will. The head, however, does not bear the fifth wound, as we know from the paradigm of the Christian mystery. It bears the crown of thorns. These thorns are nails of objectivity. The fifth wound is the wound of organic humility, which replaces the natural current of the will-to-power. This wound penetrates to the heart.

Whatever the method, the mission of organized religion and spiritual leadership is to make sure that true religion does not disappear from the world. Because without at least one person who carries the spiritual stigmata there is no guarantee that the flow of grace from above can reach the earth below. The only wound through which such power can flow is the freely opened heart and will of an authentic lover of God.

No amount of worldly pomp or pageantry can create such a person. The only lightning conductor that can harness the power of God is the loving will of a genuine *pontifex*. The word in Latin [*pons + facere*] means "bridge maker." The bridge between us and the genuinely and absolutely "other" is created through open wounds on both sides. Christianity, as is true for all great religions, holds the victory sign of the Divine breakthrough. The freedom we have been given is so powerful and so dangerous that it can lead us through every one of our five senses to a hell of our own construction. That is what freedom means: the free choice of surrender to heaven; or the construction of a hell from our own sweating selves. The secret wisdom hidden from the beginning of time is the mystery of God's love for us. And so powerful is this secret wisdom, Judaeo-Christianity maintains, that the five gates of hell shall never prevail against the formula of the five wounds.[11] This, ultimately, is the true meaning of "hospitality" that we are welcomed into the Divine household.

CHAPTER 9

BIBLICAL, ETHICAL AND HERMENEUTICAL REFLECTIONS ON NARRATIVE HOSPITALITY

Marianne Moyaert

Samuel Huntington's work concerning the clash of civilizations seems more often than not, a reality.[1] Still, there are people who attempt to offer resistance and alternative options to these conflicts. They promote a case for dialogue and encounter, hoping to stop the spiraling effect of misunderstandings, misapprehensions, annoyances and violence. It is possible that this counter-voice is a sign of tremendous naivety. Perhaps reality has already silenced this counter-voice and proves that any argument for interreligious dialogue is a hopeless venture. However, belonging to the biblical tradition, I believe that human interconnectedness takes priority over brokenness. This interconnectedness is the arena in which hope resides and this hope inspires and strengthens Christians to work toward a different world. "[Christian hope] encourages Christians not to loose sight of the final goal which gives meaning and value to life, and it offers solid and profound reasons, in which one may dedicate oneself, toward a daily commitment to transform reality in order to make it correspond to God's plan."[2] Presently, people may have a glimpse of the final reconciliation awaiting them—a reconciliation that does not depend on humanity but requests that they contribute and act toward it. Looking forward to an eschatological time in which all humans will be united, Christians are already called to search for places of peace, which strengthen them in their hope.

In view of this, I believe our world today stands in need of a spirit of interreligious hospitality that consists in transporting oneself into the sphere of meaning of a foreign tradition and in welcoming the other's narrative tradition.[3] This hospitality presumes an attitude of hermeneutical openness: believers give up part of their control and mastery to become a guest in a strange narrative tradition.[4] Precisely in this "letting go" of the familiar to make room for the unfamiliar, new and unexpected meanings can be found that give a unique depth to one's own faith commitment. It is my conviction that such a spirit of interreligious hospitality has the potential to break through the spiral of ethnocentric tendencies and assist in decreasing, or at least opening up discussions concerning, interreligious conflicts.

In my contribution I will be looking at interreligious dialogue, in particular, between the Jewish, Christian and Muslim traditions, using the Abrahamic scripture that they all have in common. I will further explore this notion of interreligious hospitality through the works of the French philosopher, Paul Ricoeur.

I. Hospitality as a Theological and Ethical Virtue

Ricoeur's work has taught me that *taking long detours* via narrative traditions
has the potential to evoke new meanings within my own tradition. With this
in mind, I will take one step back from the difficult challenge of understanding
interreligious hospitality and begin by focusing on an in-depth reflection on the
scriptural notion of hospitality. To that end, I will turn toward the patriarch
Abraham, who is known in Judaism, Christianity and Islam because of his
generosity, hospitality and great sense of justice. Only after having revealed the
various ethical and theological layers regarding *the virtue of hospitality* within
the biblical notion in general, as well as through the narrative of Abraham in
particular, I will then turn to the context of religious plurality and the question
why *interreligious hospitality* presents a hopeful and creative response to the
enigmatic situation of religious diversity.

1. ABRAHAM AND THE VIRTUE OF HOSPITALITY

One of the most striking examples of hospitality in the biblical tradition is
recounted in the story of Abraham at Mamre (Gen. 18:1-33). This is a difficult
story, with many layers of meaning.

The story opens with Abraham sitting at the entrance of his tent, when
God appears (18:1). In Eden, God had walked together with the first human
beings. After their eviction, he had only rarely shown himself, but here He
turns up, rather unexpectedly, during the hottest part of the day, to pay a visit
to Abraham. Almost at the same time three wayfarers enter the scene (18:2).
What follows is a detailed narrative in which Abraham displays himself as an
excellent host. He really goes out of his way to welcome his guests and to make
them feel at home in his tent:

> "Now let a little water be fetched, wash your feet, and rest yourselves under the tree.
> I will get a morsel of bread so you can refresh your heart. After that you may go your
> way, now that you have come to your servant." They said, "Very well, do as you have
> said." Abraham hurried into the tent to Sarah, and said, "Quickly make ready three
> measures of fine meal, knead it, and make cakes." Abraham ran to the herd, and
> fetched a tender and good calf, and gave it to the servant. He hurried to dress it. He
> took butter, milk, and the calf which he had dressed, and set it before them. (18:4-8)

This passage bears witness to the generosity of Abraham's hospitality: he spares
no effort in ensuring that his guests would be comfortable, while at the same
time minimizing his efforts, thus trying to reassure his guests that they are no
burden at all.[5] Abraham shows himself to be very sensitive to the needs of
his guests. By downplaying his efforts, he accentuates their dignity. For that
matter, he does not eat himself, so that he can take even better care of them.
This is a story of utmost Eastern hospitality. Superabundance and simplicity
go together. Because of this story Abraham has become the prototype of

hospitality.[6] Likewise in the Islamic tradition, it is understood that Abraham sets the example for what it means to be hospitable to strangers. That is why he is called father of hosts—*abû l-dhifân*.

Usually the story of Abraham at Mamre is divided into three parts:

1. Gen. 18:1 Abraham sits at the entrance of his tent when God pays him a visit.
2. Gen. 18:2-15 Abraham looks up and sees three men. He drops everything and hurries to give them a hospitable welcome. The men stay for lunch and they tell Abraham that he and Sarah will have a child within the year, which they will call Isaac. Sarah laughs, when overhearing the message, but God reassures Abraham.
3. Gen. 18:16-33 The men get up and travel toward Sodom, and the dialogue between God and Abraham on the fate of the city takes place.

When dividing the story in this way, it becomes clear that Abraham and God are the main characters in parts one (Gen. 18:1) and three (Gen. 18:16-33) of the story. In the second part of the story (Gen. 18:2-15), God moves to the background, and the three wayfarers and Abraham play the central role.

In understanding this story, an important and at the same time complex question concerns the precise relation between the visitors, Abraham and God. Why does the story shift from God as Abraham's visitor and conversation partner (18:1/18:16-33) to the three wayfarers, without a word of explanation? Who are these visitors? What is their relation to God, if any? How can we understand the triangle between these three parties? As we will see later, these questions are crucial for understanding the radical and even the un-heard of character of Abraham's hospitality.

Many possible interpretations of this story have been suggested, all trying to tackle the difficult question regarding the relation between God, Abraham and the visitors. The most helpful interpretation for our purpose is the reading of Chief Rabbi Jonathan Sacks. Though Sacks' reading is in one way the most obvious, it is also a very provocative interpretation. Some may even find it an outrageous reading of the narrative. According to Sacks, this story does not mention angels: God himself visits Abraham. The three visitors are precisely what the story says they are: wayfarers, who happen to be so fortunate that they pass by Abraham's tent at the warmest moment of the day. This interpretation is somewhat bold, because it implies that Abraham lets God wait while he entertains some tired nomads.

Textually, Sacks' interpretation is based on an alternate reading of the third verse: "He said: 'If I have found favour in your eyes, my lords/my Lord, do not pass your servant by.'" This verse is quite enigmatic, because the Hebrew shifts between singular and plural.[7] Because of this shift, it is open to two interpretations.[8] According to the first interpretation Abraham is talking to the three wayfarers (my lords), asking them not to leave but to stay as to enjoy his warm hospitality. The second interpretation is more radical, saying that

Abraham is not talking to the three visitors (my lords), but rather to God (my
Lord). In this case the verse would read as follows: "Please God, have a little
bit of patience. When I am done welcoming these three strangers, I'll come
back."[9] The difference between both interpretations turns on one vowel. In the
first interpretation, the *nun* of the word A-D-N-Y (Adonai), carries a *patach*.[10]
In this case, the word simply means "my lords," and would thus refer to the
three visitors. In the second interpretation, ADNY carries a *kametz*. In this
case, the word represents the name of God. This means that the term is sacred.
Sacks follows the second line of thought. This interpretation would imply that
Abraham, seeing the three visitors, asked God to wait while he took care of the
visitors with the greatest possible generosity. So Abraham leaves God where
He is, to give hospitality to the three wayfarers. Even in the midst of Abraham
having what might seem to be odd priorities, God appears unbothered by
Abraham's decision. He does not request or make Abraham remain and listen
but instead allows Abraham to make the choice of hospitality. God waits (at
least that is what we suspect) patiently until Abraham's visitors resume their
travels. Abraham acts as though it is a normal activity to leave God waiting.

This story teaches that the value of hospitality to strangers overrides the
concerns of God himself. God prefers that we attend to strangers in need
rather than attend to him. He can wait. Greater is hospitality than welcoming
the Divine presence. This story also teaches that hospitality takes precedence
over the spiritual enjoyment of an intimate encounter with God. Apparently
Abraham withdrew from an intimate encounter with God for the sake of his
guests. According to the Talmud this is indeed the correct prioritization.[11] The
halakha takes precise account of this behaviour: "The reward of escorting a
visitor from one's home is the greatest of all rewards for hospitality. This is a
law set in place by *Avraham Avinu* and the charitable ways which he made his
lifestyle. He would give wayfarers food and drink and would escort them on
their way" (Mishne Torah. Hilchot Evel. 14:2). On an even more fundamental
level, this story tells us that the ethical virtue of hospitality has a theological
bearing: God reveals himself in the face of the other. God comes into view as
a God incognito, to whom we do or do not offer hospitality. God shows and
conceals himself in the stranger, without knowing who we are dealing with,
we discover in surprise and only later the attitude with which we have met
God.[12] Where one welcomes the stranger, one welcomes God. Where one
makes room for the other, one resides in God's presence. Chief Rabbi Jonathan
Sacks concludes:

> With this interpretation of the narrative structure of Genesis 18, Jewish tradition
> expressed one of its most majestic ideas. There is God as we meet Him in a vision,
> a mystical encounter in the depths of the soul. But there is also God as we see His
> trace in another person, even a stranger, a passer-by; in Abraham's case, three Arab
> travellers in the heat of the day. Someone else might have given them no further
> thought, but Abraham ran to meet them and bring them rest, shelter, food and
> drink. *Greater is the person who sees God in the face of the stranger than one who*

sees God as God in a vision of transcendence, for the Jewish task since the days of Abraham is not to ascend to heaven but to bring heaven down to earth in simple deeds of kindness and hospitality.[13]

After having attended to the three wayfarers, God simply continues where he left off. Finally he reveals the purpose of his visit, telling Abraham about his plans for Sodom (18:20-21). Abraham's reaction is well known: he is outraged:

> Abraham drew near, and said, "Will you consume the righteous with the wicked? What if there are fifty righteous within the city? Will you consume and not spare the place for the fifty righteous who are in it? Be it far from you to do things like that, to kill the righteous with the wicked, so that the righteous should be like the wicked. May that be far from you. Shouldn't the Judge of all the earth do right?" (18:23-25).

Again, Abraham confronts God boldly. First, he lets God wait while he takes care of his guests, and then he challenges God. In the name of justice, Abraham protests against God's plans. And God accepts this moral candor.

It is clear that Abraham is a man of mercy, kindness and righteousness. He sets himself up as advocate of all just people in Sodom and Gomorrah. In doing so, he realizes his true calling: to be a host for strangers, and advocate for those who are threatened to become victims of ruined circumstances. He sets out to resist exclusion and injustice. God's message to Abraham and Abraham's hospitality are different facets of the same story. Both in welcoming strangers in need and in standing up against God, Abraham shows himself to be a man who incarnates the virtue of kind justice. "Abraham is the man on earth who epitomizes kindness to all. Independent of who you are, you are invited into this home, unquestioningly, you are escorted back into the desert."[14]

2. HOSPITALITY AS AN ETHICAL AND THEOLOGICAL VIRTUE

We can learn a number of theological and ethical lessons from this story with regard to the virtue of hospitality. The first lesson concerns the ethical relationship between universality and particularity, especially concerning the treatment of *strangers*. In the biblical tradition, the tension between universality and particularity is of utmost importance: with the focus, here, being that universality precedes particularity. In biblical language: creation precedes election. Every human person is created in the image of God. As such, humanity is one large family, and all human beings are brothers and sisters. This interconnectedness, which points at the universal perspective, precedes the particular election of Abraham. Within biblical tradition, this implies that tribal attachments take second place compared to the universal commitment to all of humanity. The tension between universality and particularity resounds between identity (concern for what is known and familiar) and openness (concern for the stranger). This tension, which I will later address, takes a central place within interreligious dialogue. According to biblical tradition, identity and openness do not mutually exclude one another. Inclusion is essential and the affirmation of one's particular commitment of faith should never promote the exclusion of others. This becomes eminently clear when turning to the story of Abraham at Mamre, where the tension between universality and particularity climaxes.

The story begins with Abraham sitting in his tent during the heat of the day. Abraham is recovering from the circumcision that he underwent a few days before, a procedure that symbolized the covenant he made with God (Genesis 17). A physical sign has been engraved on his body as visible evidence that his identity, and the identity of his community, are determined by their relationship with God. There is no doubt that Abraham felt deep pain from this in his body. Sitting during the hottest part of the day, Abraham was panting and moaning. At the same time, Abraham was only beginning to become conscious of his particular, newly cut, identity. He was starting to realize what his incorporation into this new covenant would entail, particularly regarding rights and duties. Soon after his body is branded, as a sign of a particular calling, he is challenged. Unannounced, three strangers enter his life. How should he react? Will Abraham, from now onwards, only concern himself with those who have been included in the covenant? Does his particular commitment exclude a universal perspective? Will he give his election an exclusivist interpretation? Does he understand the covenant in terms of a closed symbolic community? Will God become another tribal god? This narrative deals with these questions and it also depicts relevance toward a pluralist context.

The story tells that Abraham has understood that particularity does not exclude universality and that his election, rather, entails a responsibility for humanity at large. Confronted with the three strangers, which visit at a rather inconvenient time—he is in pain, it is hot and God is waiting for him[15]—Abraham does not hesitate to act toward what is expected of him. He drops everything, he even lets God wait and *runs* toward the three wayfarers to welcome them.

Abraham's hospitality expresses that "God's covenant is ultimately for the sake of bringing the blessings of righteousness and holiness to all human beings. His privileged relationship with God must not lead Abraham (or his clan) to xenophobia, undue 'homophilia' or injustice."[16] Responsibility for the other precedes election. Election is not the same as tribalism, on the contrary, it contradicts it. Emmanuel Levinas phrases this thought as follows: "Election is not a privilege, and Abraham understands this. It belongs to the dignity of humanity to be elected and thus to bear responsibility for another. Anyone who is elected, has more responsibility than others. He can not flee this responsibility."[17] In the biblical tradition, the relationship between humanity and their fellow beings affects their relationship with God. To turn away from a fellow human in need equals to turning, in a way, from God. Different to Cain who asked "Am I my brother's keeper," and was subsequently banished from God's presence, Abraham understands the priority of theological meaning of human responsibility. His audacious resistance against God's plans for Sodom and Gomorrah likewise shows that he is well aware of his covenantal duties.

Different from Noah who simply endorses what God asks him to do, Abraham argues with God. He takes the fate of the Sodomites at heart, even though they do not belong to his covenantal clan. Abraham "fulfils the true nature of his election, namely by not only acting justly himself but by also standing up for justice, and thus going against injustice, in whatever form it may take, even when it appears in a context of justice."[18]

Abraham's life shows how the virtue of hospitality is deeply connected to friendship with God. Where strangers are hospitably welcomed, God is present to uphold worldly commandments as hospitality is the highest possible form of religion, and vice versa; a prayerful life can never result in disregard of neighborly love. For every believer standing in the Abrahamic tradition knows that a stranger, asking for hospitality, is not necessarily an intruder, nor an enemy (though both are always possible),[19] but that it can also happen that he/she is a messenger from God. The other might be someone who has been put on one's path by God and who helps to guide one toward the path of God. When love of the Divine presence leads us to love our neighbor, and when loving our neighbor brings us back to the Divine presence, this circular motion of love is where God dwells. Then the tent, in which the strangers are welcomed, becomes a sacred tent, a *mishkan*. In Hebrew this word is related to two other words; *shekhinah*, meaning divine presence, and *shakhen*, meaning a neighbor. Welcoming others is not merely good manners and a sign of civility, it is an expression of faith and an act of worship of God.[20] Here conversation becomes a form of prayer.

Let me add one more thought. In biblical imagery, strangers are sometimes seen as the representatives of God's future. They are ambassadors of a new heaven and earth. That is why hospitality refers to eschatology, realized already on this earth and in this time. In allowing strangers to become friends, hospitality symbolizes the eschatological communion. Cardinal Daniélou expresses this thought as follows:

> One can say that a civilization takes a decisive step, and perhaps the most decisive step, on the day that the foreigner, the enemy, becomes a guest. Yes, it is on that day that human community has been created. Previously, these humans were battling each other like animals in the prima forest, but on that day when the stranger is seen as a guest and instead of being held in execration, is invested with the conspicious dignity of a brother in humanity—on such a day, one can say that something has changed in this world.[21]

Hospitality anticipates a time when all people will form a communion in the presence of God and is a foretaste of what is yet to come. That is why we can call hospitality a state of peace, which affirms people in their hope for the future and gives them the strength to help build that future already today. Hospitality is one way to presently *heal the world*. The hope for the future brings responsibility into the present.

II. Interreligious Hospitality: recontextualizing an age-old virtue

"Because of his generosity, Abraham was the first human being who could enjoy God's presence after the eviction from Eden."[22] Recently the virtue of hospitality, embodied by Abraham, has been rediscovered and reinterpreted in view of the context of religious plurality.[23] The central idea is the following: just as we should be hospitable toward the stranger looking for shelter, likewise, we should treat with hospitality the religious other who is looking for recognition regarding his/her particular religious differences. The appropriate attitude toward the religious other is not that of passive tolerance, which far too often degenerates into indifference,[24] but rather that of an active concern. In this perspective, hospitality emerges as a model for interreligious dialogue, especially between the so-called Abrahamic traditions—Judaism, Christianity, Islam—who have the inspiring example of their common forefather Abraham.

According to the French philosopher Paul Ricoeur, perhaps more than ever before, the world, marked by cultural and religious plurality, needs to recall the age-old virtue of hospitality. Ricoeur regards hospitality primarily as a form of hermeneutical openness, which challenges growing tendencies of closure, exclusivism and isolationism.

1. THE RESURGENCE OF TRIBALISM: PARTICULARITY AT THE COST OF UNIVERSALITY

Religious plurality may invoke conflicts, tensions and tribalism. Especially when there is "the protective withdrawal" of each religion "into its own linguistic tradition."[25] The clash of civilization seems to be confirmed: plurality becomes a curse with no equal. According to Ricoeur, this protective withdrawal is prompted by a fear of otherness, which is actually a fear of losing one's own identity.

People wrestle with the question as to how their age-old traditions can survive in a context of secularization and pluralization. In the midst of change, they may look for something that is permanent, unchanging and ahistorical. They may search for a cultural essence, a core of values that must remain untouched or something that is indisputable and non-negotiable. With a desire for certainties, cultural identities are reduced to an enumeration of "substantial characteristics."[26] Subsequently, these substantial characteristics have to be protected against loss of meaning, excavation and relativization—all dangers coming from outside. As a result to their insecurity, believers act as "security guards who stand at the door of their religion to make sure that its identity and integrity are not violated by another religion."[27] Because of this fear, many people find it particularly appealing to withdraw behind the closed doors of their own symbolic community. To protect my own identity, I am never at home *enough*, safe *enough* or protected *enough* against the strange other.

This uncertainty results in the inability to deal with complexity, nuance *and* strangeness. Otherness is opposed to identity and is perceived as a potential threat. This antithetical structure (identity↔otherness) does offer a sense of clarity, but this is a clarity that is based on fear of the other and is provided for at the cost of the other. This "clarity" does not allow for a more complex and ambiguous relationship with one's own faith, nor with the other or the other's faith. The concern here for the preservation of identity is nothing more than conservatism: "If we cling to the need for identity in this sense, we are anxious if it escapes us."[28] Ricoeur calls this "the temptation of identity" or *la déraison identitaire.*[29] The fear of losing one's own identity results in the sacralization of one's religious tradition, the outcome of which is the refusal of what is foreign as a challenge and the cherishing of what is known and familiar. Here the curse of Babel is felt.[30]

Moreover, whenever identity and otherness are placed in such an antithetical schema, claims to particularity are made at the cost of the universal perspective. It is forgotten that, regardless of the particular groups of which they may be members, people belong to the same "large family." The concern for the "tribal" arises at the expense of our involvement with everyone.

Over against the antithetical scheme of tribalism (identity↔otherness) Ricoeur places the virtue of hospitality as a model to integrate identity and otherness. In view of the clash of civilizations, what we need today are indeed people who are capable of moving between traditions and who are prepared to welcome religious strangers; people who see themselves as sojourners in search of truth rather than as possessors of the one truth. The fact that Ricoeur harks back to the virtue of *hospitality* is meaningful, especially in view of the aforementioned tension between unity and universality. Often expressions such as "to show humanity and to show hospitality" are used as interchangeable. This verbal equivalence between humanity and hospitality signifies that at the foundation of hospitality is the recognition that we all belong to the human family.[31] Hospitality is showing a concern for a concrete other, because he/she is human. The strange other is not the *totaliter aliter* but the one who is welcomed in his or her alterity "as similar in humanity."[32] It concerns an attitude of active receptivity: it is making room for the stranger in one's own space—it is the strange other received into one's home in a way that does justice to the otherness of the other. The otherness of the other is never lifted, asymmetry persists, but this asymmetry never takes on problematic forms.

2. ON THE HERMENEUTICS OF NARRATIVE HOSPITALITY

In view of religious and cultural plurality and the resurgence of tribalism, Ricoeur reinterprets the common understanding of the virtue of hospitality. According to common understanding, hospitality concerns people in need— people who need a place to rest and to regain their strength. When hospitality is suggested as a model for interreligious dialogue, the age-old virtue of hospitality takes a new twist. What is asked for in interreligious dialogue is hospitality for another who is *not* in need. The religious other does not request a roof over his/ her head, he/she is not looking for food. He/she does not really want help but wants to be heard and understood and to be taken seriously as a conversation partner.

That is why Ricoeur speaks about narrative hospitality as a practice in which interreligious and intercultural exchange of narratives is taking place. Narrative hospitality is "taking responsibility, in imagination and in sympathy, for the story of the other through the narratives which concern that other."[33] Believers are called "to enter into the world of the other, to discover what it looks like and feels from the vantage point of the person whose world it is."[34] Thus, this reciprocal practice can be understood as a sort of laboratory in which believers open themselves up to the other, or the "visitor" (like Abraham) and learn to see that there exists other ways of *being-in-the-world*. By venturing into the world of the other our imaginations can think differently and our practical lives find rejuvenating new orientations.[35] Thus, narrative hospitality offers new and surprising interpretations of known and less known stories.

Narrative hospitality challenges native speakers of this or that tradition who have appointed themselves not only as the "guardians" but also as the only true possessors of their tradition. Such "pretensions to self-sufficiency, the refusal to allow the foreign to mediate, have secretly nourished numerous ethnocentrisms, and more seriously numerous pretensions to cultural hegemonies."[36] People of differing faiths "constantly face the challenge of resisting the reification of a founding religious event (Creation, Incarnation, Revelation, Manifestation, Sermon, Martyrdom) into a fixed dogma."[37] When this reification occurs, one's faith identity not only becomes immutable but also incommunicable.

> A rigid and arrogant conception of cultural identity prevents us from perceiving the corollaries of this principle mentioned above: the possibilities of revising every story which has been handed down and of carving out a place for several stories directed towards the same past.[38]

Over against reification and property claims, Ricoeur places narrative flexibility, which implies welcoming strangers and adversaries and allowing for a plurality of narrative perspectives. As Richard Kearney puts it:

> Multiple perspectives need not betray the unique singularity of a confessional event; on the contrary, they may eloquently testify to its exfoliating richness and inexhaustible suggestiveness. And this faithful testimony may in fact be deepened as we extend the circle of reference to include further perspectives from other religious confessions.[39]

Ricoeur emphasizes that this hospitable exchange of narratives is not a threat to tradition, on the contrary:

> Tradition means transmission, transmission of things said, of beliefs professed, of norms accepted, etc. Now such a transmission is a living one only if tradition continues to form a partnership with innovation. Tradition represents the aspect

of debt which concerns the past and reminds us that nothing comes from nothing. A tradition remains living, however, only if it continues to be held in an unbroken process of reinterpretation.[40]

Here, the importance of exchanges of narratives and plural readings comes into the picture. New and unexpected readings coming from unusual readers liberate narratives from repetition. Such innovative readings do not reject what lies in the past, rather they open the past into the future:

> [T]he past is not only what is bygone—that which has taken place and can no longer be changed—it also lives in the memory thanks to arrows of futurity which have not been fired or whose trajectory has been interrupted. The unfulfilled future of the past forms perhaps the richest part of a tradition. The liberation of this unfulfilled future is the major benefit that we can expect from the exchange of narratives.[41]

Narrative hospitality allows the participants to move away from what is, into the realm of what might be. It creates a hopeful perspective on how things might be *different*. Though conflict is real, communion could be too. Might this praxis of mutual hospitality not give us an "eye-opening experience of roads not taken? Some of these roads we will be relieved not to have travelled—and this is valuable self-knowledge. But in other roads we may see terrain we wish our traditions had guided us into but did not, and we may discover otherwise hidden potentialities in our own worlds."[42]

III. Scriptural Reasoning: meeting in Abraham's tent

Unfortunately, Ricoeur has not pushed through his thoughts on narrative hospitality. He gives us a glimpse of what he means, but without elaborating on it. In trying to give Ricoeur's model of narrative hospitality more body, I now turn to an interreligious praxis, embodying the same hospitable spirit, namely the praxis of *scriptural reasoning*. I further develop Ricoeur's plea for narrative hospitality as a plea for Jews, Christians and Muslims to gather around their scriptures and their accompanying traditions of interpretation and application.

1. BECOMING GUESTS IN EACH OTHER'S NARRATIVES

Scriptural reasoning aims at building interreligious communion through a praxis of reading and studying the sacred texts together. I understand this interreligious praxis as a form of intertextual hermeneutics. Scriptural reasoning presupposes a sensitive concern for the concrete other and his/her scripture. This entails, on the one hand, "acknowledging the *sacredness of the other's scriptures to them* (without having to acknowledge its authority for oneself)." On the other hand, "the 'native speakers' need to acknowledge that they do not exclusively own their scriptures."[43] Scriptural reasoning presents itself as a praxis of mutual hospitality, in which each is both host and guest in relation to the others. "Yet this is three-way mutual hospitality: each is host to the others and guest to the others as each welcomes the other two to their 'home' scripture and its traditions of interpretation."[44]

Let me quote Nicholas Adams at length as to draw a clear picture of this praxis of narrative hospitality:

> The typical study is oriented to at least one text in each of the three Abrahamic traditions. There are thus typically at least one person from each of the traditions. There are thus typically at least three texts and three persons engaged in study. If scriptural reasoning were a teaching environment, one would expect the Jewish scholar to expound the Hebrew, the Christian to expound the Greek and the Muslim to expound the Arabic texts. It might be a question of proceeding person by person, text by text, perhaps with questions for clarification. But that is not quite what happens in scriptural reasoning . . . Instead of one-by-one procession of speakers, the group will choose to focus on one of the texts, and all participants will engage in its interpretation, generally beginning with the plain sense . . . Once the plain sense has been satisfactorily identified, understanding this to mean satisfactory for the time being, the discussion moves on to questions concerning how the text might be interpreted to address particular situations either in the past or in the present . . . Some may have a deep knowledge of how a text has been interpreted, others may have a thorough grounding in the range of meanings associated with particular words and concepts, and others still may have a wide-ranging grasp of comparative economics. It is thus a most interesting kind of learning environment.[45]

2. PITCHING A TENT

Following the example of Abraham, scriptural reasoning takes place in "a tent" understood as a temporary shelter, open to unexpected visitors.[46] Clearly the notion "tent" has "scriptural resonances of hospitality and divine presence and with the whole Middle Eastern culture of nomads and desert travel in which the Abrahamic scriptures are rooted."[47] According to David Ford, a tent is also connected with travel between places. It evokes the idea of the "in-between," of moving in between "spaces." In view of the clash of civilizations, we need people who are capable of moving between traditions and who are prepared to welcome religious strangers; people who see themselves as sojourners in search of God's truth rather than as possessors of the one truth. We need people who are prepared to pitch a tent as a place of encounter.

To become a guest in another tradition and to bring home some of the insights from that tradition into one's own narrative realm, does not leave one's own tradition unaltered. One's own religious language will be affected by this exchange. Shifts in meaning are almost certain and what is seen as strange might become something that is more deeply understood. Scriptural reasoning relies on people who are not afraid to re-interpret past traditions in view of the future, people who understand their faith commitment as a spiritual journey rather than as assenting to clear-cut doctrines, people who resist the temptation

> always to speak empathically in the indicative and imperative moods, when it might be more appropriate to use the interrogative mood, or the exploratory subjunctive mood of "may be" or "might be," or the optative mood, the "if only" of desire to see face to face in the future while acknowledging that now we see through a glass darkly.[48]

A tent is by design a temporary shelter. It is open to the elements, temporary, insubstantial, in short, it provides little real shelter. Thus it reminds us of our reliance on the will of God in a hostile world. Ultimately, it is with God that we must look for shelter. Scriptural reasoning is a wisdom-seeking practice, guided by God's Spirit. Instead of looking for safety and security in repeating past interpretation traditions, scriptural reasoning is ultimately about relying on God and trusting that building community today is worth more in God's eyes than clashing over the one true interpretation of his revelation.

3. THE HOPE FOR THE FUTURE

Scriptural reasoning believes both in the necessity and the possibility of strengthening the bonds in the family of Abraham, by gathering around the different sacred scriptures. When Jews, Christians and Muslims become guests in each other's narrative traditions, this gathering might be considered as more than a mere hermeneutical enterprise. Theologically speaking, God is at stake. He is the ultimate orientation of reading for Jews, Christians and Muslims alike.

> The ultimate desire is to hallow the name of God, to bless, praise and thank God, to acknowledge that God is great, compassionate, forgiving, holy, and has whatever other perfections are expressed in worship, to relate to God all that we are and think and hope and do, and read and live in ways that please God.[49]

Reading in the presence of *strange guests* places one in the presence of God. In all of this, Abraham sets the example. As any form of hospitality scriptural reasoning is a form of prayer and worship of God who is always greater. God cannot be sedimented in one or another tradition. The multiplicity of texts and *the conflict of interpretations* attest to his greatness. To worship God does not mean to hold on to the past in a rigid way, but to set the past free in new readings.

What brings Jews, Christians and Muslims together is not simply their deep reverence for sacred texts, but also the ethical command to repair the world (*tikkun olam*). Just as hospitality and justice are two dimensions of friendship with God, so too, scriptural reasoning is primarily a form of hospitality aimed at healing the world.[50] Especially in view of the conflict nature of inter-Abrahamic relations, narrative hospitality shows its redemptive character: to bring peace

where there is conflict; to constitute communion where there is division; to
bring understanding where there is misrecognition. However, it does not have
the power nor the intention to change the world in an immediate way. It is not a
form of politics, it is rather a religious praxis. Its redemptive nature exists in the
fact that it temporarily brings an end to interreligious struggle. As Kepnes puts
it bluntly, "in the 'tent of meeting,' people whose communities are otherwise
at war with each other, are sitting down in peaceful conversation."[51] Here, the
three Abrahamic traditions temporarily defer their sibling rivalries to become
guest in each other's rich narrative traditions. In doing so, this practice offers
a horizon of hope, which temporarily eases the struggling hearts of Jews,
Christians and Muslims and thus opens a utopic perspective of what could be.
As a rare state of peace, scriptural reasoning has the power to transform future
relations between the Abrahamic traditions. In this sense, I believe, it is one of
the ways Jews, Christians and Muslims can answer the call to work together
for the Kingdom of God in the full consciousness that this will not come about
through human hands alone.

III

Buddhist Perspectives

CHAPTER 10

THE AWAKENING OF HOSPITALITY

John Makransky

When Richard Kearney explained Boston College's "Hosting the Stranger" project, he mentioned two kinds of response to the stranger: *hospitality* or *hostility*.[1] He noted that the Latin roots of these terms are *hospes* and *hostis*, both of which mean "stranger," while *hospes* can also mean "friend" and *hostis* "enemy." To welcome the stranger, Richard Kearney argues, implies a real risk, a wager as to how hospitality may be wrestled from hostility.

I want to focus on another dimension of our experience of the "stranger" that may epistemologically precede the potential for hostility to which Kearney alluded. The overwhelming majority of beings, billions of humans and other creatures, look and feel to me like strangers in the sense that they don't seem to matter nearly as much as myself, my friends or my relatives. On a daily basis, the strangers all around me don't automatically evoke from me the spontaneous loving concern that I feel for dear ones and intimate friends. Unless the stranger provides a specific reason, unless he justifies his worth to me in some specific way, I do not spontaneously esteem or appreciate him. That is my experience, and I invite you to explore whether yours is similar. Buddhist philosophers have argued that this feeling of apathy to strangers is common to human beings and subconsciously conditions all our social interactions and social discourse. Yet, they argue, however normal this attitude of apathy toward strangers may feel to us, it is out of touch with reality. It flows from a thorough misperception of self and others. Indeed, one important purpose of Buddhist practice is to awaken from the illusion that one's world is mostly populated by people who (unlike one's dear friends or relatives) don't really matter.

Recently I was travelling with my family on an interstate highway and stopped at a rest stop to use the facilities. Interstate rest stops have very large restroom facilities to accommodate many people. In a rush with my two sons, I hastily walked to what I thought was the men's washroom. Near the entrance, I noticed a woman inside, washing her hands. "How strange," I thought. "A woman in the men's washroom!" As I continued to enter, she looked at me with surprise and then gestured the way to the exit. "How odd," I thought. "Although she is in the wrong washroom, she motions me away!" As I continued to enter, I noticed several more women milling around. "What are all these women doing here?" I wondered. That's when I heard my sons' voices behind me: "Uh, Dad, do you realize that you are walking into the women's room?" My perception that those women were the ones who had walked into the wrong washroom—that they were foreigners, the *strangers* here—was completely false. Yet this false perception felt so real. Was this incident a fluke or was it an especially vivid example of how my mind generally tends to falsify my experience of others, making them look more distant, other, and strange than they really are?

In Buddhist cultures the story is told of a remarkable interchange between the Buddha and a young woman named Kisa Gotami. Gotami was a village woman who longed to have a son. Having finally given birth to a baby boy, she was overjoyed. But as a toddler, her son became seriously ill and suddenly died. Gotami, mad with grief, carried her son's body on her hip as though he were alive and went through her village pleading with every one she met, "Please give me medicine for my son!" Astonished by her behavior, a few people mocked her, asking, "What medicine can there be for the dead?" But an old man took pity on her and suggested she see the Buddha who was teaching near their village.

Hurrying to the Buddha, a renowned sage, with the hope that he might have magical powers, she beseeched him, "Please, blessed one, give me medicine for my son!" The Buddha recognized Gotami's spiritual potential, and replied, "Go back to your village and visit every abode. At each home where nobody grieves for the dead, fetch a mustard seed, then return to me with those seeds." Gotami excitedly returned to her village. At the first house she declared, "The blessed one has instructed me to get mustard seeds from every home where nobody grieves for the dead. Please give me mustard seeds for my son's medicine." But the householder replied, "Alas, Gotami, we grieve for our little daughter who died last summer." Gotami went to the next house, made the same declaration, and received this reply, "Alas, Gotami, we grieve over our dear son who died last year." At the next house she was told, "Alas, Gotami, we grieve for our beloved parents."

Visiting home after home, her search continued until she had gone to every home in the village without receiving a single mustard seed. Then it struck her—"*Everyone* in the village, indeed, every single being undergoes grief like my own!" At that moment her anguish transformed into an intense empathy for all beings in their grief of loss. And Gotami's longing to be free of distress became a powerful wish for all to be free. It dawned on her, "*This* is what the Buddha, in his compassion for beings, has seen!"

Soon after, she felt ready to hold the funeral rites for her son. When she returned to the Buddha, he smiled and asked, "Gotami, have you brought me mustard seeds?" "Oh blessed one," she replied, "I am done with mustard seeds. Just give me refuge." The Buddha welcomed Gotami into his monastic community, where, it is said, her great compassion for beings empowered rapid progress on the Buddha's path of awakening.

What does this story imply about the construct of "stranger" and the potential for human connection beyond the construct? Gotami felt isolated in her grief as if her pain and loss were unique to her, as if all other people must be *strangers* to such intense personal pain. By inhabiting that mental construct, she became estranged not only from her neighbors but also from her fuller personhood, her innate capacity for empathetic connection, the underlying potential of wisdom and love that the Buddha embodied in the story. By practicing the Buddha's "mustard seed" instruction, Gotami discovered her grief need not isolate and estrange her from others but could reveal her deep connection to all other beings, a more fundamental reality than her narrow constructs of self and other had previously permitted to be seen. All those other beings are *not* strangers, she realized, but part of her larger family—the family of beings who are undergoing the sufferings and joys of living and dying with her. Declaring, "This is what the blessed one in his compassion has seen," she, like the Buddha before her, had begun to know others in the basic nature of their experience as profoundly like herself and her child—as not really strangers at all. By allowing the people of her village to reveal this to her, she was reconnected with her own fuller humanity, her fundamental being. She was no longer such a stranger to herself.

Gotami's story raises a basic question for us. Why should so many others appear like strangers to us, given how much we have in common with them all? If I put down this piece of writing, walk outside among crowds of people on a nearby street, those I've had a few pleasant interactions with are categorized the moment I see them as "my friends" (deserving loving concern), those I've had a few unpleasant interactions with are categorized as "adversaries" (not deserving of loving concern), and the vast majority, whom I haven't met, are labeled "strangers" (appearing to have little value or importance at all).

Although other people do not experience *themselves* as what my self-concerned labels reduce them to, I tend not to notice that distinction. It appears as if the unknown person passing me on the street really was just the "stranger" my mind makes of him or her, nothing more—not a parent, sibling or child beloved by others, not a full human being with all the hopes, fears and struggles that humans are undergoing. As a mindfulness exercise from Buddhism, I would invite the reader to do similarly. Look around you in a setting where a few people are known to you and the vast majority of them are not. If, as Gotami discovered, we have so much in common with all those others—all of us wishing for happiness and well-being, all undergoing sufferings, grief and death in this world—why should most others commonly appear to us as if they weren't just as profoundly human and fully dimensioned as ourselves and our dear ones?

Buddhist epistemology looks into this question. Our experience at every moment, Buddhist philosophers have noted, is utterly impermanent—an ever-changing flow of sensations, thoughts and feelings. The basic awareness that takes expression in those shifting experiences is completely open, transcending all narrow frames of reference. So if we were able to look directly into our own awareness, say Buddhist teachers, we would find no substantial entity, no unchanging self—just momentary sensations, thoughts and feelings that flow continuously from the openness and cognizance of that basic awareness.

Within that openness and cognizance is the innate capacity to sense our deep connection to all other beings, to recognize our deep interdependence, our similar wants and needs, and to sense others as one's greater self or larger family.

Due to primal ignorance, the Buddha taught, a sub-conscious movement of grasping in our minds tries to fill up the utter openness of our basic awareness, and concretize the transience of its experiences, by constructing a very narrow, substantial and unchanging sense of self. In that way, our minds hide from the vast, ungraspable mystery of experience as it really is. Our chains of thinking work hard to interpret each situation in ways that would make this shifting, narrow, thought-made sense of self feel like a concrete, substantial, permanent entity. In sum, Buddhist philosophers have argued, although our thoughts help pattern our experience coherently through labels like "me" and "you," thereby enabling us appropriately to act and relate to others, there is no unchanging, substantial self to be found in our experience of the sort that our chains of thinking keep trying to establish.

And as the mind creates such a narrow and mistaken sense of self, it also creates correspondingly narrow and mistaken impressions of other beings. Those who make our sense of self feel substantial, real and valued at any moment are grasped as dear, as exclusively deserving love, "my friends." Those who seem to undercut our ego-construct of self are grasped in that moment as inherently dislikable, adversaries not deserving love but aversion or hatred. Billions of other beings—human and animal—that don't seem to affect our ego-construct of self at the moment, are routinely dismissed as "strangers" who don't seem to matter enough to love or hate, or even to warrant our notice. This egocentric conditioning of mind supports and is further supported by the social conditioning that identifies one's self with one's ethnic, social and religious group, frequently constructing entire groups as "stranger" or "enemy."

This brief summary of the etiology of "stranger" and "adversary" in Buddhist epistemology sheds light on the basic purpose of Buddhist practice. Buddhist practices are intended to help the individual learn to release the grip of individually and socially conditioned self-grasping by relaxing into the boundless openness of basic awareness that is prior to constructions of separateness from others, of distance, of strangeness. For, it is argued, the fundamental awareness of our minds, which is prior to constructs of self versus other, has the innate power to sense all others as like ourselves in the most essential ways—in our wish to be well and happy, in our wish to be free of distress, and in our capacity to realize our intimate connection to all others. Gotami's story is so often repeated in Buddhist cultures because it so vividly demonstrates that human possibility. The purpose of Buddhist practice, then, is to awaken our potential to know and love others beyond constructs of otherness, and from that recognition, to mirror and evoke the same potential in others, as the Buddha did with Gotami.

For that purpose, Buddhist practices include philosophical analysis, phenomenological investigation of experience, cultivation of meditative concentration and insight, ritual and devotional practices, ethical practices, and more.

Alternatively, the essential practice can unfold from a very simple form of guidance, like the Buddha's "mustard seed" instruction for Gotami. That instruction exemplified both universal and particular aspects of human transformation. The path of awakening that Gotami entered addressed a *universal* human problem (egocentric construction and reaction), in the *particular* and personal way needed for that individual.

Another Buddhist story, this one from Japan, sheds further light on the deluded construction of "stranger," the reality of deep relatedness that it obsucres, and the possibility of awakening from the delusion to the reality.[2] One evening a Zen monk named Shichiri was chanting sacred texts when a thief entered with a sword, demanding his money or his life. Shichiri said, "Don't disturb me. You can find the money in the drawer," and resumed chanting. A little later Shichiri called out, "Don't take it all, I'll need some to pay taxes soon." The intruder collected most of the money and was about to leave, when he heard Shichiri call out, "Don't you thank someone when given a gift?" The man, chuckling at Shichiri's strange request, thanked him and left. A few days later, the man was captured by the authorities, then confessed a number of robberies that he had committed, including Shichiri's. When Shichiri was called to court as witness, he declared: "This man is *not* a thief, at least as far as I am concerned. I gave him the money and he thanked me for it." After spending time in prison, the man returned to Shichiri to become his disciple.

The story of Shichiri and the thief incorporates several elements of Buddhist philosophy that were noted above. The thief, like most of us, assumes that he is reading his concepts of self and other off of a reality outside of himself; as if the labels that the thief uses—"thief" and "victim"—refer to unchanging, fixed identities established in the very being of persons. In reality, according to Buddhist analysis, such identities are not inherent and fixed but only constructs, generated moment by moment from the thoughts and actions of the people involved. Because the intruder is committed to his mental construct of self and other as inherent strangers and adversaries, separate and unrelated, they appear as such to him. Because Shichiri is committed to the reality of deep human relatedness that is always present prior to such constructs, everything he does undercuts the intruder's perspective while expressing a profound human connection. In doing so, Shichiri also demonstrates his faith in the thief's capacity to awaken to the reality.

"Don't disturb me. You can find the money in the drawer." Shichiri's words are gruff but relational, expressing authority and permission, like a father responding to a son who has asked for his allowance. "Don't take it all, I'll need some for taxes" implies that the amount is set by mutual need and obligation, as in a family. "Don't you thank someone when you are given a gift?" are the words of a gruff, loving father when teaching his child essential social skills. Speaking from his awareness of the deep human connection prior to all constructs of separateness and distance, Shichiri's language spontaneously reconstructs their relationship as an interaction of family members.

Upon leaving Shirchiri's apartment, the intruder doesn't yet realize what

Shichiri has done. The law-court scene is a literary trope—whatever Shichiri says, however outlandish, is the sworn truth. Shichiri declares in court "This man is *not* a thief, at least as far as I'm concerned . . ." How could that be, the people in the courtroom must have wondered. But from Shirchiri's perspective, since identities are constructs, and his mind does not construct the man's relationship to him as "thief-victim," Shichiri is not a victim and therefore the man cannot be a thief. As in Gotami's moment of insight, Shichiri recognizes others not as strangers but as fully dimensioned human beings, part of his larger family, whatever their confusions and misbehaviors. It becomes clear now that Shichiri's actions expressed a compassionate recognition of the suffering that the intruder, and by implication all of us, undergo when we act upon our mental falsifications of self and other. He had faith in the potential of this hardened criminal (and by implication all of us) to become aware of our underlying relatedness and innate compassion.

While in prison, the man had much time to ponder Shichiri's actions. Shichiri, by viewing the man not as a stranger but as a son, interrupted the man's construction of himself and others as inherently estranged. Shichri's actions were also a means of communication, speaking to the man's own latent capacity to awaken to what Shichiri had previously realized—that no one is a stranger. With the gift of prison time to reflect on these things, the man—like Shichiri, Gotami, the Buddha and countless others before him—found himself taking up the responsibility to realize his deeper personhood for the sake of all. He became Shichiri's disciple.

As a literary figure, this man represents us all.

CHAPTER 11

BUDDHISM AND HOSPITALITY

EXPECTING THE UNEXPECTED AND ACTING VIRTUOUSLY

Andy Rotman

We can learn quite a bit about Buddhist understandings of hospitality by examining one of the terms frequently found in Indian Buddhist Sanskrit texts and commonly translated as "hospitality." The term, *atithisatkāra*, means "doing" (*kāra*) something "good" or "virtuous" (*sat*) for a "guest" (*atithi*). This etymology raises two interesting questions for an investigation into Buddhist ideas of hospitality. First, what constitutes a good deed (*satkāra*)? This is a crucial question for Buddhist ethics. Second, what do we mean by "guest"? The term *atithi* has a complex etymological history, with important implications for Vedic and astrological studies, but two etymologies are most common, and both of them are illuminating. We can understand the term as deriving from the Sanskrit root *at*, which means "to go constantly," "to walk," "to wander." Hence, someone who is *atithi* is "on the move." He or she isn't a permanent resident in one's home; rather, that person is a visitor, one who is passing through. *Atithi*, however, can also be understood as the antonym of *tithi*, which denotes a specific time—an auspicious one, at that. In this sense, *atithi* refers to "one who has no fixed time for coming" or "one who has arrived outside the auspicious lunar days." In other words, it refers to someone who has arrived unexpectedly, at a random time; or worse, at the wrong time.

Though there is an abundance of material in Buddhism about *planned* giving—what to give to the monastic community, where to give it, when to give it, and how much merit such offerings will generate for the donor—the category of *unplanned* giving has received less attention. Yet, this category of unplanned giving is addressed explicitly in Buddhist narrative literature. Accounts in these materials of Buddhist laymen and laywomen interacting with Buddhist monks, who all too often arrive unexpectedly and at what seems to be the wrong time, form a template for Buddhist hospitality more generally. Even today, among Indians of all faiths, there is a common saying, *atithi devo bhavaḥ*, meaning "the *atithi*—the guest—is god." I have heard this said by my friends and teachers in India, whether Buddhist, Hindu or Jain, when I or someone else arrived unexpectedly and tea and biscuits were quickly conjured. I have also heard this said by strangers on trains and buses, when they shared food with me or I with them.

The way one treats a guest, I have been told, says a lot about one's relationship with the divine. While writing about the logic and practice of Hindu worship in central India, Lawrence Babb explains, "the entire sequence [that constitutes pūjā] . . . has one overall purpose: to make the [god or] goddess feel like a welcome guest."[1] Worshipping the god or goddess is a form of hospitality, and hospitality is a form of worship. Hence, the *atithi* is to be treated as a god. But what does one do when an *atithi*, a guest, arrives unexpectedly at an importune time? What actions in such a situation are virtuous? What, in the end, are the component parts of hospitality?

In addressing these questions, I will consider a number of stories from the *Divyāvadāna*, or "Divine Stories." The text is a vast compendium of Indian Buddhist narratives written in Sanskrit from the early centuries of the Common Era. Its stories have since spread throughout Asia, as both narrative and narrative art, leaving an indelible mark on Buddhist thought and practice. Many of these stories were incorporated into the monastic code of the branch of Buddhists known as the Mūlasarvāstivādins, and this canonical text was later transmitted to Tibet, China and beyond. As a result, scores of generations of Buddhists in Asia have considered these stories "the word of the Buddha" (*buddhavacana*), and have repeatedly recited, reworked, painted and sculpted them. These are, in short, some of the most influential stories in the history of Buddhism.

Many of the stories in the *Divyāvadāna* feature accounts of people who, suddenly and unexpectedly, meet up with the Buddha; one of the senior monks in his order, such as Mahākāśyapa, Mahākātyāyana and Mahāmaudgalyāyana; or a solitary buddha, an awakened being, like the Buddha, but who doesn't found his own monastic community. All of these figures are *arhats*, a term that comes from the Sanskrit root *arh*, meaning "to be worthy" or "to deserve." An *arhat*, therefore, is someone who is "worthy" and "deserving." But worthy and deserving of what? The answer, according to the *Divyāvadāna,* is that they're worthy and deserving of offerings (*dakṣiṇeya*), food offerings in particular, by Buddhists and non-Buddhists alike.

An *arhat* is a particularly good field of merit (*puṇyakṣetra*) for devotees to "plant" an offering. "Thus," as John Strong notes, "any good (or bad) action directed toward [such a being] can have positive (or negative) karmic results beyond all expectations."[2] In "The Story of Meṇḍhaka," for example, during a famine, with stocks of food nearly depleted, the householder Meṇḍhaka, his wife, son, daughter-in-law, servant and maid happen to meet a solitary buddha, and each of them give him the last bit of food that they possess. They then make fervent aspirations for more food, all of which are fulfilled *immediately*. When the king hears of this, he exclaims: "Oh! This field is so fertile and faultless! A seed sown today bears fruit today as well!" (Divy 135.12–13).[3] Since the solitary buddha constitutes a particularly fecund field of merit, the karmic results of their respective offerings are obtained on the same day. As the Buddha explains:

> If, monks, beings were to know the result of charity and the consequence of offering charity as I know the result of charity and the consequence of offering charity, then at present they would never eat the very last remaining mouthful of food without giving it away or sharing it, if a worthy recipient of that food were to be found. (Divy 298.2–7)

Intrinsic to these encounters is an exchange—laypeople offer food to monastics, and monastics in turn offer those laypeople merit. This "food for merit" exchange is made explicit in "The Story of Sahasodgata." A solitary buddha who is traveling through the countryside arrives at a park on the outskirts of a town but then decides to go elsewhere. A householder happens to see him and says, "Noble one, why are you turning back? You are in want of food, and I, of merit. Take up residence here in this park and I'll support you with alms with no interruption" (Divy 312.15–16).

But there is a problem: solitary buddhas, such as those in "The Story of Meṇḍhaka" and "The Story of Sahasodgata," cannot be *sought out* as the recipients of offerings. They live "in remote areas," as the texts tell us (e.g. Divy 88.14–15; 132.21), and they like to roam, following the famous prescription from one of the Pali suttas (*Sutta Nipata* I.3; *Khaggavisana Sutta*) to "wander alone like a rhinoceros." It is their offering to the laity that they come and accept the laity's offerings, providing them a chance to transform their gifts into merit.

Moreover, in addition to living in remote areas, Buddhist monks of all kinds tended to be "on the move." In the era before permanent monastic settlements, which probably occurred in the early centuries of the Common Era, monks would "walk" and "wander" (*viharati*) for nine months of the year and then settle somewhere for the three months of the rainy season, when travel was difficult, to study and meditate. These settlements came to be known as vihāras, since they were places in which monastics could do just what they did when it wasn't raining: "live," "pass time," and, to be sure, "walk about."

The "walk about" component of their lives was crucial. Monastics have always been dependent on the largesse of the laity for their food, and during this period of Buddhism monasticism, monastics would normally go on an alms round each day to find food for themselves. This was the case whether they were wandering the countryside or settled in a vihāra. They would wander from home to home, generally without predestination, until their bowls were full, accepting whatever food they happened to receive. That was their main meal for the day.

Although lay people could make arrangements to invite the Buddha or the full monastic community to one's home for a meal—a practice amenable to the very rich, such as kings, but out of the question for the poor and middle class—one could not invite a single monk to one's home, at least not according to the earliest strata of material. One could not, therefore, simply invite a senior-most monk to one's home and feed him, even though he was worthy of offerings. Moreover, those spiritually advanced monks who were *arhats* were often the most peripatetic. They would wander constantly, from one region to the next, not domesticated by monastic structures.

This left the average layperson in a quandary: how could someone of ordinary means afford to feed the entire monastic community or just find a single monk to feed, especially one who was eminently worthy? The *Divyāvadāna* offers no easy answers, nor do other Indian Buddhist texts. There simply aren't many chances for a layperson to make food offerings. What is stressed, however, is that one should make the most of any such opportunity that arises, even if one isn't particularly prepared to do a "good deed" for the "guest" who suddenly appears.

Some of the most famous stories in Indian Buddhism address this problem. Probably the most famous of all concerns King Aśoka, the great Indian monarch from the third century BCE, whose empire stretched from present-day Afghanistan to Bangladesh and whose conversion to Buddhism and righteous rule are still remembered through his famous pillar inscriptions. The life story of King Aśoka is told in great detail in the *Divyāvadāna*, stretching back to a previous life of Aśoka, when he was a boy named Jaya in the city of Rajagṛha, and extending to his last days when, imprisoned by his heir-apparent son, he gave away all his possessions to the monastic community. Central to this narrative is the offering he made when he was the boy named Jaya, for we are told that this very offering culminated in his becoming a great monarch and, in the end, a great patron of Buddhism.

As we read in "The Story of a Gift of Dirt":

> The Blessed One arrived at the main road [in Rajagṛha]. Two little boys were there. One was a son from a very prominent family, and the other a son from a somewhat less prominent family. They were playing at building houses in the dirt. The first of them was named Jaya (Victory), and the second was named Vijaya (Conquest). Both of them saw the Buddha, whose body was adorned with the thirty-two marks of a great man and who was a sight one never tires of seeing. The young boy Jaya, thinking, "I'll give him some barley meal," threw a handful of dirt into the Blessed One's begging bowl. Vijaya approved of this by respectfully folding his hands together.
>
> As it is said:
>> He saw the greatly compassionate self-made one
>> whose body radiated a halo a fathom wide.
>> With a resolute face, and instilled with faith,
>> he offered some dirt
>> to the one who brings an end to birth and old age.
>
> After making this offering to the Blessed One, Jaya then proceeded to make a fervent aspiration: "By the root of virtue, may I become king and, after placing the earth under a single umbrella of sovereignty, may I serve the Lord Buddha."
>> The Sage perceived the boy's disposition,
>> and knowing that his fervent aspiration was proper,
>> saw that the desired result would be attained
>> because of the power of his field of merit.
>> He therefore accepted, with compassion, the proffered dirt.
>
> And so, that seed of merit that was to ripen into Aśoka's kingship was planted. (Divy 366.5–23)

There are some notable features of this story that tell us a lot about Buddhist notions of hospitality. First, the intention of the giver is important. Aśoka, in his former incarnation as Jaya, sets the intention to give some barley meal as an offering, even though he has none to give and, instead, offers the Buddha a handful of dirt. Dirt is not food, and as such the gift has very little utility. Yet Jaya had a good "disposition" (*bhāva*), in large part, no doubt, because he is blessed with faith.

Faith is like the price of admission into the system of Buddhist morality—not faith *in* Buddhist morality per se, but the faith that admits and empowers one as a Buddhist. Faith is the seed money that allows one to invest in a Buddhist future. It allows one to buy in, creating the possibility for "spiritual growth." To use the analogy of a card game, faith is like the chips one receives to ante up for a first hand. While one can perform good or bad deeds without faith, one does so not as a Buddhist, and the rewards are limited. To be a Buddhist, faith is a requisite. And once one has faith, one can participate in the Buddhist moral economy, readily accruing moral value through good deeds.

The value of the deed that Jaya has performed is apparent by the success of his "fervent aspiration" (*praṇidhāna*), which the Buddha affirms was "right" or "proper" (*samyak*). The accrued merit from the offering is both "root" and "capital," the basis for future good deeds and attainments, and the purchase-power for current ones. Roots of virtue, Luis Gomez observes, "are like roots (*mūla*) because, once performed, they remain as the basis for future virtue, and, if properly cultivated, grow, mature, and bear fruit."[4] In this case, as our narrator the Buddha explains, Jaya's offering functioned as a "root" that helped him develop into a world-conquering monarch. (Actually, the text calls it a "seed of merit," combining two different agricultural metaphors, that of "roots" and "seeds.") Yet the term *mūla* also refers to one's capital or financial principal. To use a certainly false cognate, *mūla* here really is the moola, Jaya's bank of virtue that allows him to "cash in" for a fervent aspiration.

Second, the recipient of one's offering is important. Jaya gives and, as a result, receives, yet the rate of return is exceptionally good—universal monarch for handful of dirt—because the recipient of his offering is the Buddha, who is an excellent "field of merit" (*puṇyakṣetra*) in which to plant merit-seeds.

Third, the value of the object that is given is important, though one might not know it from this story. Nevertheless, "The Mahāyāna Sūtra On the Topic of Giving" simply lists 37 gifts and their results, with no mention made of the proper intention or recipient. For example,

> [10.] He gives a gift of food that results in his being free from the cravings of hunger.
> [11.] He gives a gift of drink that results in his being free from thirst everywhere in all his lives [yet to come]. (Divy 482.13–16)

Buddhist materials often minimize the value of one or more of these variables as a way of emphasizing the worth of the other (or others). In the "Story of Candraprabha," for example, an evil brahman asks King Candraprabha for his head, so the king decapitates himself and offers his severed head to the brahman. The value of the offering is negligible. The brahman, after receiving the king's head, simply tosses it aside, unsure of what to do with it.[5] The field of merit constituted by the recipient is also negligible. It's a barren field for sowing seeds of virtue. What is emphasized, however, is the power and propriety of the king's intention. Good donors have good dispositions in general, and good intentions when they make offerings.

The importance of good intentions, as opposed to offerings with great use-value, is shown quite graphically in an episode from "The Story of a Woman Dependent on a City for Alms." In the story, a leprous beggar woman wandering for alms happens to see the venerable Mahākāśyapa, who "instills faith through his body and through his mind" (Divy 82.13–14), and decides to make him an offering.

> Then the venerable Mahākāśyapa, understanding her thoughts with his mind, held out his begging bowl. "If you have anything to spare, my sister, please put it in my bowl."
>
> Cultivating faith in her mind, she poured [some rice-water] into his bowl. Then a fly fell in. She began to take it out when one of her fingers fell off into the rice-water. She reflected, "Although the noble one, out of respect for my feelings, hasn't thrown [this rice-water] away, he won't partake of it."
>
> Then the venerable Mahākāśyapa, understanding her thoughts with his mind, right before her eyes, sat down against the base of a wall and began to eat.
>
> She reflected, "Although the noble one, out of respect for my feelings, has partaken of this, he won't think of this food as a proper meal."
>
> Then the venerable Mahākāśyapa, understanding her thoughts, said this to that woman who was dependent on the city for alms: "Sister, I am happy! I can pass the whole day and night on the food [that you have given me]."
>
> She became very excited. "The Noble Mahākāśyapa has accepted alms from me!" Then, while cultivating faith in her mind for the venerable Mahākāśyapa, she died and was reborn among the gods in the heaven known as Tuṣita ("Contented"). (Divy 82.13–14)

If the leprous beggar woman's offering of rice-water (with finger) were to be judged by its use-value, even though Mahākāśyapa managed to make a meal of it, she no doubt would have earned very little merit. With the enumeration of offerings and their rewards in the previously mentioned "The Mahāyāna Sūtra On the Topic of Giving" as a benchmark, an offering of some rice-water wouldn't merit rebirth among the Tuṣita gods. While the woman may have been just one small offering away from attaining the karmic threshold that would allow her such an auspicious rebirth, the emphasis here is on how faith can elevate even a mundane offering into something, karmically speaking, very valuable.

Guests offer the devotee an amazing opportunity. While Mahākāśyapa received a meal, the leprous beggar woman secured herself a place in heaven. The donor, as such, is the biggest beneficiary. Mahākāśyapa gave her the gift of being able to give to him. Giving, as such, is its own reward, especially if one gives out of faith and (or) gives to a worthy recipient.

To whom, then, should one make offerings? Everyone, for one never *really* knows what kind of person one stands before, whether the beggar in your presence is a thief or a saint or a god. For example, later in "The Story of a Woman Dependent on a City for Alms," Śakra, the lord of the Trāyastrimśa gods, hears that the leprous beggar woman, as a result of her offering, has been reborn in the Tuṣita heaven, one heaven above his, and he gets jealous. He tries to entice Mahākāśyapa, whom he knows likes to give the gift of receiving alms from the poor, to accept his offering as well so that he too can achieve a large reward of merit. Śakra, we are told, "magically created a dilapidated, broken-down house in which crows lurked, on a road where poor people lived. Then he magically transformed himself into a weaver dressed in hempen rags and wearing a rumpled turban, with cracked hands and feet" (Divy 83). Even gods can be beggars and vice versa.

This past week, in one of my classes, I was screening a film on hijras, members of a "third gender" on the subcontinent, whose repertoire of behaviors blurs the distinctions between man and woman, Hindu and Muslim. Though they are social outcastes in many ways, shopkeepers routinely offer them alms, in part because hijras are thought to have the power to bless and curse, but for other reasons as well. In response to the question of why he gives alms to hijras, one shopkeeper in the film, explains, "You never know what external form souls will take when they appear before you." A hijra might be a god, too.

For a person of faith, the chance to make an offering to a guest is a tremendous opportunity to earn merit and plant new roots of virtue. And so, one must treat "the *atithi*, the guest, as a god," offering him whatever one can: the very last morsel of food in one's possession, as the Buddha advises; some rice-water, if that's all one has; or a handful of dirt with the hope that it will suffice—by dint of a good disposition, faith, and some wishful thinking—as a handful of barley meal. Hospitality is a very effective way to progress on the spiritual path.

Hospitality of this kind, it should be noted, continues to be an important concern and practice for both Buddhists and Indians. Recently, the Government of India's Ministry of Tourism has taken up the saying *atithi devo bhavaḥ* and introduced the Atithi Devo Bhavah Program. According to their website—atithidevobhavah.com—"The concept [guest as god] is deep-routed in modern progressive India. Even [the] Government of India believes in the concept."[6] Considering the enormous numbers of migrants that attempt to flee persecution and inequity each year, I can only hope that more countries come to believe in the concept as well, greeting and welcoming those "on the move," even those dressed as beggars who arrive at inopportune times. That would truly make the world a better place.

IV

Islamic Perspectives

CHAPTER 12

THE DEAD AND THE CITY

THE LIMITS OF HOSPITALITY IN THE EARLY MODERN LEVANT[1]

Dana Sajdi

To Be "Damascene": the openness and closeness of identities

An appellation, the strongest marker of identity, can be misleading. Certainly, the sobriquet "al-Nabulusi" ("of the city of Nablus") in the name of one of the most famous scholars and Sufis of the eighteenth century, `Abd al-Ghani al-Nabulusi (d. 1731), is confusing to the unknowing. The man was not from Nablus. It was Damascus where he was born and bred, and where he taught, composed his books, epistles and poetry, got severely depressed for seven years, and received his mystical revelations. Despite having been thoroughly Damascene, al-Nabulusi wrote of himself, "I am the Damascene, I am the Indian, I am the Turk, I am the Sicilian."[2] This ingathering of sobriquets constitutes a truly globalized vision where the Self is spacious enough to include the Other. (Henceforth, "self" and "other" will be in lower case and without quotation marks).

One of the contemporaries, students and colleagues of al-Nabulusi was a certain Muhammad Ibn Kannan (d. 1740). While not of the spiritual and intellectual stature of al-Nabulusi, he was, nevertheless, one of the known teachers and notables of Damascus, and the leader of an important mystical order. Ibn Kannan wrote an unusually loquacious chronicle about the events he witnessed in his beloved city. At a certain point in the chronicle, Ibn Kannan mentions the arrival of a community of immigrants, about 400 in number, from the city of Balkh (in today's Afghanistan). Ibn Kannan, being a notable of the town, performed his duty of going to visit and welcome the Balkhi newcomers—the would-be Damascenes. Of his encounter with the Balkhi community, he wrote:

> Whatever they (the community) earn is given to their leader and is not dispensed to them even as inheritance . . . they call his wife "the lady," and they are like servants to her and walk with her in retinue. Their obedience to their leader is not equalled by that accorded to the greatest ruler . . . no one is seated in the assembly of the leader except his deputy or the prayer-leader. *They have customs that do not make sense to the people of this land.*[3] (My emphasis.)

Thus, in sharp contrast to al-Nabulusi's identification with almost random ethnicities (Indians, Turks and Sicilians), Ibn Kannan's observations about the Balkhis is one of significant difference between self and other. Even when the other, in this case, are fellow Muslims, their customs remain illegible to the Damascenes.

It is arguable that the differences in attitudes of al-Nabulusi and Ibn Kannan have to do with the specific discursive space that each of the authors chose to use. The former expressed an inclusive cosmopolitanism in *mystical poetry*, the very space of idealization and the metaphysical, while the latter offered bounded and sealed identities in *historical prose*, the place of the real and the tangible. However, the argument of this paper is that a definite attitude toward the other is, to say the least, difficult to locate in the early modern Levant, and may require the examination of a variety of spaces beyond the discursive and the literary into the social and even the urban physical space. Furthermore, one should not stop at the world of the living, but venture beyond it into the subterranean world of the dead. Even in these other spaces, the other is never fully identifiable and the self is open to redefinitions. But before we embark on the discussion, a definition of terms is in order.

According to the *Oxford American Dictionary*, one of the definitions of "hospitality" is "the friendly or generous reception and entertainment of visitors, guests, or strangers." It is the "stranger" element that is of significance since hospitality can only be complete or true if it is directed at the stranger. After all, allowing one's sister into one's house is not hospitality at all, as the sister, in more ways than one, is none other than the self. She is *family*, the *familiar*. Here, I use "familiar" in its original Latin derivation, which indicated both *family* and *household* (again, according to the *Oxford American Dictionary*). Thus, in this essay, I examine hospitality as a process in which the *stranger* is rendered *familiar* through an act of reception in or/and sharing of one's household or place. In other words, it is the release of exclusive ownership of a place to the other, the ideal of which is expressed in the Arabic proverb, "the house is yours" (*al-bayt baytuka*).

Strangers in Life and in Death?

"The house is yours" is an ideal that the aforementioned Ibn Kannan tried to enact by his reception of the Balkhi strangers, a Muslim community who entered *his* space, the city of Damascus. Despite assumed familiarity and shared vocabulary derived from the fact of a supposedly all-encompassing "Islamic tradition," Ibn Kannan was estranged by the behaviour of the Balkhis. Further, this moment of estrangement/unfamiliarity is borne out of precisely a process of, or an attempt at, familiarizing the stranger. Thus, it is a moment of simultaneous inclusion and exclusion.

This tension between inclusion and exclusion exists in yet another space in the early modern Levantine city: the cemetery. In the sources of the period, the frequent mention of "the Graveyard/Tombs/Side of the Strangers" as a topographical feature in both Damascus and Aleppo is puzzling to the modern scholar.[4] In the naming of the topographical feature, the "stranger" is made immediately familiar not only by the very process of appellation, but also by being literally granted a place, a physical space that is, in the city's "underground." So, what is the use of "the Graveyard of the Strangers"? Is it to exclude or include? To peripheralize or to make part and parcel of the urban landscape? To release ownership of the city or to secure it?

This essay is an attempt at understanding these slippery moments of tension between inclusion and exclusion of the stranger-citizens of Damascus and Aleppo. While the reader may expect for the mystery of the "Graveyard of the Strangers" to be unraveled, the point of this paper is primarily methodological. Can we really locate a definite Islamic/Muslim attitude toward the other? Is it at all helpful to refer to Islamic canonical texts in our search for a certain Islamic hospitality or lack thereof? Is Islam really schizophrenic, possessing an open mystical vision on the one hand, and closed legalistic practice on the other? Indeed, the entire point of this exercise is to carry out a close sociological examination of a few historical moments, an exercise that is meant to render the foregoing questions moot. In order to do this, we must first re-visit the worlds of al-Nabulusi and Ibn Kannan.

The Scholarly Webs in Life, in Text and in Death

The protagonists in this inquiry *per force* are the `ulama' (sing. `alim, literally, "the knowing"), such as al-Nabulusi and Ibn Kannan. They are "scholars of religion," most of whom, in the early modern period, were also mystics (or Sufis). They are the protagonists simply because they happen to be the main authors of texts in the pre-modern Islamic world, and texts happen to be the main sources for the modern historian. But the fact of the scholars' almost exclusive propriety of textual space in itself is telling as will become presently. But, who really are the scholars?

A short definition would be "clergy," but such a translation is inaccurate because they were much more and perhaps much less than the Christian clergy. They were the transmitters and producers of knowledge (religious, historical and even literary), they were interpreters of divine law, and as such, they were dubbed "the heirs of the Prophet" in a formula attributed to the Prophet himself. In short, the scholars were a social group that commanded moral and social authority. In their occupation of administrative and judicial offices (such as judge, jurisconsult, etc.), they, or more precisely, some of them, also constituted a part of the political elite. They were a multi-competent, literate part of the urban population who functioned as a crucial link between state and society, and their identity straddled both.[5] While they were discursively and socially hegemonic, they were not an isolated part of the community. Rather, because of their social position, they were the organic and natural leaders of the urban community and existed at every socio-economic class. In other words, the scholars were culturally and socially (even sartorially) distinct, but they permeated the entirety of urban society.

But, what do these scholars and their texts have to do with the topic of "hospitality"? As in the anecdote of the encounter between Ibn Kannan and the Balkhi community, it was the notables among the scholars who were endowed with the authority to decide whom to open the door to. In other words, they were the gatekeepers of society. How then did these scholars, being the natural leaders of the community, integrate, that is, include; or estrange, that is, exclude themselves/others in their textual and social practices?

The simple and straightforward answer is that the scholars safeguarded the community by the establishment of social hierarchies of place and situation, which occurred in a very complicated fashion and on various levels and in a variety of spaces. Let us take an example from an entry in the same chronicle authored by Ibn Kannan. Here, the author is describing the inaugural lecture of the teaching cycle in one of the colleges of Damascus:

> On Thursday, our master Muhammad Afandi al-`Imadi started the teaching cycle at al-Sulaymaniyya College . . . the lesson was attended by the notables. On his (`Imadi's) right sat al-Shaykh Muradi, then al-Shaykh Abu al-Mawahib al-Hanbali—the Hanbali jursiconsult of Damascus, then our master the scholar al-Shaykh Muhammad Afandi al-Ustuwani al-Hanafi. On his [that is, Muhammad Afandi al-Muradi's] left sat our master Abu al-Safa Afandi Ibn al-`Arif—the Hanafi jurisconsult of Damascus, and directly next to him was `Abd al-Rahman al-Qari, the teacher of the Zahiriyya College, then his cousin Muhammad Afandi al-Qari, the teacher of the Balkhiyya College. As for the Shafi`i jurisconsult our master al-Shaykh Ahmad Afandi al-Ghazzi, he sat in the line behind the revered teacher, and as for our Shaykh al-Mulla Ilyas, *he sat in the line of the students because it was in his habit to detest fame and haughtiness.*[6] (My emphasis.)

Thus, the savants—teachers, jurisconsults and judges—are meticulously organized in a neat hierarchy where each is assigned a seating position commensurate to his social position. In other words, these scholars define themselves in relation to one another in a familiar and familiarizing vocabulary of a closed seating arrangement. It is noteworthy that this seating arrangement takes place in a college and indeed some of the illustrious savants are associated with known urban institutions (especially the colleges mentioned in the quoted passage), each of which is a physical landmark. Thus, this seating arrangement is not only a microcosm, and a reduction to the essence of the scholars' social world, but also, in as much as the scholars are associated with institutions, the arrangement inscribes the scholars in the urban topography.

But, what is most remarkable about this passage is the behavior of Mulla Ilyas, another famous scholar and mystic. His act of abandoning the scholarly circle and joining the row of the students may seem puzzling at first. But the act and its immediate comprehension and interpretation by the author, Ibn

Kannan, help us decode the social vocabulary of the seating arrangement. Mulla Ilyas's abandonment is meant as an expression of humility, an act to counter fame. It is to *un-fame*, that is, to render himself unfamiliar, or not immediately recognizable in the community of scholars. Of course, this act of abandonment due to humility is mere pretense. Mulla Ilyas leaves the hierarchy because he no longer has any use for it. He is above and beyond hierarchies and relative definition. He is a league of his own, so to speak. Thus, his act could be posited as one of rejection of hospitality and a refusal to partake in the social space of the scholars. Let us keep in mind Mulla Ilyas's attempt, as pretentious as it is, to de-familiarize or estrange himself. It may be that this deliberate act to become or remain a stranger is but a strategy of incorporation and integration. To Mulla Ilyas we will return later.

Let us move from the realm of actual social practice to that of the text as a parallel practice. If the definition of the scholar is related to his knowledge of God and things Divine, his social definition comes from his tireless practice of writing himself to himself, that is, to inscribe himself in text. The audience of the text is, naturally, other scholars. This tendency to record the self (as a social and cultural group) finds full expression in the genre of the biographical diction- ary. This genre is a sort of *Who's Who* made up of obituaries/necrologies of typically deceased scholars.[7] A typical entry would include a scholar's academic achievements: what they studied, who they studied with, where they taught, who were their students, what their colleagues thought of them, and where they were buried. In as much as it locates individuals in social and physical spaces, the biographical dictionary maps out the social world of the scholars—their teachers and disciples and associates—and defines them in hierarchies that establish their relative positions in that world.

It is also noteworthy that the obituary inscribes the scholar, not only in the social world, but also in the urban topography. The obituary in the biographical dictionary notes the institutions with which the scholar was associated, includ- ing the colleges where he studied and taught, if relevant the dervish lodge where he stayed, the mosque in which the prayer of the deceased was said before his burial, and his burial place. Thus, the biographical dictionary, even more than the practice of seating arrangement, establishes the scholars as a community within an urban topography and identifies each scholar within that community.

But the scholars' strategies of identifying, or rendering familiar, are not lim- ited to seating arrangements in life and inclusion into textual space, but also extend to the world of the dead. The "underground," too, has social significa- tion. The dead, too, have a definite address. Let us look at a few entries about burial places in the chronicle of Ibn Kannan:

On the 23rd of Muharram 1124/1712, al-Sayyid Fadl Allah al-Fustuqi . . . died in Damascus. The prayer of the deceased was held in the (Umayyad) Mosque. He was buried in Mount Qasyun, by the grave of al-Qumayni, across from the grave of the saint Muhammad al-Shayyah, to the west of al-Zaynabiyya and al-Rukniyya colleges.[8]

The meticulousness in the description of the physical location of the grave of the deceased scholar is striking. The grave is marked not only by urban institutions, the colleges, but also by the burial sites of others. In this case, the mention of the names of the two "dead neighbors" is important since both were famous saints. In other words, al-Fustuqi's new abode is not neutral but thoroughly blessed. Let us look at another example. This time, however, the deceased is a member of the immigrant Balkhi community, whom we have encountered earlier:

> Al-Sayyid Rafi` al-Yazbaki . . . died of the epidemic (i.e. the plague) in his house to the west of al-Ward Mosque. The prayer of the deceased was performed at the mosque, and he was buried in Mount Qasyun in the burying plot of the commoners, outside the plot of his Shaykh. No one is buried within (the plot) except for Shaykh Muhammad and the tailor, Ishaq. Everyone else is buried outside and around the plot.[9]

By now, a clear pattern emerges: in the neighborhoods of the dead, there is a social hierarchy. To be buried in the "public burying plot in Mount Qasyun," as in the case of the Balkhi, is markedly different in status from being buried in a private plot, or being surrounded by illustrious neighbors, as in the case of the above-mentioned al-Fustuqi.

So, the immediate question is: is the fact that the Balkhi was a recent immigrant to Damascus responsible for his failure to acquire a more prestigious burial spot? The social significance of al-Yazbaki's burial in the public plot is revealed when one compares his funerary address with that of yet another immigrant but of a different ethnicity: the Indian Badr al-Din al-Ghawth al-Naqshabandi, who died in 1726:

> The pious and cultivated saint, al-Shaykh al-Imam Badr al-Naqshabandi, came to Damascus in 1094 [Hijri calendar] and lodged in the Qishani hospice to the east of the Umayyad Mosque along with his cousin Hidayat Allah. He was virtuous, devout, quiet, upright and unswerving. He is author of the *Kitab al-jawahir al-khams* ("The Book of the Five Gems"). He was ill with dropsy and swelling for a year. The prayer of the deceased was said over him at the midday prayers in the (Umayyad) Mosque. He was buried in Eastern Graveyard, *on the Side of the Strangers*, next to his cousin Hidayat Allah.[10] (My emphasis.)

Badr al-Din is an immigrant who, despite residing in Damascus for 40 years, and despite all of his obvious social standing, remained unassimilated even in death and was buried in a plot set aside for strangers. Al-Yazbaki (the one from Balkh), at least, seems to have assimilated sufficiently into Damascus society to be buried not as a stranger but as a Damascene, albeit a commoner in a public plot.

So, what does this elaborate underground hierarchy of commoner, strangers and saints signify? Is it that the immigrants, despite being Muslim scholars and mystics, were kept on the peripheries of these dense and complex hierarchies, and limited only to the "Graveyards of the Strangers"? Are the gestures of hospitality shown by Ibn Kannan to the new Balkhi community on their arrival merely a nod to the ideal of hospitality to strangers? Are the words of al-Nabulusi ("I am the Damascene, the Turk, the Indian, the Sicilian") hollow? Is it that the Levantine scholars kept themselves locked and interlocked in a closed web of social, textual and burial practices? Were they never able to familiarize the strangers and incorporate them into the self? And what of the Graveyard of the Strangers? The clue may lie in the odd behavior of Mulla Ilyas, who, it will be remembered, abandoned his glorified position among the teachers to join the students.

The Saint and the City

It is important to note that Mulla Ilyas *chose* to abandon the hierarchy of the scholars. His choice was out of pretense of humility, albeit one that derived from the fact of his established fame and uncontested authority. Is it possible that the various scholars and mystics that have been encountered in the city of the dead, had, in the manner of Mulla Ilyas, chosen to leave the hierarchies (a decision that, no doubt, they made when they were still alive)? Does the choice indicate that the scholar-mystic had become too famous or too familiar to play the game of "musical chairs" in the subterranean seating arrangement? A relatively recent study by Heghnar Zeitlian Watenpaugh is suggestive.[11] So, let us now turn from Damascus in the eighteenth century to Aleppo in the late sixteenth century and the life of the antinomian mystic, Abu Bakr Ibn Abi al-Wafa (d. 1583).

Abu Bakr stunned the city of Aleppo with his strange habits. He was an antinomian mystic who displayed the most extreme of the antisocial practices accustomed from the category of mystics known as "possessed." This trend of deviant "possessed" mystics appeared as a distinct social movement by the late thirteenth century in Central Asia and the Middle East and continued well into the eighteenth century, if not beyond. Watenpaugh describes them as follows:

> Having rejected settled life, they roamed the countryside and violated the space of the city to flaunt their outrageous behavior. This included an eccentric appearance in society where self-presentation functioned as a marker of identity: they inverted social hierarchies and disregarded Islamic law.[12]

And Abu Bakr was not slack about behaving in typical antinomian fashion. However, what is relevant for us is Abu Bakr's choice of dwelling and burial place. It was in the extramural wilderness, in none other than the Tombs of the Strangers (*turab al-ghuraba'*) that was where the mystic chose to live and die.[13] Watenpaugh argues that the antinomian Sufi connection with cemeteries was a realization of the Prophetic injunction "Die before you die," where the mystic behaved like a corpse, which included dwelling in graveyards. And thus, Abu

Bakr lived and died in the graveyard in expectation and realization of his saintly status. His grave became not only a site of veneration, but with the passage of time, it acquired a monumental mausoleum with a lodge for mystics attached to it. Indeed, Watenpaugh's main goal is precisely to demonstrate how the construction of the edifice for the dead saint ushered the transformation of the wilderness that is the graveyard into the urbanity of the city.

So, like Mulla Ilyas, Abu Bakr *chose* to be unfamiliar. It is perhaps because of his strangeness and non-assimilability that he was accepted into the urban topography. Abu Bakr chose to live outside the city, but the city itself extended its borders to include him (albeit after his death). It is his very strangeness that led to cosmopolitan urbanity.

Conclusions: who is the Damascene?

Let me offer a few statements and attempt to draw connections: Mulla Ilyas was too famous to remain in the circle of scholars and chose to sit among students—the commoners. The Indian mystic, al-Naqshabandi, well known for his scholarship but especially mystic piety, was buried in the Graveyard of the Strangers. Al-Yazbaki, the Balkhi, who came from a community whose manners, according to Ibn Kannan, were "strange to the people of [his] lands," was buried next to his master in the Graveyard of the Commoners. Abu Bakr, the strange dervish/saint, lived and died in the Graveyard of the Strangers, effectively causing wilderness to turn into civilization.

Did al-Yazbaki (the Balkhi) act in the manner of Mulla Ilyas? Was he also too famous to join the hierarchy? Did he *choose* to be buried with the commoners because he "detested fame and haughtiness"? Was the Indian mystic merely a tamer version of Abu Bakr, the antinomian? He insisted on remaining a stranger. Is the Graveyard of the Strangers really the Graveyard of the Blessed? Does the Graveyard of the Strangers actually represent the heart of urbanity, hence, normative religious life?

While there are no definite answers, it has become clear by now that the self and the other/the familiar and the stranger are neither absolute nor mutually exclusive categories. The other has a *choice* not to participate, or to employ precisely his difference/strangeness in order to be incorporated, in the least seamless of ways, into the self. The self may will to accept the other, but may become estranged in the very attempt. In short, as soon as there is an encounter between the self and the other, both are immediately changed.

It has also become clear by now that these encounters are not particularly Islamic. While the protagonists were Muslim and their cultural forms were also unmistakably Islamicate, no Quranic injunction or prophetic tradition can explain or determine Ibn Kannan's reaction to the Balkhis. Theirs was merely a human encounter. Nor can one detect a Sufi attitude as opposed to a legalistic attitude in the encounters, as all the protagonists, despite variations, were "practicing Sufis" (if such a term may be used).

Ultimately, to be Damascene (or Aleppan) is also to be Turk, Indian, Sicilian and yes, Balkhi. But this inclusive identity does not constitute a simple openness, or a seamless aggregation of a myriad of sobriquets indicating a variety of cities and ethnicities. It is a complex, often difficult, dynamic process of negotiation among the living, and between the living and the dead. Dead or alive, Damascenes interacted, both as natives and as strangers (and sometimes as both), in textual, social and burial practices to partake in the city; to make the city, sometimes in ironic, strange ways, hospitable to them.

CHAPTER 13

SOME REFLECTIONS ON HOSPITALITY IN ISLAM

Joseph Lumbard

Among the many virtues of the Islamic world that visitors often remark upon is the great hospitality. When I first lived in Morocco as a young student study-ing Arabic, I was overwhelmed by the hospitality that I received. I was often welcomed into the homes of people I had never met before with a degree of generosity and hospitality that went far beyond what I had experienced in the homes of some people I had known for many years. Of the many memories that I have from this, my first adventure into the Muslim world, there is one that is most dear to me.

One evening between the sunset and evening prayers I was sitting in the courtyard of the famous Qarawiyin Mosque in the old city of Fes. I was scheduled to leave the country in just a few days and was enjoying this last opportunity to absorb the *barakah* or blessing that permeates this magical place. As I sat, an old man who was serving water to everyone in the courtyard came up to me and looked me over. "Muslim?" he asked with a stern expression. I answered in the affirmative. *"Abūka Muslim?"* (Is your father a Muslim?) he asked. I replied, "No." *"Ummuka Muslim?"* (Is your mother a Muslim?); again, I replied, "No." At this, his face was transformed from that of the stern inquisitioner who had first approached me to a childlike joy. He began to cry, got down on his knees, hugged me, and kissed me. Then, with what appeared to be great difficulty, he got back up. To my horror, he grabbed a cup of water from the bucket he had been passing around, and with the expression of a young toddler presenting a gift to his or her parent, held the water out to me and said, *"Bismillāh,"* "In the name of God." I knew I would get sick, but I also felt that I had to accept. And indeed, the generosity and hospitality of this old man was something that I quite literally carried home with me, unfortunately, in the form of giardia. Nonetheless, this has always been one of my most cherished memories. For in his instant of joy that man felt that he had to do something to offer hospitality to the stranger. With nothing on him and probably with few possessions other than the bare necessities, there was only one thing, a cup of water. Yet at the same time, I had learned something during my time in Morocco that I often forget elsewhere, namely that hospitality is a two-way street. Not only is extending hospitality toward family, friend and stranger considered a moral imperative, so too, accepting hospitality from others, however mean their circumstances may be, is a moral imperative. It is a way in which we manifest mercy toward one another, for each act of mercy in which we partake is a reflection of God's mercy. As a famous *ḥadīth*, or saying of the Prophet Muhammad, that is known to all students of *ḥadīth* states: "The merci-ful [human beings] are shown mercy by the Merciful. Be merciful to those on earth, and He who is in heaven will be merciful unto you."[1] Conversely, another *ḥadīth* says, "God is not merciful to one who is not merciful to people."[2] In this sense, the kindness and mercy that human beings convey to one another can be seen as one of the ways in which God's "mercy embraces all things" (7:156).

In many ways, the hospitality I experienced through this humble old man and through many others like him is an extension of the hospitality that the Prophet Muhammad practiced and that he enjoined upon his followers. Once when asked, "What is faith (*īmān*)?" the Prophet replied, "The giving of food and the exchange of greetings."[3] Conversely, he is reported to have said, "There is no good in one who is not hospitable."[4] In many ways, this understanding of hospitality derives from pre-Islamic times, for in pre-Islamic Arabia generosity and hospitality were considered to be among the chief virtues of a noble Bedouin. Many verses of pre-Islamic poetry enjoin or boast of reckless hospitality, wherein one spends lavishly and wantonly to honor the guest. One could see how in a desert environment such an emphasis on hospitality might develop, for with the serious harm of traveling in harsh desert conditions a single act of hospitality could be the difference between life and death. Nonetheless, Islam called for moderation of profligate hospitality, while still emphasizing the importance of honoring the guest and providing charity. The key difference, however, is that it must be done with humility, such that the right hand knows not what the left hand does. In this way, the Quran enjoins charity and hospitality without excessive indulgence or condescension, as in 17:26-17: "Give unto the kinsman his due, and [unto] the indigent and the traveler, but do not squander wastefully. Truly the wasteful are the brethren of satans, and Satan is ungrateful to his Lord."[5]

From pre-Islamic times until today, one of the vilest of insults in Arab lands has been to call someone stingy, miserly or inhospitable. Such attributes are presented in the Quran as major moral flaws,[6] the most famous instance being 107:1-7:

> Hast thou seen the one who denies religion?
> That is the one who drives away the orphan,
> And does not urge feeding the indigent.
> So woe unto performers of prayer
> Who are heedless of their prayers,
> Those who strive to be seen,
> Yet refuse small kindnesses.

According to all commentators, these verses address the stinginess exhibited by hypocrites, who *only came to the prayer lazily, and only spent reluctantly* (9:54). The reference to *small kindnesses (mā'ūn)* is seen by most commentators as an allusion to utensils or tools that people might share and lend to one another, such as a pot, a bucket, or other items of this nature. Expanding upon this, many commentators also say that refusing small kindnesses indicates refusing hospitality toward guests.[7] In this sense, to refuse hospitality is viewed as a manifestation of hypocrisy.

The Quran also speaks repeatedly of the need to be generous and give charity.[8] Among the most important of such exhortations are the following verses:

> They ask thee what they should spend. Say, "Let whatever of your wealth you spend be for parents, kinsmen, orphans, the indigent, and the traveler. Whatever good you do, truly God knows it." (2:215)
>
> Those who spend their wealth by night and by day, secretly and openly, shall have their reward with their Lord. And no fear shall come upon them, nor shall they sorrow. (2:274)

Providing for the poor has also become a major part of all major Muslim feasts, such as the end of Ramadan and the feast of the Hajj (Q 22:28).

Such generosity is undoubtedly an important part of hospitality, but it is not necessarily hospitality in and of itself, and the Quran in fact says very little about hospitality in a direct manner. Nonetheless, there are several verses the revelation of which is said to have been prompted by an act of hospitality. An example of this is verse 59:9:

> And those who settled in the land and [abided in] belief love those who emigrated to them and find in their breasts no need for that which they were given, preferring others over themselves, even if they be impoverished. And whosoever is shielded from the avarice of his soul, they are the prosperous.

It is said that this verse was revealed when Muhammad entrusted one of the Folk of the Bench (that is the poor people who lived outside the Prophet's Mosque in Madīnah) to the care of a man from among the Helpers (those Muslims who had lived in Madīnah before the Muslims of Makkah had emigrated there). The latter took the former to his family and asked his wife: "Do we have anything [to feed him]?" She said: "We do not have anything except the children's food." He said: "Put them to sleep and then bring me the food. And when you put the food down, turn the lamp off." She did as her husband requested. The Helper offered what he had to his guest. The following morning he took him back to the Prophet, who said: "Indeed, the dwellers of the heavens are amazed at what you two have done." Then verse 59:9 was revealed.[9]

Two aspects are fundamental to this verse: the first is that of "preferring others to oneself," a virtue that comes to be known in the later Islamic tradition simply as *īthār* or "preference." The second is to be shielded from the avarice of one's own soul. We will return to these after mentioning a few *ḥadīth*, that is, sayings of the Prophet Muhammad, that flesh out the Quranic discussion of hospitality. In many sayings attributed to the Prophet Muhammad and his companions, courtesy and hospitality are presented as central virtues of Islam. Perhaps the best known of these is one wherein the Prophet was asked, "What is the best part of Islam?" To which he responded, "Offering food and extending the greeting of peace to those you know and to those you do not know."[10] Conversely, his servant Anas bin Mālik (d. between 91–93/709–712) reports, "A house which is not entered by a guest is not entered by angels."[11] And another well-authenticated saying of the Prophet enjoins neighborliness and hospitality upon all believers: "May he who believes in God and the Last Day do no harm to his neighbor, and may he who believes in God and the Last Day honor his guest, and may he who believes in God and the Last Day say what is good or keep silent."[12]

The virtues of generosity and hospitality are so deeply rooted in Islam that one finds them cited as virtues that attested to Muhammad's qualification to be a messenger of God. In the story of the very first revelation, Muhammad is said to have been awestruck at receiving words from God and to have doubted his own sanity, saying, "I fear that something may happen to me." But his wife Khadijah comforted him by replying, "Never! By God, God will never disgrace you. You keep good relations with your kith and kin, help the poor and the destitute, serve your guests generously, and assist those afflicted by calamity."[13]

In examining this understanding of hospitality within Islam, it should be remembered that it is presented as a two-way street. Not only must one open one's home and one's heart to family, friends and strangers, so, too, accepting invitations is considered to be among the most important acts of generosity in Islam. In this vein, a famous *hadīth* equates declining an invitation with religious disobedience: "He who has not accepted an invitation has disobeyed God and His prophet."[14] It is reported that Muhammad would accept the invitation of both the bondsman and the pauper.[15] And just as one should not base the acceptance of an invitation on the social standing of the host, so too, the quality of the food should not be considered. As the Prophet Muhammad is reported to have said, "Were I invited to eat trotters, I would accept, and were I to be given lamb, I would accept."[16] Expanding upon such *hadith*, Abū Ḥamid al-Ghazālī (d. 505/111) tells the story of Ḥasan bin ʿAlī (d. c. 50/728/9), a figure esteemed in both Sunnī and Shīʿī Islam, who was invited by a group of beggars to eat the breadcrumbs they had found on the ground. He said, "Yes, God does not like those who are proud." Then he dismounted and ate with them, after which he invited them to a meal in his home, where he placed the best food before them and again sat to eat with them.[17] This emphasis upon accepting invitations is so prevalent within Islam that several sayings of the Prophet Muhammad even enjoin one to break a voluntary fast (not the fast of Ramadan, which is obligatory) in order to accept the hospitality offered by another. Some even go so far as to say that the reward for breaking an intended supererogatory fast is two-fold, as one receives the reward for the intended fast and the reward for having cut the fast short in order to gladden the heart of one of God's servants.

Within these accounts we see not only a teaching about the importance of hospitality, but about humility, the respect that one must have for others, and the virtue of "preferring others over oneself," known simply as *īthār* (preference), mentioned in verse 59:9. On the one hand, *īthār* is defined as placing the rights of others before one's own rights.[18] On the other hand, it can be seen as placing that which pleases God above all else.[19] Through this virtue of *īthār*, one can look more deeply into the fundamental principles that, from an Islamic perspective, lead God to demand hospitality of us. For from an Islamic perspective, God would not enjoin particular attitudes or actions upon human beings if these did not correspond with our true natures and were not in conformity with the nature of reality as such. With *īthār*, we see that true hospitality, not ostentatious display that is often mistaken for hospitality, is grounded in humility and in the effacement of the ephemeral self. For placing the rights of others above one's own and preferring what pleases God to all else is to recognize that the human "I" is not a reality unto itself and that the human ego is not its own master. Through a realization of this fundamental reality of the human condition, one manifests the two virtues necessary for true hospitality, effacement and generosity: effacement of the ephemeral self, the web of passions and desires that one often mistakes for the true "I"; and generosity toward others because they, too, have as much right to an "I." For in the final analysis, every "I" belongs to God and none other. As the Quran affirms over and again, *unto God belongs whatsoever is in the heavens and the earth* (4:126, 131, 132, 170, 171; 31:26; 53:31).

So central is the notion of recognizing the right of the other, that a famous *ḥadīth* states, "None of you believes until you desire for your brother what you desire for yourself."[20] Lest one interpret this as applying only to Muslims, Yaḥya bin Sharīf al-Nawawī (d. 1278), regarded by many as one of the greatest scholars of Islamic history, declares, "This should first and foremost be understood as universal brotherhood, such that it includes the Muslim and the non-Muslim."[21] From the perspective here enjoined, recognizing the rights and needs of others alongside the rights and needs of oneself is essential for faith to be complete. Here one finds the greatest challenge of hospitality. It is easy enough to open one's house to those to whom one inclines. But to fully open one's heart to others is among the greatest challenges of the human condition. For it demands that one combine effacement with generosity, humility with charity, and modesty with compassion. One might object that if these are indeed the requirements of hospitality, then only the saint can be truly hospitable. But as another famous saying of the Prophet Muhammad says, "Actions are in accord with their intentions and each person shall have that which he intends."[22] Part of any virtue is the intention to realize it, such that it is at once a condition and a result. In this way sincere hospitality, hospitality offered in the humble recognition that, on the one hand, we are nothing before God and that, on the other hand, every other human being bears the potential for sanctity, can be a door that opens to truth itself. Perhaps this is alluded to in another *ḥadīth*, which states: "Pride is to disregard the truth and to scorn people."[23]

The word, "the truth" in this *ḥadīth*, *al-ḥaqq*, can also be read as one of the names of God, for *al-Ḥaqq* is often employed as a reference to God and in such cases is taken to mean "the True" or "the Real." In this way the same fault that would lead one to scorn another human being is here presented as the very same fault that would lead one to disregard God. Thus the same fault that would prevent us from opening our hearts to our fellow human beings is the same fault that would prevent us from opening them to God. To turn away from another human being and to not give him or her, his or her proper due, is thus to turn away from God. For in turning away from the other one falls prey to the constant illusion that the ego is sovereign unto itself, forgetting that, as the Qur'ān says, "unto God belongs the sovereignty of the heavens and the earth" (3:189; 5:18, 40, 120; 9:116; 42:49; 45:27; 48:14). Conversely, the positive dimension of the reciprocity between openness toward God and toward others is reflected in a very subtle manner in verse 2:177 of the Quran: "It is not piety to turn your faces towards the east and west. Rather, piety is he who believes in God, the Last Day, the angels, the Book, and the prophets; and who gives wealth, despite loving it, to kinsfolk, orphans, the indigent, the traveler, beggars." Here the phrase "despite loving it" could also be translated "and out of love for Him [i.e. God]." Such that through the subtle placement of a single pronoun, the Quran alludes to the manner in which true piety requires both that one transcend attachments to the things of this world by giving them away, despite one's love for them, and that one love God by giving up one's attachments to this world "out of love for Him." This also touches upon an essential aspect of all virtue; that it must be carried out with the intention of being for God, for without faith and sincerity, all deeds are said to "come to naught," as in verse 47:32: "Truly those who disbelieve, who bar [others] from the way of God, and defy the Messenger of God after guidance has been made clear to them will not harm God at all. And He will make their deeds come to naught."[24]

Conclusion

As one can see from the manner in which I have attempted to tease an Islamic understanding of hospitality out of the sources available to us, hospitality is not necessarily a virtue in and of itself. Rather like love, it is a complex combination of many virtues whose fulfillment requires us to transcend our ephemeral selves. Moreover, one could say that hospitality is a direct manifestation of the mercy that God has shown to us, and is thus one of the ways in which "the mercy of God is ever nigh unto the virtuous" (Q 7:156). So to the extent that one might hope to be accepted into Paradise with "a welcome from One forgiving and merciful" (41:32), so too, must one be willing to extend such a welcome unto others. Perhaps this is why the image of the old man from Morocco with which this essay began has resided so deeply within me for all these years. In some way, the hospitality that he showed to me was a small glimmer of the mercy that God shows to all of us, and the welcome that all Muslims seek. And in some way the hospitality that we show to one another is a way in which we welcome God into this world more fully, making Him present within our homes and within ourselves.

Hindu Perspectives

CHAPTER 14

FOOD, THE GUEST AND THE *TAITTIRIYA UPANISHAD*

HOSPITALITY IN THE HINDU TRADITIONS

Frank Clooney

"Hospitality" of course indicates an important and inclusive human value that takes many forms in different religions and cultures. This is particularly when we go about trying to characterize the understanding and practice of it in Hindu India, a vast and ancient cultural area that includes many strands of religious identity ranged over more than three thousand years, and not inclined, in most of its forms, toward single, agreed-upon principles. In this brief essay, as in the conference presentation, I attempt no overall characterization of hospitality in Hinduism, but simply a demonstration of how one seminal text, the *Taittiriya Upanishad*, provides an important grounding for hospitality, characteristic of Hindu tradition and relevant even today. I will stay close to the *Upanishad*, and only at the end of this essay will I offer a few generalizations.

The *Taittiriya Upanishad* is one of the older of the classical Upanishads of India, from approximately the sixth century BCE. It is notable in that it is a rather clearly ordered text, in three distinct parts: the *Siksha Valli* (reflections on the art of recitation and the general dispositions of the teacher-student relationship), the *Brahma Valli* (reflections on the continuous layers of the self, from the physical to the spiritual), and the *Bhrgu Valli* (reflections on the true happiness of the self and the enjoyment of food, produced, eaten and shared). The *Upanishad* is as old a reflection on hospitality as we will find in India, and in its layer we can see the anthropological and philosophical case made for generosity with food.

The word "guest" is used twice in the *Upanishad*, both times in its first part. The first mention comes in a listing of fundamental values and right practices expected of the student who wishes also to learn properly, including righteousness, learning and teaching, truth, self-control, the performance of ritual, and several social commitments: "*Guests*, yes; but also the private and public recitation of the Veda. *Humaneness*, yes; but also the private and public recitation of the Veda. *Children*, yes; but also the private and public recitation of the Veda" (1.9).[1] The point is obviously to highlight several commonly accepted virtues—such as care for guests—but also to link them to Vedic study and recitation. Social virtues and religious practice remain interconnected.

Then, in the course of an instruction on the way of virtue after leaving the life of the student for the householder's life, we hear a famous instruction that includes hospitality: "Do not neglect the truth. Do not neglect the Law. Do not neglect your health. Do not neglect your wealth . . . Treat your mother like a god. Treat your father like a god. Treat your teacher like a god. Treat your guests like gods" (1.11.2). This language need not distract us with the question of what "gods" are like. Here, behaving toward the guest as toward a god simply marks the extraordinary respect that is also found in the worship of deities; the guest is a particular object of reverence, worthy of hospitality, high courtesy and material gifts.

The teaching on the guest does not stand alone in the *Taittiriya Upanishad*; another key theme must also be considered: the emphasis on food. Food is mentioned twice in this first section. First, when one understands properly the relationships among the parts of the mouth, articulation, and components of recitations, "he will possess offspring, livestock, the luster of sacred knowledge, a food supply, and the heavenly world" (1.3.4). Second, when the teacher is heard to pray for success and prosperity as a teacher surrounded by eager students, he asks that he be given an abundance of "clothes and cows," "food and drink." This *Upanishad*, right from the start, does not embrace a world-denying ethic, but affirms continuity between worldly values and higher and sacred truths. Food is a blessing, one that bears with it social responsibilities.

The second part of the *Upanishad* is more philosophical. It begins with a definition of Brahman, the highest reality, as being (*sat*), consciousness (*cit*), and what is endless (*anantam*), and closes with a meditation on gradations of true happiness, as multiples of the happiness of a healthy young man. After the initial definition of Brahman, the main part of the chapter is devoted to reflection on the five-fold nature of the self: as food, breath, mind, intelligence and true happiness (or bliss). The section begins by arguing that material reality—characterized as food—is that from which one begins in order to reach further or deeper states of reality:

> From food, surely, are they born; all creatures that live on earth.
> On food alone, once born, they live; and into food in the end they pass.
> For food is the foremost of beings, so it's called "all herbs."
> From food beings come into being; by food, once born, they grow.
> "It is eaten and it eats beings." Therefore it is called "food." (2.2)[2]

Food is the grounding of the observable world, and it exists of its nature as transactional, what living creates consume, and what they become. Interestingly, the famous characterization of Brahman at the beginning of chapter 3 takes the same form: "That from which these beings are born; on which, once born, they live; and into which they pass upon death—seek to perceive that! That is *Brahman*" (3.1).

After this assertion of the importance of food, chapter 2 proceeds to identify deeper levels of the self that are more than food or materiality, even if never separate from that food: within the self of food, there is a self of vital breath; within that, a self of mind; within that, a self of intelligence; and within that, a self of true happiness. These five layers of self comprise a complex anthropology that, for our purposes, is interesting because it gives an essential place to material reality described as food.

The end of chapter 2 is then given over to reflection on true happiness, multiplied over and over from the experience of a young man in full health. In the concluding summation, food is again mentioned. The person who understands this complex self and its destiny in true happiness is one who after death "first reaches the self that consists of food," (2.8) and then the four subsequent layers of self. As we shall see regarding chapter 3, the grounding realities of materiality, food and hospitality are not separable from the final goal, the true happiness. In all of this, it is important to remember, "food" marks not only the material substance that we eat, but also the socially and religiously located preparation and disposition of food, as eaten and shared.

Early in chapter 3, food is mentioned again, as the student Bhrigu meditates on the layers of self that had been proposed in chapter 2:

> After he had practiced austerities, [Bhrigu] perceived: "Brahman is food—for, clearly, it is from food that these beings are born; on which, once born, do they live; and into which they pass upon death."

In his meditation he also sees breath, mind, intelligence and true happiness as Brahman, but the insistence that food is Brahman is never denied or even attenuated; all of reality shares in this transactional and participatory manner of being.

In fact, in the final portion of chapter 3, the reflection on food in particular recurs and is expanded, in a series of reflections that bring the chapter to its conclusion:

> One should not belittle food—that is the rule. The lifebreath is food, and the body is the food-eater. The body is based on the lifebreath, and the lifebreath, on the body. Thus, this food is based on food. When someone knows this food that is based on food—he will become firmly established; he will become a man who has food, who eats food; he will become a big man on account of his offspring, livestock, and the luster of sacred knowledge; he will become a big man on account of his fame. (3.7)

This is a generously conceived fullness that affirms life in the world, keeping food and the sharing of it in a key position with respect to a complete humane and spiritual life.

The teaching is later reaffirmed twice. In 3.8, he is instructed not to reject food, because of its interconnection with water and fire, and again, its productive role in creating his prosperity. In 3.9, he is consequently instructed to produce food: "One should prepare a lot of food—that is the rule," since food is interconnected with earth and air.

The implication of all this is also, and for our purposes most importantly, an insistence on hospitality, and thus a return to the theme of the guest mentioned in the first part of the *Upanishad*. Here we read, "One should never turn anyone away from one's home—that is the rule. Therefore, he should procure a lot of food by every means at his disposal. And people will say of him: 'Food is readily available to him'" (3.10). This section ends with a moral observation, somewhat obscure but that seems simply to mean, as you give, you shall be rewarded: the generous giver of food will always have food, while the stingy will end up hungry.

The entire *Upanishad* ends with another and most striking paean to food. First, there is a reaffirmation that after death one progresses through the layers of self beginning with the self that is food, then life breath, etc. In true happiness, which has already been measured in terms of the happiness of a healthy young man, the liberated person eats "whatever he likes" and assumes "whatever appearance he likes." He travels the universe, and is also heard to sing a most remarkable final hymn that begins with the words,

I am food! I am food! I am food!
I eat food! I eat food! I eat food!

and ends this way:

I am food! I eat him who eats the food! I have conquered the whole universe! I am like the light in the firmament! (3.10.6)

The *Taittiriya Upanishad* points to the integrity of body and soul, and to the fact that the body matters. This is a non-renunciant text that values life in this world. The importance of the guest is clear.

All of this is, I suggest, a grounding of hospitality that is solidly scriptural, socially sensitive, and theologically articulate, noteworthy in highlighting the material and spiritual nature of hospitality in ancient India. Hospitality is reverence for the guest, but is also rooted in a profound theological analysis of the human condition. The equation is basic: food = true happiness = Brahman, and this turns out to be a superlative insight, as deep a basis for hospitality as we will find in ancient Indian Hinduism.

Even if the preceding insights are correct, we can still ask whether the tradition actually looked to the *Upanishad* for the sake of emphasizing and deepening respect for the guest. Whatever we might expect, though, it seems that the classical Vedanta commentators did not feel it necessary to elaborate the *Upanishad*'s stress on food and hospitality. The great Vedanta theologian Sankara (eighth century) offers a thorough reading of the *Taittiriya Upanishad*, but he is not particularly interested in the hospitality theme, but rather in the nature of Brahman. The most he will admit is that that he does see the lineage from food to Brahman (at 3.7); food is a help to knowing Brahman. Ramanuja, another great theologian, likewise handles the *Taittiriya Upanishad* in terms of the standard array of theological issues, and does not make a special point regarding the emphases on guest, food and hospitality. Neither, we can admit, rushes to offer special notice of the *Taittiriya Upanishad*'s affirmation of life in *this* world.

This is not to say that the great theologians did not see the importance of hospitality or did not appreciate the social and religious dimensions of food; rather, they may well have simply accepted these values, and rooted them in other kinds of texts that would outline proper hospitality, while using the *Upanishad* to establish other points regarding Brahman and the self.

But we do have a good modern instance where the *Taittiriya Upanishad* is put to apt use, in chapter 8 of *Annam Bahu Kurvita*,[3] "Anna [Food]: the first manifestation of Brahman." *Annam Bahu Kurvita*—prepare a lot of food—is, as we have seen, taken from the *Upanishad* 3.9.1. The general theme of the volume is that there is a long tradition of the sharing of food in India and of the celebration of material prosperity, and consequently a deep commitment to hospitality.

While the book surveys a larger range of Vedic and orthodox texts, the relevant eighth chapter is largely an exegesis of the *Taittiriya Upanishad*'s three sections (against the background of analysis of the earlier *Taittiriya Upanishad Brahmana*). I will not repeat all the passages already cited above from *Taittiriya Upanishad* chapter 3, but give just this section on 3.10, because of its interesting variant translation:

> The *anuvaka* [verse] begins by further elaborating the discipline of anna with the injunction that a guest should never be turned away from the door. And the seer continues with the insistence that a seeker ought to obtain a plenty of food somehow or the other, so that no guest ever needs to return un-sated from his door: "Do not turn away anyone who comes seeking your hospitality. This is the inviolable discipline for the one who knows. Therefore, obtain a great abundance of anna [food], exert all your efforts to ensure such abundance; and welcome the guests with the announcement that the food is ready." (*Taittiriya Upanishad* 3.10)[4]

Bajaj and Srinivas see in the *Taittiriya Upanishad* a sufficiently clear justification of hospitality, which they support by offering a series of later stories illustrative of extraordinary hospitality, families giving away their last bit of food, saintly figures offering their own bodies as food, etc. Near the end of the book, there is a poignant reflection by the memories of hospitality in a twentieth-century family, where cooking and eating were always accompanied by attention to the needs of others who needed to eat. It is remarkable in its detail and meticulous care for the sharing of food:

> Not long ago, when mother would sit down to prepare rotis [simple flat breads], we, the children of the house, gathered around the hearth and watched. She would take the first ball of dough, touch it with a little ghee, and give it to one of us, to run into the street, find a cow and put the ball of dough in her mouth. Only then

would mother put the griddle on the fire; and next she would take a rather small bit of dough, dip it in ghee, wipe the griddle with it, and leave it on the side, to be offered to the ants or the crows later. The next full ball of dough was rolled into a roti and put on the griddle. But this first roti mother would cook only on one side, touch it with it a little mustard oil, and then it was the turn of another one of us to run and offer it to a dog. The next two rotis were cooked and kept aside for the gurudvara along with a bowl of the day's vegetable curry or dal. Later, the wife of the gurudvara priest would come and collect her share. She collected such offerings from perhaps forty houses, and that would have probably sufficed for her family as well as the occasional guest who sought shelter in the gurudvara. We were young then, and our appetite used to be sharp. But howeverso hungry we might have been, we had to wait for mother to take out the share of the cow, the crow, the dog and the gurudvara, before being served. And, in spite of the gnawing feeling of hunger in our stomachs, it somehow felt good to wait.[5]

Bajaj and Srinivas add more trenchant comments on the decline of the culture of hospitality, due not only to urbanization and the waning of the intimacies of village life, but also the arrival of colonialism and the British destruction of older and more holistic social patterns. At book's end, they conclude:

We shall be liberated from the sin [of failing to grow food in abundance and share it] only when we begin to take the classical injunction of *annam bahu kurvita* seriously, and begin to grow a great abundance of food again . . . With care and application these lands can produce the abundance that classical India cherished, and in the process can enliven large numbers of Indians who have been forced into economic idleness because of the idleness of the land . . . But we cannot continue to be indifferent to the hunger around us until the abundance arrives. Because, as classical India has taught with such insistence, hungry men and animals exhaust all virtue of a people . . . In fact, not only the nature in the abstract, but every individual grhastha [householder] bears the sin of hunger around him. We have been instructed, in the authoritative injunctions of the vedas, that anyone who eats without sharing, eats in sin . . . (208–9)[6]

Hospitality, grounded in analysis of food and the social realities of cooking and sharing, is an ancient Indian tradition that is also grounded in the memories of people alive today. The contemporary issues of political and economic import, set in the context of a postcolonial rethinking of tradition, enable us to look back with a fresh eye to older texts such as the *Taittiriya Upanishad*.

This brief excursion into the *Taittiriya Upanishad* and its heritage is by no means all that can be said about hospitality in the Hindu context, but it is one of the most fundamental and important sites that we must take into account. The Upanishads have mattered deeply in Indian culture, and the characteristics evident here can be generalized, albeit cautiously. First, hospitality, like life in general, has very much to do with food, while both the preparation and sharing of food and the practices of hospitality are firmly rooted in ancient

Indian culture, even in its Vedic configuration. Second, food is not merely a material thing—what we put in our mouths—but is also the symbol or sacrament of the material stuff of our lives in this world, lives that are very a matter of eating and, in various ways, being eaten. Third, this eating that is sharing is always connected with the ever-present likelihood of the guest who will come unexpectedly—*a-tithi*—and nevertheless expect to be fed. With these features of hospitality in place, larger and more ambitious sketches of Hindu views of hospitality can be ambitioned, as marked by a spiritual and material sensitivity that respects the body, the family and community, and the inseparability of higher spiritual insights from more basic rules about food and its sharing.

CHAPTER 15

GOD AS GUEST

HOSPITALITY IN HINDU CULTURE

Swami Tyagananda

Prayer is generally the first natural and conscious response in a person who has had some kind of religious awakening. The awareness of our human limitations and mortality is generally enough to turn us in the direction of, and seek help from, a power or a person who is not bound by those limitations. As a form of "receiving," prayer is a movement from God toward human beings. When a prayer is answered, the heart is filled with gratitude. Worship is an expression of gratitude to God, expressed through love, praise and offering of anything that one holds dear. As a form of "giving," worship is a movement from human beings to God. How does this movement from human beings to God manifest in daily life?

Hindus view everything as permeated by God's presence,[1] so hospitality becomes an act of worship. God is the only possible guest, encountered inside a temple through ritual worship, and outside the temple through karma yoga or selfless service to others, seeing them as manifestations of God. Saints and mystics have experienced the presence of God through both ritual worship and selfless service, attesting to the power and authenticity of these practices.

God as Guest in Ritual Worship

In Hindu forms of worship, God is the divine guest and rituals recreate, mostly symbolically, the kind of hospitality that is generally offered to an honored guest in India. Among the things that are offered are an honored place to sit, words of welcome, water for washing hands and feet, water to drink, water for bathing, clothes, ornaments, sandal paste, flowers, incense, light and food. The offerings themselves are symbolical and are accompanied by appropriate Sanskrit mantras. More important than the symbolical offering and the chanting of mantras is the focusing of the mind on God with love, devotion and faith.

Another form of Hindu worship, called *ārati*, involves waving of light, water (poured from a conch shell), cloth, flowers and a fan, ritually recreating a respectful welcome to the honored, divine guest. The five items that are offered correspond to the five primary elements that the Hindu texts view as the building blocks of the material world: fire, water, space, earth and air, respectively. In this form of worship, God is both a personal guest and a cosmic presence, welcomed simultaneously in one's home as well as in one's heart.

God as Guest in the Practice of Karma Yoga

The presence of God is encountered not only inside temples but also outside them. Hindu texts have proclaimed that the divine is present in everything and everyone. Helping others can be more than simply "helping others." It can also include acknowledging and worshiping the presence of God in their hearts. Hospitality thus becomes not merely an act of service but also worship.

When work becomes worship, helping others is transformed into service of God in everything and everyone.[2] It involves giving of oneself freely without seeking anything in return. Hindu texts categorize "giving" into three types:

> The *sāttvika* gift is one that is given with no expectation of return, in a right place and to a worthy person, with the idea that it is good to give. The *rājasika* gift is one that is given with an expectation of return, or with an eye on the result, or given with reluctance. The *tāmasika* gift is one that is given at the wrong place or time, to unworthy persons, without regard or with disdain.[3]

The *sāttvika* gift is the one that qualifies as karma yoga. Vivekananda spoke glowingly about the spiritual benefits of serving others in the spirit of karma yoga:

> Although a man has not studied a single system of philosophy, although he does not believe in God, and never has believed, although he has not prayed even once in his life, if the simple power of good actions has brought him to that state where he is ready to give up his life and all else for others, he has arrived at the same point to which the religious man will come through his prayers and the philosopher through his knowledge; and so you may find that the philosopher, the worker, and the devotee, all meet at one point, that one point being self-abnegation. However much their systems of philosophy and religion may differ, all mankind stand in reverence and awe before the man who is ready to sacrifice himself for others.[4]

Two Stories

I shall conclude with two stories: one from Hindu mythology and the other from recent history. The story from mythology highlights the dual role of God as guest and teacher. Disguised as a wandering mendicant, Krishna visits a wealthy family, who welcome him warmly and offer him hospitality that matches both their devotion and prosperity. When it is time to leave, he blesses his host profusely, promising him even more wealth and glory. Krishna's next visit is to a poor widow, whose only possession is a cow. She too welcomes him with great devotion but all that she can offer him is a glass of milk. When it is time to leave, Krishna blesses her and tells her that her cow will die soon. Arjuna, who has accompanied Krishna to both the places, is horrified. He asks Krishna, "Your wealthy hosts lacked nothing and yet you blessed them with even more wealth. Whereas your blessing to the poor devotee accompanied the ominous news that she will lose her cow. This is unfair and unacceptable." Krishna smiles and tells Arjuna, "My wealthy host is insanely attached to his wealth and his reputation; he has a long way to go before he becomes spiritually awakened. On the other hand, this poor devotee is already far advanced on the spiritual path. The only thing that is separating her from the highest freedom is her attachment to her cow. I removed the hurdle from her path." The insights that this story provides are obvious. God can enter our lives in any form and at any time, often in most unexpected circumstances. The blessing that the divine guest bestows upon us can be difficult to decipher at first glance.

My second story is of a relatively recent origin: it happened in southern India, where I lived in the early 1990s. A cyclone had wrought enormous damage in and around the Tirunelveli district of Tamil Nadu. A monk of the Ramakrishna Order and a few volunteer members visited the affected area and were temporarily accommodated in a classroom of a school that had partially escaped the destruction. They had reached the place late in the evening after a long train journey. Exhausted, they had gone to sleep right away. Early next morning there was a knock at the door and they were surprised to see a middle-aged person with a bag filled with food. He said that he had a dream the previous night when a woman appeared and told him, "Go feed my children who have just arrived." The dream was so vivid that he woke up with a start and narrated the dream to his wife in the morning. She first asked him to just forget about it but when she saw how affected he was by the dream, she felt it would be good if something were done about it. They learnt that some people had arrived from Chennai the previous evening and were staying in the school next door. To get the dream out of his mind, they decided to give some food to those strangers and be done with it. As the man was speaking with the swami and his companions, he noticed the picture of Sarada Devi on the small temporary altar the group had set up in the classroom. At once his face lit up and he exclaimed, "That's the woman I saw in my dream last night!" Baffled at what was unfolding before them, the swami and his group were crying tears of joy and gratitude.

Life offers infinite opportunities to extend hospitality in one form or another. In a worldview that has God's presence pervading all existence, God is not only the divine guest but also the host. Hospitality is worship for those who understand its inner significance and potential.

NOTES

Notes to Introduction

1 Foreigner/Stranger/Other, by Ana Vieira, shows how the stranger mediates between host and guest and can also manifest itself in the double sense of *hostis*—namely friend or enemy, an occasion of hostility or hospitality

2 Paul Ricoeur, *On Translation*, trans. Eileen Brennan (New York: Routledge, 2006), 23.

Notes to Chapter 1: Hospitality in Translation

1 Jacques Derrida, *The Gift of Death*, trans. David Wills (Chicago: University of Chicago Press, 1995), 66.

2 Jacques Derrida and Anne Dufourmantelle, *Of Hospitality*, trans. Rachel Bowlby (Stanford: Stanford University Press, 2000), 25.

3 Ibid., 15.

4 Ibid., 75.

5 Jacques Derrida, *Memoires: For Paul de Man*, trans. Cecile Lindsay, Jonathan Culler and Eduardo Cadava (New York: Columbia University Press, 1986), 35.

6 Derrida and Dufourmantelle, *Of Hospitality*, 83.

7 Derrida, *Gift of Death*, 66.

8 Ibid.

9 Jacques Derrida, *Points . . . Interviews, 1974–94*, ed. Elisabeth Weber, trans. Peggy Kamuf et al. (Stanford: Stanford University Press, 1995), 209.

10 Derrida, *Gift of Death*, 66.

11 Jacques Derrida, *Deconstruction in a Nutshell: A Conversation with Jacques Derrida*, ed. John D. Caputo (New York: Fordham University Press, 1997), 17.

12 Derrida, *Of Hospitality*, 127.

13 Paul Ricoeur, *On Translation*, trans. Eileen Brennan (New York: Routledge, 2006), 8.

14 Ibid., 22, 23.

15 For more interesting information on the case of Nabokov's translation of Pushkin and Nabokov's correspondence with the reviewers of his translation, among others, see Edmund Wilson, "The Strange Case of Pushkin and Nabokov," *The New York Review of Books*, 4 (12), July 15, 1965, 3–6. See also Brian Boyd, "*Eugene Onegin*," in *Vladimir Nabokov: The American Years* (Princeton: Princeton University Press, 1991), 318–55.

16 Ricoeur, *On Translation*, 6.

17 Ibid., 22.

18 Ibid., 10.

19 Ibid., 8.

20 Walter Benjamin, "The Task of the Translator," in *The Translation Studies Reader,* ed. Lawrence Venuti (New York: Routledge 2004), 76.

21 Ricoeur, *On Translation,* 22.

22 Ibid., 5.

23 Ibid., 10.

24 Ibid., 29.

25 Ibid., 13.

26 Ibid., 33.

27 Ibid., 24.

28 Paul Ricoeur, "Religious Belief: The Difficult Path of the Religious," in *Passion for the Possible,* eds. Brian Treanor and Henry Isaac Venema (New York: Fordham University Press, 2010), 38, 39.

29 Ibid., 39.

30 See Richard Kearney, *Stranger, Gods and Monsters* (London: Routledge, 2003); *The God Who May Be* (Bloomington: Indiana University Press, 2001); *Anatheism* (New York: Columbia University Press, 2010). Also of interest are: *Phenomenologies of the Stranger: Between Hostility and Hospitality* (Fordham University Press, 2011), eds. Richard Kearney and Kascha Semonovitch, in particular the introductory essay, "Foreigners, Strangers, Others"; *Traversing the Heart: Journeys of the Interreligious Imagination,* eds. Richard Kearney and Eileen Rizo-Patron (Brill, 2010); "Beyond Conflict: Radical Hospitality and Religious Strangeness," in *Philosophy and the Return of Violence: Studies from this Widening Gyre,* eds. Christopher Yates and Nathan Eckstrand (Continuum, 2011); "Towards a Poetics of the Stranger—Hospitality or Hostility," in *The Seamus Heaney Lectures,* Dublin, 2010, ed. Andrew O'Shea; and "Ricoeur's Hermeneutics of Hospitality," Plenary Paper at the International Conference, "Paul Ricoeur and Hermeneutics of the Just," University of Lisbon, July 7–10, 2010.

31 Richard Kearney, *Anatheism: Returning to God after God* (New York: Columbia University Press, 2010), 50.

32 Ibid., 51.

Notes to Chapter 2: Western Hospitality to Eastern Thought

1 Jacques Scheuer, "Détournement de biens spirituels? Un point d'éthique des relations interreligieuses," *Revue Théologique de Louvain* 40 (2009): 305–23.

2 See Mark Siderits, *Personal Identity and Buddhist Philosophy: Empty Persons* (Abingdon: Ashgate, 2003); Jay Westerhoff, *Nāgārjuna's Madhyamaka: A Philosophical Introduction* (Oxford University Press, 2009).

3 For instance, Bartholomäus Ziegenbalg's pioneering works on the religion of Malabar, written in 1711–13, were rejected for publication by August Hermann Francke on the grounds that missionaries should be extirpating heathenism, not spreading it in Europe; they were published only in 1791. See Helmuth von Glasenapp, *Das Indienbild deutscher Denker* (Stuttgart: Koehler, 1960), 167.

4 *Oeuvres complètes* VII (Paris: Flammarion, 1978), 470–1.

5 Roger-Pol Droit, *L'Oubli de l'Inde: Une Amnésie Philosophique* (Paris: Presses Universitaires de France, 1989; 2nd ed., Paris : Le Livre de Poche, 1992).

6 See Helmuth von Glasenapp, *Kant und die Religionen des Ostens* (Kitzingen am Main: Holzner, 1954).

7 Friedrich Schlegel, *Kritische Ausgabe* 8 (Munich: Schöningh, 1975), 111, 309.

8 See Ursula Oppenberg, *Quellenstudien zu Friedrich Schlegels Übersetzungen aus dem Sanskrit* (Marburg: Elwert, 1965).

9 Friedrich von Schlegel, "On the Language and Philosophy of the Indians," in *The Aesthetic and Miscellaneous Works of Friedrich von Schlegel*, trans. E. J. Millington (London, 1900), 526.

10 See Carmen Dragonetti and Fernando Tola, *On the Myth of the Opposition between Indian Thought and Western Philosophy* (Hildesheim: Olms, 2004), 19–22.

11 Arthur Schopenhauer, "Paralipomena," 184, *Sämtliche Werke* 4 (Stuttgart/ Frankfurt: Cotta/Insel, 1963), vol. 5, 469. Schopenhauer clung doggedly to this source, and unreasonably suspected that the translations made directly from the Sanskrit had introduced theistic, Europeanizing distortions; see Wilhelm Halbfass, *Indien und Europa* (Basel/Stuttgart: Schwabe, 1981), 123.

12 Halbfass, *Indien und Europa*, 129.

13 Ibid., 132. "He seems in contrast with Hegel to represent a much greater openness, a much greater readiness to recognize philosophical insights in foreign dress and to acknowledge Indian tradition in its proper value and autonomy. Yet we also found that in his approach to Indian tradition he proceeds much more selectively than Hegel . . . quite explicitly making his own metaphysics the yardstick of evaluation" (ibid., 135).

14 Ernst Behler, "The Contemporary and the Posthumous," *Surfaces* 4 (1994), www. pum.umontreal.ca/revues/surfaces/vol4/behler.html.

15 F. W. J. Schelling, *Studium Generale* (Stuttgart: Kröner, 1954), 119–20.

16 Review of Wilhelm von Humboldt's "Über die unter dem Namen Bhagavad-Gita bekannte Episode des Mahabharata," *Gesammelte Werke* 16 (Hamburg: Meiner, 2001), 19–75; here, 33–4.

17 See Wilhelm von Humboldt, "Über die Bhagavad-Gita," in *Gesammelte Werke* 5 (repr., Berlin: de Gruyter, 1968), 168–72.

18 Bradley L. Herling, *The German Gītā: Hermeneutics and Discipline in the German Reception of Indian Thought, 1778–1831* (New York: Routledge, 2006), 235, citing Saverio Marchignoli, "The *Bhagavadgita* as a Forgotten Source for European Aesthetics," in *Frontiers of Transculturality in Contemporary Aesthetics,* ed. Grazia Marchiano and Raffaele Milani (Turin: Trauben, 2001).

19 See Jens Halfwassen, *Hegel und der spätantike Neuplatonismus* (Bonn: Bouvier, 1999).

20 G. W. F. Hegel, *Vorlesungen über die Philosophie der Weltgeschichte* (Hamburg: Meiner, 1968), 351.

21 Ibid., 347.

22 Ibid., 353.

23 Von Glasenapp, *Das Indienbild*, 57–9.

24 Hegel, *Vorlesungen über die Philosophie der Weltgeschichte*, 365.

25   Roger-Pol Droit, *Le Culte du néant: Les philosophes et le bouddhisme* (Paris: Éditions du Seuil, 1997), p. 95; this nihilist picture of Buddhism was not supported by more recent sources such as H. T. Colebrooke and Abel Rémusat.

26   G. W. F. Hegel, *Vorlesungen über die Philosophie der Religion* (Hamburg: Meiner, 1974), 2, 124. For the source, *Allgemeine Historie der Reisen*, see Reinhard Leuze, *Die ausserchristlichen Religionen bei Hegel* (Göttingen: Vandenhoeck & Ruprecht, 1975), 64.

27   Max Walleser, trans. *Die Mittlere Lehre des Nāgārjuna* (Heidelberg: 1911).

28   Droit, *Le Culte du néant*, 21.

29   Leuze, *Die ausserchristlichen Religionen bei Hegel* , 79. H. T. Colebrook, "Essays on the Philosophy of the Hindus," *Transactions of the Royal Asiatic Society* 1 (London, 1827), 19ff., 92ff. and 439–67, and 2:1–40. Hegel used only the first two essays, on the Samkhya and Nyāya philosophies; the third is on Mimamsa and the fourth on Vedanta.

30   See Halbfass, *Indien und Europa*, 119–21, 166, and the quotations from Schwegler, Fries, Zeller, Sigwart, Michelis, Erdmann, Dühring, Überweg, von Hartmann, Windelband, Lewes, Burnet and Russell, 173–6.

32   Von Glasenapp judges that "he was not someone open to the world, capable of entering with loving understanding into all foreign paths of thought" (*Das Indienbild*, 39); he produced only a "caricature" of India, after taking on a task for which he lacked the prerequisites (ibid., 40). Halbfass demurs, claiming that Hegel is valuable as an observant witness of the birth of Indology (*Indien und Europa*, 105).

33   Herling, *The German* Gītā, 236. "Hegel's thought . . . was by its very nature always already non-identical to itself (and thus began to register the way Western thought in general was non-identical to *it*self): the concept's movement is a universal that is ultimately impossible to determine or specify once and for all" (ibid., 205). "Hegel's interpretation of Indian religious concepts shifts and changes: it displays all of the marks of an already present, disruptive exteriority—the self-sameness of Hegel's system simply could not be maintained, nor can the self-sameness of his 'Orientalist' identity" (ibid., 206).

34   Helmuth von Glasenapp, *Die Philosophie der Inder* (Stuttgart: Kröner, 1958), 452.

35   See also Jan E. M. Houben, "Bhartrhari's Perspectivism," *Beyond Orientalism: The Work of Wilhelm Halbfass and its Impact on Indian and Cross-Cultural Studies*, ed. Eli Franco and Karin Preisendanz (Amsterdam and Atlanta, GA: Rodopi; Poznan Studies in the Philosophy of the Sciences and the Humanities 59), 317–58.

36   Von Glasenapp, *Die Philosophie der Inder*, 452.

37   Paul Deussen, *Allgemeine Geschichte der Philosophie mit besonderer Berüchsichtigung der Religionen. Band I* (in three parts, Leipzig: Brockhaus, 1899–1908). Heroically, he completed the matching history of Western philosophy despite the loss of his sight (1911–17).

38   See Reinhard May, *Heidegger's Hidden Sources* (New York: Routledge, 1996).

39   Martin Heidegger, *Unterwegs zur Sprache* (Pfullingen: Neske, 1959), 144.

40   Ibid.

41   Ibid., 90.

42 See J. S. O'Leary, "Heidegger and Indian Philosophy," *Beyond Orientalism: The Work of Wilhelm Halbfass and its Impact on Indian and Cross-Cultural Studies,* ed. Eli Franco and Karin Preisendanz (Amsterdam and Atlanta GA: Rodopi; Poznan Studies in the Philosophy of the Sciences and the Humanities 59), 171–203, with Professor Halbfass's reply, 309–13.

43 Jean-Yves Lacoste speaks of "the pagan overtones of the 'return to the matter itself'" (R. Kearney and J. S. O'Leary, eds, *Heidegger et la question de Dieu* (Paris: Presses Universitaires de France, 2009), 17). Jean Beaufret claimed that Heidegger's concern with "the phenomenon of the world" put him in opposition to "monotheism" and "Christian dogmatics" (ibid., 52–3). However, this is directed not against the scriptural vision of God and creation but against its metaphysical interpretation insofar as it has become estranged from the phenomena.

44 See Vatican II's Declaration on the Relation of the Church to Non-Christian Religions (*Nostra Aetate*), in *Vatican Council II: The Conciliar and Post Conciliar Documents,* ed., Austin Flannery (Northport, NY: Costello, 1982), 738–42. See also the Dogmatic Constitution on the Church (*Lumen Gentium*), 16–17; the Decree on the Church's Missionary Activity (*Ad Gentes*); the Pastoral Constitution on the Church in the Modern World (*Gaudium et Spes*), 22 (ibid., 367–9, 813–62, 922–4).

45 John Paul II, "Redemptoris Missio: On the permanent validity of the Church's missionary mandate," Libreria Editrice Vaticana, www.vatican.va/edocs/ENG0219/_INDEX.HTM#fonte.

46 These terms are used by Paul F. Knitter, *Introducing Theologies of Religion* (Maryknoll, NY: Orbis, 2002). See also Peter Phan, "Universal Salvation, Christian Identity, Church Mission," *The Japan Mission Journal* 64 (2010):3–20.

Notes to Chapter 3: Interreligious Hospitality and its Limits

1 Paul Ricoeur, *On Translation* (London and New York: Routledge, 2006), 23–4.

2 Martin Marty, *When Faiths Collide* (Oxford: Blackwell, 2005), 124–48.

3 Catherine Cornille, *The Im-Possibility of Interreligious Dialogue* (New York: Crossroads, 2008), 17–210.

4 Amos Young, *Hospitality and the Other: Pentecost, Christian Practices, and the Neighbor* (Maryknoll: Orbis Books, 2008).

5 In Post-Exilic times, this openness to the stranger became qualified by Levitical codes of purity. See Daniel Smith-Christopher, "Between Ezra and Isaiah: Exclusion, Transformation and Inclusion of the Foreigner in Post-Exilic Biblical Theology," in *Ethnicity and the Bible*, ed. Mark Brett (Leiden: Brill, 1996), 117–42.

6 Young, *Hospitality and the Other,* 152. Amos Young also argues that such an inclusive interpretation "fits better with the earlier Matthean reference to the invitation extended to "both good and bad" to fill up the banquet seats refused by the other invited (Jewish) guests, so that it involves the gentiles as a whole" (ibid., 152).

7 Pierre-François De Béthune, *Par la foi et l'hospitalité* (Clerlande: Publications de Saint-André, 1997).

8 Marty, *When Faiths Collide*, 129.

9 Ibid., 128.

10 Young, *Hospitality and the Other*, 118–60.

11 Ibid., 139.

12 Marty, *When Faiths Collide*, 128–9.

13 A visit to the temple of the International Society for Krishna Consciousness is a mandatory part of my course on the Hindu-Christian dialogue. No amount of study of the meaning of Krishna in the Bhagavadgita and in the Puranas can replace the immediate contact with believers and participation in their chanting and religious services. Students invariably remark that such a visit makes all the difference in their understanding of Krishna devotion.

14 Young, *Hospitality and the Other*, 136.

15 To be sure, religions have built on and borrowed from teachings and practices from other religions throughout history. But this has occurred by consciously or unconsciously denying any religious influence or by completely rejecting the original meaning of such teachings and practices.

16 Young, *Hospitality and the Other*, 133.

17 Ibid., 140.

18 Ibid., 133.

19 Ibid., 142.

20 Ibid., 149.

Notes to Chapter 4: Departus

1 See Richard Kearney, *Anatheism: Returning to God After God* (New York: Columbia University Press, 2010), 38.

2 For a useful problematization of the translation of *ācara* as custom and its relation to dharma in practice see Donald R. Davis Jr., "Dharma in Practice: Ācara and Authority in Medieval Dharmasastra," *Journal of Indian Philosophy* 32 (2004): 813–30. The *Dharmasastras* are traditionally represented as having three parts: *Ācara* (or the rules and norms); *Vyavahara* (judicial procedures); *Prayascitta* (atonements). The four main *Dharmasutra* texts (of Apasthamba, Gautama, Baudhayana and Vasista) are supposed to be related to the Vedas, but as Davis writes, they are in fact more historically derived from norms established by elites (ibid., 814). These Sutras are followed by the more well-known *smritis* of Manu, Yajnavalkya, Narada, and Vishnu. There are also the endless commentaries and exegeses on the *shastras* and the *smritis*, which render the *Dharmashastras* as a whole one of the most formidable aspects of Hindu practical theology.

3 The term "community" in India is a catch-all referring to both *varna* (caste) and *jati* (sub-groups), and "communalism" and its derivatives such as "communal feeling" refer to the narrow and discriminatory attitude of preferring the claims of one's own group over another's perhaps more justified ones.

4 "Atithidevobhava," Taittirya Upanishad 1.11.2 is translated by F. Max Müller as "let thy guest be unto thee like a God." *Bhava* is translated here as the imperative form of *bhu*—to be, but it can also be impersonal.

5 I shall be quoting from the *Upanishads*, parts 1–2, trans. F. Max Muller (New York: Dover Publications, 1962). These two volumes reproduce Max Muller's translations that constitute volumes 1 and 15 of the *Sacred Books of the East* series.

6 It must be acknowledged that the *Taittirya Upanishad* is not a source text for hospitality, or for that matter other duties of the householder. To take up the theme of hospitality in earnest in one or any of its facets within Hindu culture, one must turn to other texts such as the *Grihya Sutras* and the *Dharma Shāstras*.

7 This is my unscholarly layperson's translation. Max Muller translates thus:
   "Do not neglect the (sacrificial) works due to the Gods and Fathers! Let thy mother be to thee like unto a god! Let thy father be to thee like unto a god! Let thy teacher be unto thee like unto a god! Let thy guest be to thee like unto a god!" (I.11.2). Muller translates pitr as fathers, but pitrkarya refers generally to the death rites for one's progenitors. Also, the tense of the mood of the verse is impersonal not imperative.

8 See Ṣankara's commentary of this verse as translated by Swami Gambhirananda, *Eight Upanishads: With the Commentary of Sankaracarya* (Calcutta: Advaita Ashram, 1957), 323–8. (I derive the original Sanskrit text from this edition.)

9 The terminology of "inner self," "soul," "spirit," etc. as translations of *purusha* should be subjected to careful scrutiny for not only do they carry unexamined presuppositions, but they cause confusion with other ontological terms such as *atman, bhuta, aham*, etc. In this essay, I translate *purusha* as soul and *preta* as spirit. Another possible translation for *preta* would be ghost, but the word has acquired such strong connotations in the Indian context that is better avoided.

10 With all due respect to Ṣankara, who in his commentary, of course, posits a hierarchy of these multiple essences, the *Upanishad* itself in its most straightforward reading celebrates the food-body—the so-called "outer" sheath. However, this emphasis in the text makes the *arche* as such impossible to discern—is it *Brahman, ananda*, or *annam*?

11 Perhaps there is a correspondence here with Richard Kearney's discussion of what he terms "the Christian wager" (i.e. Mary's ability to welcome the angel), but I cannot pursue it here. See his *Anatheism*, 23–6.

12 This theme receives a fuller elaboration with reference to Derrida's discussion of hospitality in my essay "Departures," written for the volume *Phenomenologies of the Stranger*, edited by Richard Kearney.

13 In the Western tradition, perhaps it is Spinoza (alone?) who can be said to partially approximate this worldview. I am thinking not only of the famous expression "*Deus, sive Natura*" (*Ethics*, IV Preface, 153) but also his explanation of "*Natura naturans*" and *Natura naturata*" (I, p29s, p. 51–2). However, reading Julie Klein's essay "Nature's Metabolism: On Eating in Derrida, Agamben, and Spinoza" in *Research in Phenomenology* 33 (2003): 186–217, clarified for me that rather than Spinoza himself, it is perhaps the manner in which his thought has been appropriated by thinkers such as Giorgio Agamben and Gilles Deleuze and perhaps also Antonio Negri that are more truly proximate. Derrida's own refusal of "substance dualism" is undoubtedly another powerful point of connection.

14 While this may or may not be official doctrine, this was the explanation that I was given by our family priest.

15 Consider here Derrida's critique in *Aporias* of Heidegger's "decision" about the

anteriority of an existential analysis of death and the necessity of its excluding "all consideration about the beyond and the here . . . It is on this side, on the side of *Dasein* and of its here, which is our here, that the oppositions between here and over there, this side and beyond, can be distinguished" (ibid., original 98; trans. 52). It is also in this context that Derrida writes the following sentence, which could well have served as my epigraph: "I would say that there is no politics without an organization of the time and space of mourning, without a topolitology of the sepulcher, without an anamnestic and thematic relation to the spirit as ghost [*revenant*], without an open hospitality to the guest as *ghost* [in English in the original], whom one holds, just as he holds us, hostage" (ibid., 112; 61–62).

16 See David Knipe's excellent essay "*Sapindikarana*: The Hindu Rite of Entry into Heaven," in *Religious Encounters With Death: Insights from the History and Anthropology of Religions,* ed. Frank E. Reynolds and Earle H. Waugh (University Park: Penn State University Press, 1977), 112, 114, 121. A minor but popular festival is *Kanu,* celebrated around January, a little after the harvest festival. On this day, women of the household make rice in seven colors, which they set out in seven rows of seven *pinda* balls on leaf plates. One is told that this is meant to nourish the "small life," namely the birds, little animals, even the insects. The significance of animal death and dying/perishing with reference to Hindu ritual would be very interesting to explore from the point of view of Derrida's critique of Heidegger in *Apories* (Paris: Éditions Galilée, 1996), translated by Thomas Dutoit as *Aporias* (Stanford, CA: Stanford University Press, 1993), which includes as well a questioning of the impossible border that runs between cultures and disciplines.

17 I suggest that the crossing of the threshold in the funeral rite between "this side" and the "other side" that is enjoined upon the main "sacrificer" (the one who performs the rituals), which renders him "impure," complicates the scenario of sacrifice as such as consecration proper.

18 Jonathan Parry, "Death and Digestion: The Symbolism of Food and Eating in North Indian Mortuary Rites," *Man* 20, 4 (Dec 1985): 612–30.

19 See also the *Vishnu Shastras* XXII, 1–6 for a caste-based differentiation of the length of the rites. *The Institutes of Vishnu,* vol. 7, trans. Julius Jolly (Delhi: Motilal Banarsidass Publishers, 1965), 87–97.

Notes to Chapter 5: Misgivings about Misgivings and the Nature of a Home

1 Richard Dawkins, Daniel Dennett, Sam Harris, Christopher Hitchens.

2 A partial list (of translated, English editions) would include: *The Other Heading* (Bloomington, IN: Indiana University Press, 1991); *Specters Of Marx: The State Of Debt, the Work of Mourning, and the New International* (New York and London: Routledge, 1994); *The Gift of Death* (Chicago: University of Chicago Press, 1995); *The Politics Of Friendship* (London and New York: Verso, 1997), and *Rogues: Two Essays on Reason* (Palo Alto, CA: Stanford University Press, 2005). See also the collection *Acts Of Religion,* edited by Gil Anidjar (New York and London: Routledge, 2002).

3 See especially *Of Hospitality* (Palo Alto, CA: Stanford University Press, 2000), and also "Hostipitality" in *Acts Of Religion*.

4 A record of its past and upcoming events, as well as video recording of its meetings, seminars, artistic presentations, and conversations can be found at http://www.bc.edu/schools/cas/guestbook. It is directed by Richard Kearney of Boston College.

5 *Of Hospitality*, ibid, 75ff.

6 "Hostipitality," *Acts of Religion*, ibid, 360–65.

7 "Hostipitality," 364 Cited in Westmoreland, Mark W., "Interruptions: Derrida and Hospitality," *Kritike*, 2:1, June 2008, 1–10, 4.

8 See inter alia *Of Hospitality*, 75–83, and 121ff; *The Gift Of Death, The Politics Of Friendship*, and *Adieu To Emmanuel Levinas* (Stanford: Stanford University Press, 1999).

9 Ideas to be found prominently in *Levinas' Otherwise Than Being Or Beyond Essence* (The Hague: Nijhoff, 1981).

10 This may be a slight overstatement, but it does seem to me that this is Derrida's intention in *Adieu To Emmanuel Levinas*, particularly in its last ten pages or so (113–123). That Derrida manages, remarkably, to express these doubts in deeply moving, respectful, and elegiac prose does not obscure his fundamental misgivings.

11 This fine paper, originally presented by Edward Kaplan on a panel as part of the Guestbook Project, is reprinted in this volume. It contains abundant citations of relevant biblical and rabbinic texts and clear analyses, and so allows me to take the luxury here of presuming some familiarity with Jewish conceptions of hospitality on the part of my readers.

12 There are many studies of this decisive period in Jewish history. For two excellent overviews, see Shaye Cohen, *From The Maccabees To The Mishna* (Louisville, KY: Westminster John Knox, 2006), and Lawrence Schiffman, *From Text to Tradition: A History of Second Temple and Rabbinic Judaism* (Hoboken: Ktav Publishing, 1991).

13 In Gampel, ed., *Crisis and Creativity in the Sephardic World: 1391–1648* (New York: Columbia University Press, 1997), 3–22.

14 The fecundity of Derrida's work on hospitality can easily be seen here, since so many more topics naturally arise at this point. For instance, is Derrida condemning the specificity of "place," and of language, of cultural identity, and so on? To reply formally that such a question represents merely a misunderstanding of deconstruction, which is of course far more than mere negation, does not impress in this case. For in fact "place," cultural identity, language, and so on require active cultivation, innovation, and care if they are to survive. On this see for instance Edward Casey's impressive *The Fate of Place* (Berkeley, CA: University of California Press, 1997). Granting that deconstruction is far more than mere negation, in what way is it a contribution to the active work needed to nurture the enormous diversity of human and cultural phenomena we still possess, but which may well be increasingly threatened? On another front, while it may be incorrect to accuse Derrida of nothing more than a higher neutrality, the distances to which he is willing to go to preserve the possibility of *disengagement* from phenomena in which most human beings have been and continue to be deeply engaged can

sometimes, frankly, strike one as akin to something like neurosis, rather than philosophy. For a moving example of this, see his powerful ruminations on his own Jewish identity, "Abraham, The Other," in *Judeities: Questions For Jacques Derrida*, eds, B. Bergo, J. Cohen and R. Zagury-Orly (New York: Fordham University Press, 2007), 1–35. This essay of Derrida's, with its explicitly tortured sense of Jewish identity, will make emotionally challenging reading for many committed, engaged Jews today.

Notes to Chapter 6: The Open Tent

1 My biblical quotations are taken from *Etz Hayim, Torah and Commentary*. Copyright The Rabbinical Assembly, 2001; see Joel Rembaum, "Dealing with Strangers: Relations with Gentiles at Home and Abroad, 1377–82.

2 *Maxwell House Passover Haggadah* (New York: General Foods Corporation, 1989), 9.

3 *Etz Hayim*, p. 1379. "The non-Israelite in the biblical sources who most closely approaches the status of the Israelite is the *ger*, 'the resident alien.' Although originally from another nation, the *ger* chooses to live among the Israelites in their land. The *ger* is to be treated with loving kindness because Israel, having been strangers in a strange land (Egypt), understands the *ger*'s plight" (See Exod. 22:20; 23:9; Lev. 19:33-34; Deut. 10:19; 24:1-18).

4 For a traditional view see Meir Zlotowitz, *Succos: Its Significance, Laws, and Prayers*, 2nd ed. (Brooklyn, NY: ArtScroll Mesorah Publications, 1995).

5 *Succos* (ArtScroll), 95.

6 Ibid., 97, Note.

7 Joseph Telushkin, *Jewish Literacy* (New York: William Morrow and Company, 1991), 534–36.

8 Abraham Heschel, "On Prayer," *Moral Grandeur and Spiritual Audacity*, ed. Susannah Heschel (New York: Farrar, Straus & Giroux, 1996), 258.

9 Ibid., 258-9.

10 Ibid.

Notes to Chapter 7: Sukkot

1 Jill Robbins, ed., *Is It Righteous to Be: Interviews with Emmanuel Levinas* (Stanford University Press, 2001), 92.

2 Ibid., 141-2.

3 See Robert Bernasconi, "Only the Persecuted . . . : Language of the Oppressor, Language of the Oppressed," in *Ethics as First Philosophy*, ed. Adrian T. Peperzak (London: Routledge, 1995), 78.

4 In fact, coincidentally or otherwise, both references are from 1957. See notes 142 and 143 below.

5 Emmanuel Levinas, *Otherwise than Being or Beyond Essence*, trans. Alphonso Lingus (Pittsburgh: Duquesne University Press, 1998), 182. Hereafter OB in text.

6   See Jacques Derrida, "A Word of Welcome," in *Adieu to Emmanuel Levinas*, trans. Pascalle-Ann Brault and Michael Nass (California: Stanford University Press, 1999).

7   Emmanuel Levinas, "A Religion for Adults," in *Difficult Freedom: Essays on Judaism*, trans. Sean Hand (Baltimore: John Hopkins University Press, 1990), 22. The essay is based on a talk given by Levinas in 1957 at the Abbey of Tioumoline in Morocco.

8   Ibid., 22–3.

9   For the material that follows drawn from this first colloquium I am indebted to the research of Oona Eisenstadt and Robert Gibbs. See Oona Eisenstadt, *Driven Back to the Text: The Premodern Sources of Levinas's Postmodernism* (Pittsburgh: Duquesne University Press, 2001), 201–3 and 358–9, notes 1–4, and Robert Gibbs, "Levinas, the Messianic, and the Question of History," in *Difficult Justice: Commentaries on Levinas and Politics*, ed. Horowitz and Horowitz (Toronto: University of Toronto Press, 2006), 271–84. For details of the French publication of the proceedings of the Colloquium of French Speaking Jewish Intellectuals, see Eisenstadt, 358–9, and Gibbs, 284.

10 See Gibbs, 274.

11 Ibid., 278–9.

12 Ibid., 278.

13 Ibid., 279.

14 Emmanuel Levinas, *Totality and Infinity: An Essay on Exteriority*, trans. Alphonso Lingis (Pittsburgh: Duquesne University Press, 1969), 27. Hereafter TI in text.

15 Derrida, 21.

16 Martin Heidegger, *Being and Time*, trans. John Macquarrie and Edward Robinson (Oxford: Basil Blackwell, 1962), 98.

17 Derrida, 42–3.

18 Emmanuel Levinas, *Entre Nous: Thinking -Of-The-Other*, trans. Michael B. Smith and Barbara Harshav (New York: Columbia University Press, 1998), 117.

19 Gibbs, 277.

20 Franz Rosenzweig, *The Star of Redemption*, trans. Barbara E. Galli (University of Wisconsin Press), 339.

21 Robert Bernasconi, "Strangers and Slaves in the Land of Egypt: Levinas and the Politics of Otherness," in *Difficult Justice*, ed. Horowitz and Horowitz, 253. See also Emmanuel Levinas, "Without Identity," in *Humanism of the Other*, trans. Nidra Poller (Illinois: University of Illinois Press, 2006), 61.

22 Ibid., 253.

23 Bernasconi, like many Levinasian commentators, here takes Levinas's treatment of Heidegger on the question of "enrootedness," the Site, etc. at face value. It is not possible to redress this imbalance here, save briefly to quote Derrida: "[Heidegger's] solicitation of the Site and the Land is in no way, it must be emphasised, a passionate attachment to territory or locality, is in no way a provincialism or particularism." See "Violence and Metaphysics: An Essay on the Thought of Emmanuel Levinas," in *Writing and Difference*, trans. Alan Bass (London: Routledge, 1978), 181–2 and 409, note 4.

24 Ibid., 254.

25 Emmanuel Levinas, "Nameless," in *Proper Names*, trans. Michael B. Smith (California: Stanford University Press, 1996), 122.

26 Ibid., 122.

27 See Emmanuel Levinas, "Enigma and Phenomena," in *Basic Philosophical Writings,* eds Adrian T. Peperzak, Simon Critchley and Robert Bernasconi (Bloomington, IN: Indiana University Press, 1996). The lines cited from Ionesco are: "In short, we still do not know if, when someone rings the doorbell, there is someone there or not . . .", 66.

28 Emmanuel Levinas, "Without Identity," 62.

29 See Miguel Abensour, "To Think Utopia Otherwise," trans. Bettina Bergo, in *Graduate Faculty Philosophy Journal,* vol. 20, no. 2–vol. 21, no.1 (New York: New School for Social Research), 273.

30 Richard Kearney, *Anatheism: Returning to God After God* (New York: Columbia University Press, 2010), 19.

31 See "Ethics and Politics," in *The Levinas Reader,* ed. Sean Hand (Oxford: Blackwell, 1989), 292.

32 In response to the question whether, for the Israeli, wasn't the other above all the Palestinian, Levinas replied: "My definition of the other is completely different. The other is the neighbor, who is not necessarily kin, but who can be," and also that "in alterity we can find an enemy." Ibid., 294.

33 Ibid., 293.

34 Ibid., 297.

35 Emmanuel Levinas, "Politics After," in *Beyond the Verse: Talmudic Readings and Lectures*, trans. Gary D. Mole (London: The Athlone Press, 1994), 195.

36 Salomon Malka, *Emmanuel Levinas: His Life and Legacy*, trans. Michael Kigel and Sonja M. Embree (Pittsburgh: Duquesne University Press, 2006), 92.

Notes to Chapter 8: Hospitable by Calling, Inhospitable by Nature

1   Hebrews 13:2.

2   Matthew 25:31-46.

3   "This is what I say to all who will listen to me: Love your enemies, and be good to everyone who hates you. Ask God to bless anyone who curses you, and pray for everyone who is cruel to you. If someone slaps you on one cheek, don't stop that person from slapping you on the other cheek. If someone wants to take your coat, don't try to keep back your shirt. Give to everyone who asks and don't ask people to return what they have taken from you. Treat others just as you want to be treated.

If you love only someone who loves you, will God praise you for that? Even sinners love people who love them. If you are kind only to someone who is kind to you, will God be pleased with you for that? Even sinners are kind to people who are kind to them. If you lend money only to someone you think will pay you back, will God be pleased with you for that? Even sinners lend to sinners because they think they will get it all back.

But love your enemies and be good to them. Lend without expecting to be paid back. Then you will get a great reward, and you will be the true children of God in heaven. He is good even to people who are unthankful and cruel. Have pity on others, just as your Father has pity on you" (Lk. 6:27-35).

4 Clifford Geertz, *The Interpretation of Cultures* (New York: Basic Books, 1973).

5 Cf. Emmanuel Levinas, *En Découvrant l'existence avec Husserl et Heidegger* (Paris: Vrin, 1967).

6 Emmanuel Levinas, *Difficile Liberté, essays sur le Judaisme* (Paris: Editions Albin Michel, 1963), 137.

7 Ibid., 28.

8 Frederick Forsythe, *Emeka* (Ibadan: Spectrum Books, 1982). Cf. also Emeka Odumegwu-Ojukwu, *Because I am Involved* (Ibadan: Spectrum Books, 1989).

9 James P. Mackey, *Christianity and Creation: The Essence of the Christian Faith and its Future among Religions: A Systematic Theology* (New York: Continuum, 2006), 397.

10 1 Cor. 11:26.

11 Many of these ideas can be found in my *Tarot: Talisman or Taboo? Reading the World as Symbol* (Dublin: Columba Press, 2003), which in turn was heavily influenced by *Meditations on the Tarot, A Journey into Christian Hermeticism*, trans. Robert A. Powell (Boston: Element Books, 1991). This translation from the original French edition of 1967 is published anonymously in accordance with the author's instructions.

Notes to Chapter 9: Biblical, Ethical and Hermeneutical Reflections on Narrative Hospitality

1 K. Cobb, "Introduction: Studying the Western 'Other,' Understanding the Islamic Self," in *Scripture, Reason and the Contemporary Islam-West Encounter. Studying the Other, Understanding the Self*, ed. B. Koshul and S. Kepnes (New York: Palgrave MacMillan, 2007), 1–9.

2 Apostolic Letter, *Tertio Millenio Adveniente* of his holiness Pope John Paul II to the Bishops, Clergy and Lay Faithful on Preparation for the Jubilee of the Year 2000, §46, November 10, 1994.

3 Paul Ricoeur, *Reflections on the Just* (Chicago and London: University of Chicago Press, 2007), 30.

4 Paul Ricoeur, *Critique and Conviction: Conversations with François Azouvi et Marc de Launay* (European Perspectives) (New York: Columbia University Press, 1998), 191.

5 In both Jewish and Islamic tradition it is said that Abraham's tent had four entrances, so that he could welcome guests from all quarters of the compass.

6 According to Talmud, the meals of Abraham are superior to those of Solomon. Solomon's provisions were distributed to his one thousand wives, each of which prepared meals in her own house (B. Ralmud baba Metzia 86 b). Cited in S. Schwartzberg, O.S.B. *Abraham's Hospitality to Strangers (Genesis 18) A Model for Interreligious Dialogue*, in *Bulletin* 79 (July 2007).

7 The English translation obscures the difficulties in the Hebrew text. The verbs in verse 3 are in the singular, indicating that only one of the strangers is spoken to,

whereas those in verses 4-5 are in the plural. Gen. Rabb 48:9, Rashi and Ramban explain that Abraham addresses himself to the leader of the three visitors, but that his invitation applies to all three. Another problem is the opening vocative, which is in the plural *adonai*, with a final long vocal (*kametz*), the use of which is otherwise reserved for God.

8   J. Sacks, "Abraham and the Three Visitors," in *Covenant and Conversation* 11 (November 2006).

9   Ibid.

10   Ibid.

11   Schwartzberg.

12   M. Jansen, *Talen naar God: Wegwijzers bij Paul Ricœur* (Amsterdam: Academisch proefschrift ter verkrijging van de graad van de doctor in de Godgeleerdheid, 2002), 229.

13   Sacks.

14   Rav Alex Israel, *Parshat Vayera: The Importance of Chesed*, www.yehatzvi.org/shiurim/parasha/Vayera%20-%20The%20importance%20of%20Chessed_11_06.rtf

15   There is a legend that narrates that God, the day whereon he visited Abraham "had bored a hole in hell, so that its heat might reach as far as the earth, and no wayfarer venture abroad on the highways, and Abraham be left undisturbed in his pain." See L. Ginzberg, *Legends of the Jews*, vol. 1, *From the Creation to Jacob*, trans. Henrietta Szold (Baltimore and London: The Johns Hopkins University Press, 1998), 240.

16   L. R. Kass, *The Beginning of Wisdom: Reading Genesis* (Chicago: University of Chicago Press, 2003), 316.

17   "De zon, de maan . . . en de bijbel. Ontmoeting met Emmanuel Levinas," in R. Burggraeve, *De Bijbel geeft te denken* (Leuven: Acco, 1991), 265–82, 278.

18   R. Burggraeve, "Am I My Brother's Keeper? On the Meaning and Depth of Our Responsibility," in *Ephemerides Theologicae Lovanienses* 84, no. 4 (2008), 341–61.

19   In Latin, *hospes* and *hostis* are etymologically related. As Richard Kearney puts it: "The Latin root for both hostility and hospitality is the same. And the term 'host' may in fact be used to designate one who welcomes of one who invades." In Richard Kearney, *Strangers, Gods and Monsters: Interpreting Otherness* (London: Routledge, 2003), 68.

20   P. Valkenberg, "Sharing the Lights on the Way to God: Muslim-Christian Dialogue and Theology in the Context of Abrahamic Partnership," in *Currents of Encounter* 26 (Amsterdam: Rodopi, 2006).

21   Daniélou, "Pour une théologie de l'hospitalité," in *La vie spirituelle* 85 (1951), 339–47, 340.

22   See Karen Armstrong, *In the Beginning: A New Interpretation of Genesis* (New York: Alfred A. Knopf, 1996), 62.

23   A. Race, "Hospitality is Good, But How Far Can It Go?" in *Current Dialogue* 46, no. 1 (2005): 4–8; John B Switzer, "Strangers No More: The Pedagogy of Interreligious Hospitality," in *Boston College Dissertations and Theses* (2006), http://escholarship.bc.edu/dissertations/AAI3207009; Valkenberg.

24 C. Kukathas, "Liberalism and Multiculturalism: The Politics of Indifference," in *Political Theory* 26, no. 5 (1998), 686–99.

25 Paul Ricoeur, "Reflections on a New Ethos for Europe," in *Paul Ricoeur: The Hermeneutics of Action*, ed. Richard Kearney (London: Sage Publications, 1996), 3–14, 4.

26 Paul Ricoeur, "Universal Project, Multiple Heritages," in *The Future of Values: 21st Century Talks*, ed. Jérôme Bindé, trans. Brian Verity and John Cotbett (New York: Berghahn Books, 2004), 89–93, 90.

27 P. Knitter, *Introducing Theologies of Religion* (Maryknoll, NY: Orbis Books, 2002), 183.

28 Paul Ricoeur, "Pastoral Praxeology, Hermeneutics and Identity," in *Figuring the Sacred: Religion, Narrative and Imagination*, trans. David Pellauer, ed. Mark I. Wallace (Minneapolis, MN: Fortress Press, 1995), 303–14, 308.

29 Paul Ricoeur, *History, Memory and Forgetting* (Chicago: University of Chicago Press, 2005), 81.

30 See Marianne Moyaert, "A 'Babelish' World (Genesis 11:1-9) and Its Challenge to Cultural-Linguistic Theory," in *Horizons* 36 (2009), 215–34.

31 See Fr. Pierre-François de Béthune, O.S.B., "Interreligious Dialogue and Sacred Hospitality," in *Religion East and West* 7 (2007), 1–22, 9.

32 Ricoeur was taking on thinkers like Levinas who, by insisting on the alterity of the other and "the unconditionality of hospitality" ended by making the gesture of receiving inconceivable. For the French thinker, the stranger or the refugee is to be perceived first of all in his alterity "as similar" at the risk otherwise of making the encounter between the one receiving and the one being received impracticable in a common symbolic place. For if one follows Levinas, where indeed the one receiving has the illusion of practicing hospitality (but in reality he is forcing the other to model himself on his own mode of being), or where the one being received is not forced to comply with any condition (which means the erasure of the one who is doing the receiving reduced to abandoning completely his personal convictions). Between the two Ricoeur draws a middle path, that of a practical way of effective hospitality, that escapes both the extreme of "pure receptive passivity" and the total impossibility of receiving. See Marianne Moyaert, "In Response to the Religious Other: Levinas, Interreligious Dialogue and the Otherness of the Other," in R. Burggraeve, ed., *The Awakening to the Other: A Provocative Dialogue with Emmanuel Levinas* (Dudley, MA: Peeters, 2008), 161–90.

33 Ricoeur, "Reflections on a New Ethos for Europe," 7.

34 Maxine Greene, *Releasing the Imagination: Essays on Education, the Arts, and Social Change* (San Francisco: Jossey-Bass Publishers, 1995), 3.

35 Cobb, 4.

36 Paul Ricoeur, *On Translation*, trans. Eileen Brennan and introduced by Richard Kearney (London: Routledge, 2006), 4.

37 Richard Kearney, "Interreligious Discourse – War or Peace?" in *Tolerancia: El estado de la cuestión. Toleration: The State of the Question*, ed. Miguel Giusti, Colección Tolerancia/Toleration/Tolerância, vol. I (Lima: Pontificia Universidad Católica del Perú, 2010) 195–205.

38 Ricoeur, "Reflections on a New Ethos for Europe," 7.
39 Kearney.
40 Ricoeur, "Reflections on a New Ethos for Europe," 8.
41 Ibid.
42 Cobb, 4.
43 Ford, "An Interfaith Wisdom: Scriptural Reasoning Between Jews, Christians and Muslims," in *Modern Theology* 22 (2006), 345–66, 349.
44 Ibid., 349.
45 N. Adams, "Making Deep Reasonings Public," in *Modern Theology* 22 (2006), 385–401, 395.
46 W. Taylor, *How to Pitch a Tent: A Beginner's Guide to Scriptural Reasoning* (London: Center for Reconciliation and Peace, 2008).
47 Ford, "An Interfaith Wisdom," 356.
48 Ford, "Faith in the Third Millennium: Reading Scriptures Together." Address at the Inauguration of Dr. Iain Torrance as President of Princeton Theological Seminary and Professor of Patristics, Thursday 10th March 2005, 1–15, 4.
49 Ibid., 10.
50 S. Kepnes, *A Handbook for Scriptural Reasoning* (New York: Colgate University), 9.
51 Ibid., 11.

Notes to Chapter 10: *The Awakening of Hospitality*

1 Richard Kearney is the Charles Seelig Chair of Philosophy at Boston College and Director of the Guestbook Project. This international project has organized a series of seminars and conferences on the themes of "Hosting the Stranger" and "Facing the Other in Divided Communities." For details of the various publications and documentaries produced by the Guestbook Project, including recordings of most of the papers published in this volume, based on an international conference held in Boston College (May 2009) under the title of "Interreligious Hospitality," see www.guestbookproject.com. For fuller information on the other publications related to the conferences see the editor's Introduction to this volume.
2 Retold here based on Paul Reps, ed., *Zen Flesh, Zen Bones: A Collection of Zen and Pre-Zen Writings* (Rutland, VT: Anchor Books, 1957), 41.

Notes to Chapter 11: *Buddhism and Hospitality*

1 Lawrence Babb, *The Divine Hierarchy: Popular Hinduism in Central India* (New York: Columbia University Press, 1975), 43.
2 John Strong, *The Legend of King Aśoka (Aśokāvadāna)* (Princeton: Princeton University Press, 1989), 57.
3 E. B. Cowell and R. A. Neil, eds, *Divyāvadāna* (Cambridge: Cambridge University Press, 1886).
4 Luis Gomez, *Land of Bliss: The Paradise of the Buddha of Measureless Light*

(Sanskrit and Chinese Version of the Sukhāvatīvyūha Sutras) (Honolulu: University of Hawai'i Press; Kyoto, Japan: Higashi Honganji Shinshū Ōtani-ha, 1996), 332.

5   This isn't mentioned in the Divyāvadāna version, but it is in the recension in the *Sutra of the Wise and Foolish.*

6   Government of India's Ministry of Tourism, "FAQ," http://atithidevobhavah.com/ faq

Notes to Chapter 12: The Dead and the City

1   A version of this paper was presented at "Interreligious Hospitality," (conference, Boston College, Boston, MA, February 14, 2009). I thank Richard Kearney for inviting me to write the presentation. While this essay will treat the subject of hospitality among Muslims in the Eastern Mediterranean, it does not purport to represent the entirety of the Islamic tradition, as practices and habits (as will become evident early in the essay) may have been markedly different according to region. By the "Levant" I mean the Eastern Mediterranean, or the area covering the modern states of Syria, Lebanon, Jordan, Israel and Palestine. I have opted not to use standard Arabic transliteration for simplicity, however, the *hamza* is indicated by (') and the *`ayn* by (`).

2   Usama `Anuti, *al-Haraka al-adabiyya fi Bilad al-Sham khilal al-qarn al-thamin `ashar* (Beirut: Lebanese University Press, 1980), 77.

3   Muhammd b. Isa b. Ibn Kannan, *Yawmiyyat shamiyya*, ed. Akram Ahmad al-`Ulabi (Damascus: Dar al-Tabba', 1994), 311–12. It should be noted that I will also be using the original autograph manuscript of the book under a different title cited below.

4   For example, Muhammad Khalil al-Muradi, *Silk al-durar fi a`yan al-qarn al-thani `ashar*, 4 vols. (Cairo: Dar al-Kitab al-Islami, n.d.), 2:2; Muhammad b. Isa Ibn Kannan, *al-Hawadith al-yawmiyya li-tarikh ahada `ashara wa alf wa miyya*. MSS Ahlwardt 9480, 74b; and the example in the section below, "The Saint and the City."

5   There has been much excellent work on the *`ulama'* but the classics remains Ira M. Lapidus, *Muslim Cities in the Later Middle Ages* (Cambridge, MA: Harvard University Press, 1967), and Jonathan Berkey, *The Transmission of Knowledge in Medieval Cairo: A Social History of Islamic Education, 1190–1350* (Princeton: Princeton University Press, 1992).

6   Ibn Kannan, *Yawmiyyat shamiyya*, 109.

7   The authoritative biographical dictionary of the scholars and notables of the eighteenth century is al-Muradi's *Silk al-durar* cited herein. Despite its flaws, to date, the most imaginative treatment of the biographical dictionary as a social practice is Michael Chamberlain, *Knowledge and Social Practice in Medieval Damascus, 1190–1350* (Cambridge: Cambridge University Press, 1994).

8   Ibn Kannan, *Yawmiyyat shamiyya*, 189.

9   Ibid., 314. For the biography of the deceased under the name "al-Azbaki," see al-Muradi, *Silk al-durar* 2:116.

10 Ibn Kannan, *al-Hawadith al-yawmiyya*, 74b. The editor of Ibn Kannan's

chronicle, Akram al-'Ulabi, has transcribed *ila jihat al-ghuraba'*, "on the Side of the Strangers" as *ila jihat al-gharb*, "towards the West," Ibn Kannan, *Yawmiyyat shamiyya*, 377. My reading is based on the autograph manuscript, Ibn Kannan, *al-Hawadith al-yawmiyya*, 74b. This reading also agrees with the information found in the obituary of the deceased in another source, which reads: *dufina fi maqabir al-ghuraba'*, "he was buried in the Graveyard of the Strangers," al-Muradi, *Silk al-durar* 2:2.

11   Heghnar Zeitlian Watenpaugh, "Deviant Dervishes: Space, Gender, and the Construction of Antinomian Piety in Ottoman Aleppo," *International Journal of Middle East Studies* 37 (2005): 236–565.

12   Ibid., 540.

13   Ibid., 541.

Notes to Chapter 13: Some Reflections on Hospitality in Islam

1   *Sunan al-Tirmidhī*, al-Birr wa'l-silāh, 2049. Unless otherwise noted, all *ahādīth* in this essay are cited from the most recent collections edited by The Thesaurus Islamicus Foundation (*Jamī'at al-maktab al-islāmī*, Stuttgart: 1421/2001).

2   *Saḥīḥ al-Bukhārī*, al-Tawḥīd, 7465; *Saḥīḥ Muslim*, al-Faḍā'il, 6170.

3   *Saḥīḥ Bukhārī*, al-Īmān, 12; *Saḥīḥ Muslim*, al-Īmān, 39; *Sunan al-Nasā'ī*, al-Īmān, 5000; *Sunan Abī Dāwūd*, al-Ādāb, 5194; *Sunan Ibn Mājah*, al-Aṭ'imah, 3253.

4   Aḥmad b. Ḥanbal, *Musnad*, 16778.

5   See also, Qur'ān 25:67.

6   e.g. Qur'ān 69:34; 74:44; 89:18.

7   Muḥammad b. Jarīr al-Ṭabarī, *Jāmi' al-bayān 'an ta'wīl āy al-Qur'ān*, ed. Maḥmūd Shākir al-Hirstanī (Beirut: Dār iḥyā' al-turāth al-'arabī, 1421/2001), vol. 30, 382–9; Abū 'Abdallāh Muḥammad al-Qurṭubī, *al-Jāmi' li aḥkām al-qur'ān*, ed. Muḥammad Ibrāhīm al-Ḥafnāwī (Cairo: Dār al-ḥadīth, 1323/2002), vol. 10, 439–41.

8   See for example, 2:215, 274, 280; 13:22; 22:35; 35:29; 57:7; 58:12; 76:8; 90:14-16.

9   *Saḥīḥ Bukhārī*, al-Tafsīr, 4938.

10   *Saḥīḥ Bukhārī*, al-Īmān, 28.

11   Abū Ḥāmid al-Ghazālī, *Iḥyā' 'ulūm al-dīn*, Book 11, "Kitāb ādāb al-akl."

12   *Saḥīḥ al-Bukhārī*, al-Adab, 6087.

13   This account is attested in multiple sources, among them *Saḥīḥ Bukhārī*, Bad' al-wahy, 3; *Saḥīḥ Muslim* al-Īmān, 301.

14   *Saḥīḥ Muslim*, al-Nikah, 1432.

15   *Sunan al-Tirmidhī*, al-Janā'iz, 1017.

16   *Saḥīḥ Bukhārī*, al-Nikah, 5178.

17   Al-Ghazālī, *Iḥyā' 'ulūm al-dīn*, Book 11, "Kitāb ādāb al-akl."

18   Abū Ḥafṣ 'Umar al-Suhrwardī, *'Awārif al-ma'ārif*, ed. 'Abd al-Ḥalīm Maḥmūd and Muḥmūd b. Sharīf (Caior, Maṭba'ah al-sa'ādah), 184.

19   Lisān al-dīn al-Khaṭīb al-Salmānī, *Rawḍat al-ta'rīf bi ḥubb al-sharīf*, ed. 'Abd al-Qādir Aḥmed 'Aṭā 'Abd al-Sattār (Cairo, Dār al-Fikr al-'Arabī), 4, 484.

20 *Saḥīḥ al-Bukhārī*, al-Īmān, 13; *Saḥīḥ Muslim*, al-Īmān, 179.
21 Yaḥyā al-Nawawī, *Sharḥ Ṣaḥīḥ Muslim* (Beirut, 1423/2003), vol. 1, 213–14.
22 *Ṣaḥīḥ al-Bukhari*, Bad' al-waḥy, 1; *Ṣaḥīḥ Muslim*, al-ʿImārah, 5036.
23 *Ṣaḥīḥ Muslim*, al-Īmān, 275.
24 See also, 2:217; 3:21-22; 5:5, 53; 6:88; 7:147; 9:17; 47:28.

Notes to Chapter 14: Food, the Gust and the Tattiriya Upanishad

1 Patrick Olivelle, trans. *The Upanishads* (Oxford: Oxford University Press, 1996). Other translations of the *Taittiriya Upanishad* are found in *Annam Bahu Kurvita*.
2 In the Sanskrit there is a play on words between *ad*, the root "to eat," and *anna*, the noun for "food."
3 Mandayam D. Srinivas and Jitendra Bajaj, *Annam Bahu Kurvita: Recollecting the Indian Discipline of Growing and Sharing Food in Plenty* (Chennai, India: Centre for Policy Studies, 1996).
4 Olivelle, 167–8.
5 Srinivas and Bajaj, 191.
6 Ibid., 208–9.

Notes to Chapter 15: God as Guest

1 "After creating the world, God entered inside it." (*Taittirīya Upaniṣhad*, 2.6)
2 "All this is indeed Brahman." (*Chāndogya Upaniṣhad*, 3.14.1). Brahman is the term used to denote the Divine Presence that transcends all particularities.
3 *Bhagavad Gītā*, 18.20-22.
4 *Complete Works of Swami Vivekananda* (Calcutta: Advaita Ashrama), 1.86.

Index of Names

Abensour, Miguel 84, 162
Abraham 1, 5, 13, 67–8, 70–1, 74–5, 79, 80, 85, 95–102, 104–8, 160, 163–4
Abu Bakr Ibn Abi al-Wafa 129–30
Abü Hamid al-Ghazäli 136, 168
Adams, Nicholas 106, 166
al-Nabulusi 123–5, 129
al-Naqshabandi 128, 130
al-Yazbaki 128, 130
Anas bin Mälik 136

Bajaj, Jitendra 143–4, 169
Benjamin, Walter 16, 152
Berman, Antoine 3
Bernasconi, Robert 82, 160–2
Buddha, the 26–8, 30, 110–14, 116–19, 121, 167
Burnouf, Eugène 25

D. T. Suzuki 30
Daniélou, Jean 101, 165
Derrida, Jacques 3–4, 12–14, 17, 55–60, 62–3, 74, 77–8, 81, 151, 157–61
Deussen, Paul 29, 154
Dögen 30

Ford, David 106, 166
Freud, Sigmund 94

Geertz, Clifford 89, 163
Gibbs, Robert 76, 85–6, 161
Glasenapp, Helmuth von 29, 153–4
Gomez, Luis 119, 167
Guignes, Joseph de 28

Hasan bin Alï 136
Hegel, Georg-Wilhelm 3, 24–5, 27–31, 153–4

Heidegger, Martin 3, 30–1, 77, 79, 82, 93, 154–5, 158, 161, 163
Heschel, Abraham Joshua 5, 71–2, 160
Huntington, Samuel 95

Ibn Kannan 123–7, 129–30, 167–8

Jaspers, Karl 30
Jesus 19, 32, 36, 68, 90, 93

Kant, Immanuel 3, 25, 153
Kearney, Richard 8, 19–20, 85, 104, 109, 152, 155–7, 159, 162, 164–7
Kepnes, Steven 108, 163, 166
Knipe, David 50, 158
Krishna 51, 148–9, 156

Lao-Tse 30
Levinas, Emmanuel 3–5, 12, 55, 59–60, 73, 75–86, 90, 100, 159–65

Malka, Salomon 86, 162
Marty, Martin 35–7, 155–6
Marx, Karl 94, 158
Michelet, Jules 25
Muhammad 19, 133–7
Mulla Ilyas 126, 127, 129–30

Nabokov, Vladimir 15, 151
Nägärjuna 28, 30, 152, 154
Nietzsche, Friedrich 26, 29

Origen of Alexandria 23

Parry, Jonathan 50, 158
Pierre-François De Béthune 35
Plato 78
Pope John Paul II 32, 163